D1233064

Beyond Alcoholism

Alcohol and Public Health Policy

Dan E. Beauchamp

Temple University Press *Philadelphia*

Temple University Press, Philadelphia 19122
© 1980 by Temple University. All rights reserved
Published 1980
Printed in the United States of America

Library of Congress Cataloging in Publication Data
Beauchamp, Dan E

  Beyond alcoholism.

  Bibliography: p.

  Includes index.

  1. Alcoholism—Social aspects. 2. Alcoholism—
United States. 3. Mental health policy—United States.
I. Title. [DNLM: 1. Alcoholism. 2. Health policy—
United States. WM274 B372b]
RC565.B38   362.2'92   80-15122
ISBN 0-87722-189-8

Contents

Preface

This book is about the new order for alcohol that emerged after Prohibition and the set of ideas that evolved to legitimate and sustain that order, while at the same time giving a "modern" account of alcohol problems. This new account was the concept of "alcoholism," or the idea that alcohol problems in society were, in the main, the consequence of the vulnerability of a small proportion of those who drink. There have been numerous attempts to examine the rise of the alcoholism movement, and especially to challenge its central notion that alcoholism is a disease. The principal difference here is that the focus will be on a second and equally important feature, the idea that alcohol problems are mainly personal and that, for the most part, the great majority of drinkers are immune to them.

There will not be much in this book about the very real accomplishments of the alcoholism movement. While I have not resisted the opportunity to critique the alcoholism movement's ideas about alcohol, this should not be taken as a judgment that the movement is a failure. Each cultural period gets the kinds of social problems it expects. A culture of modernity arose in this country during the twentieth century, challenging Protestant asceticism, small town morality, and the restrictions of private conduct associated with what Joseph Gusfield has called "cultural fundamentalism." Cultural modernism stood for leisure, pleasure, consumption, and the liberation of the self from the burdensome constraints of community and society.

Alcohol is not, nor has it ever been, a purely public health problem. The central point of this book is that the new status quo for alcohol, taken together with the concept of alcoholism, was developed as consistent with, and symbolic of, cultural modernism. While the alcoholic is no longer defined as morally deficient, he still is considered basically different, but different in ways that relieve him of personal responsibility for his problems. The signature of the modernist point of view on many problems of deviance is to use metaphors of illness to excuse that deviance, but at the same time ensure that everyone (including the deviant) realizes that the problem still resides principally within the deviant.

I have more debts than are possible to acknowledge. The first is to the work of Joseph Gusfield. His work on the Temperance movement and subsequent developments provides the starting place for my own analysis. My second and most substantial debt is to William Ryan and his pioneering book, *Blaming the Victim*. This book has enjoyed wide popularity. Sometimes, however, I am afraid its very popularity prevents other scholars from benefiting from the truly sophisticated and subtle insights into the mechanisms of the American mind that are contained within its covers.

In assembling this book I have had to rely on the hard work and research of dozens of individuals, some of whom I have come to know personally. Robin Room, Joe Gusfield, Wolf Schmidt, Kettil Bruun, Klaus Mäkelä, and Paul Whitehead come instantly to mind. I have learned much from each of them, both from their publications and from personal conversations. One of the best-kept secrets of social science is the exciting research on drinking habits and problems being carried on in Western nations. Hopefully, the present study will help make some of this important work more accessible.

I owe a great debt to my colleagues on the Panel on Alternative Policies for the Prevention of Alcohol Abuse and Alcoholism, of the National Academy of Sciences, established in 1978. My special thanks to Chairman Mark Moore, Peter Levison, Dean Gerstein, and Deborah Maloff of the Academy staff, and Patricia O'Gorman, David Promisel, and Lois Whitley of the National Institute on Alcohol Abuse and Alcoholism (NIAAA). Chapter 6 of this study is a shorter version of a paper I prepared for the Panel titled "The Paradox of Alcohol Policy: The Case of the 1969 Alcohol Act in Finland." I owe a great deal to the sponsorship of a World Health Organization study visit in 1976, a return in 1979 under the sponsorship of the National Academy of Sciences, and the generous assistance of the scholars at the Finnish Foundation for Alcohol Studies in making their research findings available to me.

Finally, my colleagues in public health have always enriched me with their abiding interest in the philosophy and importance of public health in the United States. Milton Terris has been especially influential, but there are many others. Over the past eight years, too many students to name have challenged and encouraged me to pursue the ideas in this book. I also owe a special debt to my colleague and friend, Patricia Barry of the UNC School of Public Health, who has heard me out with much patience on these issues for many years. Her continual interest has been a great source of support.

I know now why so many authors take care to acknowledge the large debt owed those who have helped to put a manuscript into shape. Mr. Michael Ames of Temple University Press has provided needed guidance and encouragement. Mrs. Pamela McDonald has worked for a long period of time, patiently retyping revisions, and I am deeply grateful for her cheerful assistance.

But it has been my wife Carole who has provided the decisive support. Writing a book that is out of season with prevailing common sense and sentiments can only be made easier when the person to whom one is most close provides encouragement and a sympathetic ear. I know she welcomes the conclusion of this project even more than I.

D. B.
Department of Health Administration
School of Public Health
UNC at Chapel Hill

Beyond Alcoholism

I. The Discovery of Alcoholism

On the last day of 1970, President Richard Nixon rather reluctantly signed a bill establishing the National Institute on Alcohol Abuse and Alcoholism (NIAAA).[1] Although the federal government had established a small unit within the National Institute of Mental Health in 1966 (called the National Center for the Control and Prevention of Alcoholism), beyond any doubt NIAAA represented a major shift in federal policy toward the problem of alcohol abuse. The first year's appropriation for this new agency was $13 million dollars; by 1979 that figure had increased to $175 million.[2] The intervening decade saw the establishment of numerous new treatment centers throughout the United States, growing support for prevention and occupational programs, media campaigns, the training of various categories of personnel, and the awarding of research and demonstration grants.[3]

This major federal effort may have been the culmination of four decades of work by a rather small number of individuals and organizations who, in the late 1930s and 1940s, began to advance what they called a scientific concept of alcoholism. Or, more likely, it may have resulted from the earlier success of the mental health forces and the establishment of a national network of community mental health centers and from the determination of Harold Hughes, U.S. senator from Iowa, to use his Senate seat and chairmanship of the Subcommittee on Alcoholism and Narcotics to establish a major federal emphasis on alcoholism.[4] Whatever forces actually brought about its establishment, however, the NIAAA has certainly made the problems of alcohol abuse and alcoholism more visible in our society. More and more frequently we hear that alcoholism costs society billions of dollars annually—$25 billion in 1976 and $45 billion in 1978—in lost production, illness, criminal justice costs, and family disruptions.[5] We hear even more frequently about the relationship of alcohol to some cancers, especially for the smoker, and about the serious health risks it can pose to the pregnant mother and the fetus.[6] And we are also hearing the beginnings of disputes about the relationship between per capita consumption, alcohol control policies, and such alcohol-related problems as cirrhosis.[7]

During the rather spectacular growth of federal involvement in alcoholism as a problem (and of state and local involvement as well), there has been little public debate about the concept of alcoholism itself and about the policies that deal with it.[8] The purpose of this book is to explore that concept, to examine alcoholism as a way of thinking about alcohol problems in society. The strategy of analysis is one of paradigm shift and transformation. We will look first at the shift from Temperance and Prohibition thought to alcoholism models, and review the recent and exciting revisions on the origins of our idea of alcohol addiction. The aim here is not, however, to contribute another historical or critical review. Nor is it an attempt to assess the many real accomplishments of the alcoholism movement over the past decades. Rather the aim is to explore the basic patterns of thought involved in our collective struggle to define alcohol problems. Our premise is that behind our shifting views about these problems with alcohol lies a structure and a pattern. By working to isolate that structure and by elaborating its functions, we can better understand the truly major shifts that will be required if alcoholism policy is to pass into a new phase.

"Discovering" Alcoholism

During the period following the Repeal of Prohibition a rather small and loosely connected collection of self-help and professional groups began to work actively toward the "discovery" of a new definition of alcohol problems as public problems. In an obvious reaction to the experience of Prohibition, the emphasis was going to be on a "rational" approach to the age-old problems of alcohol. Gone would be the days of heated emotions and political zealotry; the need was to discover a more reasonable and scientific approach that would work and that would have the support of the public.

At the center of this process of problem discovery was what has come to be called the *concept of alcoholism*. While this was not the first time the term alcoholism was used in connection with alcohol problems, it is accurate to say that the meanings and emphasis contained in the concept of alcoholism were specifically modern and different from previous usage.

The collection of groups advancing the concept of alcoholism will be referred to as the *alcoholism movement*. The alcoholism movement provides one of the important contemporary examples of the process by which public problems are discovered. The central problem for the movement was in fact to create a new set of explanations for alcohol problems, one that differed from Prohibitionist logic.

What occurred was eminently commonsensical and logical—deceptively so. The central and guiding assumption taken by the alcoholism movement—whether self-help groups like Alcoholics Anonymous or research groups like the Yale (now Rutgers) Center of Alcohol Studies—was that alcohol was not a problem, at least for most people.

To those in the alcoholism movement, a cursory examination of the nature of alcohol problems revealed that the vast majority of persons who drank did so without serious injury. Consequently, in all the work that followed, and until very recently, the question of why a minority drinks too much was taken to be the main issue confronting the alcoholism movement.

The process by which the modern alcoholism movement constructed the concept of alcoholism was not simply, or even mainly, a process of scientific investigation, but rather a process of collective definition. Collective definition leans heavily on existing, widely accepted, commonsense notions of reality (what Hewitt and Hall refer to as quasi-theories).[9] The case of alcoholism is perhaps the best illustration of their point that problem construction proceeds not so much by first asking what the nature and causes of problematic conditions in society are, but rather by first defining the conditions as a certain kind of problem (as distinguished from rejected and discredited theories), and then proceeding to find the various causes of the problem.[10]

This inverse way of proceeding occurs for several reasons. Principal among these is the tremendous pressure for social movements to build a "theory of conditions" for a new public problem that rests upon some measure of public consensus. In other words, the organized activity of constructing a new definition of public problems must always pay attention to what the larger environment "wants and can be persuaded to support."[11]

The alcoholism movement's central ideas cannot be understood apart from the transformations occurring in American society during the first fifty years of this century. Paradoxically, even as the drive for national Prohibition succeeded and seemed to thrive, the very forces of rising prosperity—urbanization, mass media, advertising, and the automobile—were undermining the cultural fundamentalism that sustained Prohibition. These forces for change set the stage for the "discovery" of a new theory of alcohol problems, one that would conform to a central tenet of modernism, the freedom of the individual from community controls of personal conduct. Thus, the idea that the vast majority of drinkers possessed a personal ability to control their drinking was a theory that perfectly matched the triumph of modernity.

Alcoholism as a Disease

The alcoholism movement is popularly associated with the idea that alcoholism is a disease. A chief theme of this book is that this view is only half correct. The concept of alcoholism is centrally about a substance it mostly ignores—alcohol. It is true that the movement expresses its central ideas either explicitly in terms of disease analogies or in terms that roughly correspond to ideas about disease or illness (such as addiction or loss of control). Although the alcoholism movement usually sees its views about alcoholism as modern and differing sharply from the logic of Temperance and Prohibition, nevertheless the idea that some forms of alcohol-related deviance were manifestations of a disease has enjoyed long, if somewhat confused, use over the past three centuries, both in Western Europe and the United States.[12]

According to one of the most widely cited authorities, Juan Marconi, the disease concept has been used in three basic ways that mirror the general state of science and culture that prevailed in each historical period.[13] The first phase stretches from the end of the eighteenth century to the middle of the nineteenth century. During this period, drunkenness was considered by such physicians as the Englishman Thomas Trotter "in medical language, strictly speaking, to be a disease, produced by a remote cause, and giving birth to actions and movements in the living body, that disorder the functions of health."[14] A number of works appearing in the first half of the nineteenth century supported this general viewpoint. Most argued that the disease was produced by the immoderate use of spirituous (distilled) liquor.

In the middle of the nineteenth century a second view of alcoholism arose that focused more narrowly on the physical and psychological effects of excessive drinking. This became known as *chronic alcoholism*, and emphasized the long-term effects of alcohol use on various organs of the body (such as the liver). In 1897, Richard v. Krafft-Ebing defined chronic alcoholism as "the conjunct of all the lasting disturbances of the psychic and physical functions produced by the habitual use of alcohol."[15] Actually, it was during the mid-nineteenth century that the term *alcoholism* was coined by Magnus Huss, a Swedish physician, in reference to the effects on the nervous system of excessive and prolonged drinking (of brandy). This development paralleled the shift in psychiatry to the more physiological and organic complications of disordered behavior.[16]

Finally, at the beginning of the twentieth century, a "new" view began to emerge that stressed the phenomenon of *addiction* to, or habitual craving for, alcoholic beverages. This transfer, like the other, was also in step with the shift in psychiatry from emphasis on organic complications to psychoanalytic orientations.

The idea of drunkenness as a disease caused by spirituous liquors was expressed quite early in the United States. The famous American physician of the Revolutionary period, Dr. Benjamin Rush, advocated the view that inebriety was a disease caused by the excessive use of distilled liquors.[17] Throughout the nineteenth century, and paralleling the rise of the Temperance movement, there continued to be a rather lively, if small, interest in caring for alcoholics from a disease point of view. Like the sanitariums set up by the moral reform movements for the insane and mentally ill, a number of private inebriate asylums were established. This movement really began to flourish around 1850 and, after the interruption of the Civil War, continued until the early part of the twentieth century. By 1900, there were over fifty such private and public institutions for the care of inebriates in the United States.[18]

Near the turn of the century, the first publicly funded institution was set up in Massachusetts. The *Journal of Inebriety* was founded in 1876, and continued to exist until 1914, serving as a forum for physicians interested in treating the alcoholic, most of whom were connected with the private inebriate asylums and sanitariums. Organizations like the Washingtonian movement specifically aimed at reclaiming the drunkard, although this movement was not particularly interested in the prevailing medical views of alcoholism.[19]

The established view has been that the notion of alcoholism as a disease is not a new idea but rather a "renewed" one, as E. M. Jellinek has argued,[20] but until recently most scholars still have seen the logic of alcoholism as sharply opposed to the logic of Temperance. Actually, it now seems more complicated.

Harry Levine, in a widely discussed essay, argues that the idea of addiction was not unknown to the Temperance movement, but was "discovered" prior to the origins of the movement and was widely employed in their writings.[21] Levine argues that the concept of addiction was discovered only when the idea that individuals can lose control of their behavior became socially established. Levine sees deep historical roots for the modern idea of alcoholism and especially the idea of addiction in the Temperance heritage, and argues that these two movements are more contiguous than was previously thought. Other writers have also argued that the idea of alcoholism as addiction was widely accepted in the Temperance movement.[22]

The Modern Idea of Alcoholism

The view that the alcoholism movement and Temperance held similar views about addiction will be challenged here, not so much to vindicate earlier historians but rather to argue that both lines of scholarship have focused only on part, and perhaps the least important part, of the question. The modern concept of alcoholism is not so much about the idea of addiction as it is about the idea that few people are susceptible to alcohol problems, that is that the personal control of alcohol is a fact of life for most people. The corollary question of why a minority lacks this personal capacity is, of course, directly opposed to the mode of thinking common to the Temperance movement and Prohibition, which assumed personal control was not possible. The difference in focus is best expressed in Mark Keller's discussion of the definition of alcoholism. Keller was a leading figure in the movement, the long-time editor of the *Quarterly Journal of Studies on Alcohol.*

> A medical style definition of alcoholism, which does not omit the etiological aspect, goes like this: "Alcoholism: diseased condition due to acute or chronic excessive indulgence in alcoholic liquors," *Taber's Cyclopedic Medical Dictionary* (Philadelphia: F. A. Davis Co., 1953). On analysis it is obvious that the etiology of alcoholism is said to be excessive drinking. Thus it either makes alcoholism mean such things as hangover and cirrhosis of the liver, or the "etiology" could hardly be more superficial since it does not tell anything about what the *"excessive indulgence" is "due to."* [23]

It is possible to see the major shift in emphasis represented by Keller's statement as a consequence of Prohibition. In this view, after Prohibition any social movement concerned with alcohol problems that still emphasized alcohol control was doomed. The widespread perception of Prohibition as a failure, according to this view, directly transformed our collective definition of alcohol problems from being a threat to the entire community to being a threat only to a minority of drinkers. The need was to construct a definition or explanation of alcohol problems that relegated alcohol as a substance to a relatively minor role.

The evidence of Norman H. Clark and others is that while the forces of Repeal were formidable, especially after 1926, there was a substantial bloc of opinion that wanted either to retain Prohibition or to modify its most severe aspects (one such modification might be the exemption of beer from the control system). [24] Almost all observers were surprised to find that Repeal came swiftly and completely. Unfortunately, the swiftness of change seems to have discouraged national debate on a control system that might stand as a more workable alternative to outright repeal.

Still, Prohibition was viewed by many influential groups as a disaster. The revelations of official corruption and hypocrisy, the rigidity of the prohibitionists, as well as the rapidly changing character of American society, made the whole era seem particularly disjointed. Andrew Sinclair captures this sentiment in the title of his book, *Prohibition: The Era of Excess.*[25] In their films, books, and movies, Americans in the thirties and forties saw themselves as more sophisticated, more cosmopolitan, and more secular. The excessive moralizing and emotional appeals associated with Prohibition seemed quaint and provincial. Moreover, with the coming of the New Deal and World War II, the United States began to draw more heavily upon its emergent scientific and professional elites for answers to a myriad of problems that were now seen as the responsibility of the federal government. Despite the early backing of many of the scientific and educational elite for Prohibition, most now saw the entire movement as anti-scientific and anti-rational. Finally, the calamity of the Depression made the entire issue of alcohol problems seem monumentally irrelevant.

To conclude that Prohibition set the stage for the alcoholism movement by discrediting the prohibitionists' logic about alcohol is to oversimplify. At the very time that the Anti-Saloon League and their allies were building national support for Prohibition, the United States was beginning a major transformation. From 1900 to 1950, the nation changed enormously.[26] Millions of immigrants poured into the United States, there was a dramatic shift from the rural areas to the cities, the twenties brought unparalleled prosperity, and the Depression dealt a death blow to the belief that the United States could escape the implications for managing a national economy. Central to this cultural revolution was a shift in the modal character. The ideals of frugality, hard work, sternness, and abstinence were being replaced with ideals of leisure, consumption, and pleasure. A central feature of the cultural transformation was the release of the individual from the close moral scrutiny of family, church, and community, especially in matters of personal conduct. This cultural emancipation was celebrated in book, magazine, and film.

Alcohol and the cigarette were central symbols in this drama. The values of the traditional culture were not simply erased or lost; indeed, they remained strong and endure to this date. But they were losing dominance at the moment of their triumph; the twenties and the Depression converted them into a permanent minority.[27] Almost overnight, alcohol vanished as a social problem in the media. What emerged almost timidly was a small movement that sought to "explain" why "some" people could not control their drinking.

The Alcoholism Movement: The Early Years

Shortly after Repeal, a group of physicians associated with New York City teaching hospitals and Bellevue Hospital became interested in getting foundation support for a research project on chronic alcoholism. The head of this effort was Dr. Norman Jolliffe, the chief of medical service at Bellevue Hospital, and Dr. Karl Bowman, Bellevue's chief of psychiatry.[28]

Jolliffe, Bowman, and several others (including social scientists) put together a multidisciplinary research proposal to study alcoholism. Although the proposal failed, if just barely, to win the approval of one of the leading foundations, the process of developing the proposal interested a number of other professionals in the problem. This led ultimately to the founding of the Research Council on Problems of Alcoholism in 1937. The Council shortly thereafter became an affiliate of the American Academy for the Advancement of Science.

From the very beginning, the Council emphasized that it sought the support of widely differing points of view; that its purpose was to stimulate scientific inquiry into the problems of alcoholism rather than to inflame moral and emotional passions; and that it was not a Temperance or liquor organization. The Council included many prominent members of the education, medical, psychiatric, and social sciences professions. Dr. Winifred Overholser of St. Elizabeth's Hospital was the Council president in 1940. Other noted members included Dr. Karl Bowman of Bellevue; Dr. Adolph Meyer of Johns Hopkins; Dr. Lawrence Kolb, assistant surgeon general of the Public Health Service; and Dr. Luther Gulick, a political scientist.[29]

In 1939, the Council obtained a $25,000 grant to conduct a search of the literature on alcoholism. The grant was awarded to the Department of Psychiatry of New York University, and was to be supervised by Dr. Bowman and Dr. Jolliffe. Jolliffe invited a Dr. E. M. Jellinek to head the project. At this point, Dr. H. W. Haggard of the Yale Laboratory of Applied Physiology offered the facilities of the Yale organization to assist Jellinek in conducting the study, and Jolliffe and the Council agreed.

The laboratory at Yale had been conducting studies of the effects of alcohol on the human body since 1930. The laboratory and its staff, especially Dr. Yandell Henderson and Dr. Robert Carlson of the University of Chicago, had earned some notoriety in the early thirties by stating that beer with an alcoholic content of less than 3.2 percent was not intoxicating. Prohibitionists believed that this testimony before Congress, coming during the midst of great efforts to repeal Prohibition, had been especially damaging. Consequently, many Temperance organizations were hostile to the work at the Yale Laboratory.[30]

Jellinek and Haggard assembled a group of researchers to delve into the literature, and this group became the nucleus of the Section on Alcohol Studies, eventually called the Yale Center of Alcohol Studies. These included Mark Keller, Vera Efron, Martin Gross, Giorgio Lolli, and Ann Roe. In 1940, the Yale Laboratory of Applied Physiology also began publication of the *Quarterly Journal of Studies on Alcohol*, now known as the *Journal of Studies on Alcohol*.[31]

A number of subsidiary organizations were spawned by the nucleus at Yale. The Yale Summer School of Alcohol Studies, for example, was first held in New Haven, Connecticut, in the summer of 1943, and continues at Rutgers to serve as a summer institute that brings together educators, church officials, social workers, therapists, and civic leaders interested in the scientific approach to alcoholism. The Yale Plan clinics were formed at about the same time.[32] A joint project of the Alcohol Section of the Yale Laboratory and the Connecticut State Prison Association, the clinics were formed to test the feasibility of rehabilitation in outpatient clinics of large numbers of alcoholics at minimal cost.

Another organization formed from the Yale nucleus, and the group that was to place the sharpest public emphasis on the disease theory of alcoholism, was the National Committee for Education on Alcoholism, established in 1944. The executive director of the National Committee was Mrs. Marty Mann, one of the first women members of Alcoholics Anonymous. The Advisory Board for the National Committee included the two founders of A.A., Dr. Bob Smith and Bill Wilson; novelist Faith Baldwin; and Mrs. Mary Lasker, executive secretary of the National Committee on Mental Hygiene.[33]

The National Committee was formed, in Mann's words, "to arouse public opinion and mobilize it for action."[34] The new group advocated three simple principles. First, alcoholism is a disease. Second, the alcoholic is treatable and deserves help. Third, alcoholism is a public health problem and is therefore a public responsibility.

These several groups—the National Committee, the Yale Plan clinics, the Yale Summer School, the Center of Alcohol Studies, along with Alcoholics Anonymous—formed the nucleus of the alcoholism movement. There was also a related effort to establish public programs for alcoholism, but until the entry of the federal government in the mid-sixties the tangible results in the public sector were disappointing. Sidney Cahn writes that in 1966 there were 135 specialized alcoholism clinics operating, many part time.[35] Most states by the mid-sixties had installed some form of alcoholism programs but the services offered were largely token and symbolic.

One sign, although indirect, of the limited support garnered by the alcoholism movment during the first two decades of its work was its modest academic prestige. Few big names in the academic community were identified with the movement. John Seeley, Robert Straus, and Edwin Lemert, all sociologists, were the notable, if temporary, exceptions.[36] Those who have worked long in this area—E. M. Jellenik, Selden Bacon, and Mark Keller—are known primarily as "alcohologists." Few nationally known sociologists, physicians, physiologists, or psychiatrists have ventured into the special world of alcohol studies. Those who have seem not to have tarried long.

Another disappointment was the move of the Center of Alcohol Studies from Yale to Rutgers in the late 1950s. During this period, Yale eliminated several groups that it felt were marginal to its research interests, and the Center of Alcohol Studies was one of the casualties. All of the Yale group had left by 1962.[37]

The fortunes of the Cooperative Commission on the Study of Alcohol Problems paralleled those of the Yale Center. Formed in 1961, the commission was inspired by similar and successful efforts in the field of mental health. The five-year study of the nation's mental health problems and resources, funded by the National Institute of Mental Health, culminated in a widely publicized report on mental health, *Action for Mental Health*. The report was highly influential in mobilizing support for a federally financed campaign for a network of community mental health centers.[38]

By contrast, the Cooperative Commission's efforts and its report, *Alcohol Problems—A Report to the Nation*,[39] had nothing like the same impact. First, the Commission was frustrated in its search for a director who had a nationwide reputation, and many of the most talented social scientists, such as participant Howard Becker, never published their contributions. (There is some evidence that their efforts were poorly utilized and their contribution marginal.) Similarly, when *Alcohol Problems* was issued by Oxford University Press in paperback form, it got a rather wide distribution among church audiences, but failed to create the same kind of impetus for federal action that seems to have flowed from the mental health report. *Alcohol Problems* promised a follow-up volume that would contain specific policy recommendations, but this has not been forthcoming.

The Rutgers Center continues to conduct the Summer School of Alcohol Studies and to emphasize an extensive, and important, bibliographic effort. A sharp increase in federal support during the 1970s greatly increased its research capacities. Prior to this decade, its chief sources of support were the Brinkley Smithers Foundation and tuition.

Likewise, the National Council on Alcoholism (as the National Committee for Education on Alcoholism is now called) has enjoyed only marginal influence. Like A.A., for many years it was forbidden by its organizing charter from legislative action. A major source of its funds is also the Smithers Foundation; by the mid-sixties the Council rated its fund-raising efforts as poor and noted that, despite the large size of the alcoholism problem, the Council ranked fifteenth among national voluntary health and welfare organizations.[40]

There was a significant change in the public response to the problem with the entry of the federal government into the field of alcohol problems in the mid-sixties and the founding of the NIAAA in 1970. Part of this new emphasis (maybe most) is due to the efforts of

Senator Harold Hughes. An acknowledged recovered alcoholic and a member of Alcoholics Anonymous, Senator Hughes came to the Senate in 1968 after a highly successful stint as governor of Iowa. Shortly after his arrival in the Senate, a Special Subcommittee on Alcoholism and Narcotics was formed in the Committee on Labor and Public Welfare, and Hughes was named chairman. He lost little time in holding nation-wide hearings on alcoholism, and on December 31, 1970, President Nixon signed the first major federal legislation in the field of alcoholism. These new initiatives have in themselves created significant pressure to modify the concept of alcoholism, in part because of the growing recognition of its limited political appeal.

Constructing the Concept of Alcoholism

There is perhaps no better way to begin to chart the formulation of the essential elements of the concept of alcoholism as a new definition of society's alcohol problems than to turn to a 1947 lecture given by Dr. Selden Bacon before the Yale Summer School of Alcohol Studies.[41] Bacon was a central figure in the movement. A sociologist who joined the Section on Alcohol Studies in 1943, he was the director of the Rutgers Center of Alcohol Studies until 1976 and has been a leading spokesman through the years for a public policy based on the disease concept. His lecture, which distills the ideas hammered out in the first seven years of the Yale efforts, contains a precise outline of the issues confronting a successful alcoholism policy and an accurate long-range plan for the next twenty years of the alcoholism movement.

In his speech, Bacon displays a shrewd understanding of the political realities of formulating new policies. He notes that the policies of the Yale group must be carefully drawn in view of those who would be watching. Besides those groups presently dealing with the alcoholic such as the prisons, mental institutions, and the courts, whose perspectives and orientations would also have to be taken into account, Bacon warns against the creation of "unnecessary enemies," such as "moderate drinkers in general, restaurant associations, social work agencies, and the legal profession," all of whom might be opposed to alcoholism, but would not support an "anti-alcohol" drive. Others who might be offended include "A.A., the medical profession, and public health officers."[42] Bacon did not need to add the liquor industry among those "powerful, prestigeful, and organized groups."

Bacon also saw that policy innovation must be formulated in such a way as to avoid cooptation by other groups. Here Bacon shows appreciation for a peculiar dynamic of policy communication: one must communicate shared understandings to build support. But these understandings must be sufficiently distinct and different to prevent their being absorbed by other powerful organizations in the environment. Besides (although Bacon did not specifically mention this point), there is the danger of attracting unwanted and damaging support. An anti-alcohol campaign would not only offend prestigious and powerful groups, it would also invite the embarrassing support of organizations, such as Temperance leagues, whose legitimacy has seriously declined.

In view of the various audiences for alcoholism policy innovation, what view of alcoholism was to be communicated to the public? Bacon suggested that it might be appropriate first to consider what alcoholism was *not*. Actually, along with other spokesmen for the alcoholism movement, Bacon saw three separate and rather distinct sets of social realities. The first was social (moderate, normal) drinking. The second was alcoholism. The third was a sort of residual group in which alcoholism was present but was usually not the principal causal agent. This category would include drunken driving, skid row pathological drinking (nonaddictive), public drunkenness, boisterous behavior, and heavy or excessive drinking. In this residual category, alcoholism might be present, but it was not equivalent with, or perhaps even significant for, such behavior.[43]

From the very beginning of the alcoholism movement, the almost unanimous position was that moderate or "social" drinking and alcohol itself were not the problem. This message was constantly and emphatically signalled by the various publications coming from the Center of Alcohol Studies and its representatives. Even though alcoholics could not exist without alcohol, the uncontrovertible evidence of millions of normal drinkers was seen as prima facie evidence that alcohol or drinking did not cause alcoholism. The executive director of the National Committee for Education on Alcoholism, Marty Mann, stated in one of her first public pronouncements that the alcoholism movement was "a rational approach—which in no way need enter—in fact should not enter—the controversial field of alcohol as a beverage."[44] Bacon noted in 1947 that of the estimated 65 million drinkers in the country, more than 60 million experienced no problem.[45] Similarly, in 1958 Keller noted that alcoholism "involves drinking and, almost always, drunkenness; but not all drinking or drunkenness involves alcoholism. There are people who occasionally or even with some frequency drink to excess and become more or less intoxicated, and who nevertheless are not alcoholic. And of course the vast majority of drinkers are not alcoholics."[46] Robert Bales, whose seminal 1946 article on culture and alcoholism is one of the most widely quoted in the literature, likewise argues that high rates of alcohol consumption do not necessarily mean high rates of alcoholism.[47]

The recurrence in the alcoholism literature of the litany, "alcohol is not the problem" and "the vast majority of persons drink without problems," deserves very serious attention by students of alcohol policy. It is easy to forget what a sharp change this represents. For almost one hundred years drinking was seen as increasingly problematic, and was eventually defined as disruptive of the entire social order. Then, in a very short period after Repeal alcohol and its use had been legitimated within the new dominant national culture. The alcoholism movement, however, cannot to any significant extent be credited with what was actually a major cultural and economic transformation of the American landscape. The central achievement of the alcoholism movement was to present a set of explanations that fit the new situation and new set of cultural values. The new area of definition was *loss of control.*

Losing Control over Alcohol

Nearly three decades after the beginnings of the alcoholism movement, Nils Christie and Kettil Bruun were to observe that, while with alcoholism we talk about "bad users," with other drugs we talk about "bad substances."[48] The way this occurred is easy to understand. The vast majority of adults in most advanced industrial societies, and certainly in the United States, drink alcohol beverages, at least occasionally. Most of these drinkers do not experience problems with alcohol. Hence, it seems only natural to ask: What is it about certain people that causes them to experience problems?

The answer given almost universally by the major figures in the alcoholism movement has been that the problem users lack some attribute that the nonproblem drinking majority possesses. This attribute is in most cases termed an ability, capacity, or control; most commonly the alcoholic has lost "control" over alcohol. Other definitions refer to being powerless or losing the power of choice over alcohol.

The powerlessness explanation is exemplified by the First Step of the "Twelve Steps" Alcoholics Anonymous recommends to recovering alcoholics: "We admitted that we were powerless over alcohol—that our lives had become unmanageable."[49] Similarly, in her *Primer on Alcoholism*, Marty Mann defines alcoholics as those individuals who have lost the "power of choice" over their drinking.[50]

Another cluster of attributes can be illustrated by the work of Mark Keller, who has been responsible for a number of influential definitions of alcoholism. In 1960, Keller defined alcoholism as a "psychogenic dependence on or a psychological addiction to ethanol manifested by the inability of the alcoholic consistently to control either the start of drinking or its termination once started."[51] The report of the U.S. Cooperative Commission on the Study of Alcohol Problems appearing in 1968 likewise defined alcoholism as a "condition in which an individual has lost control over his alcohol intake in the sense he is consistently unable to refrain from drinking or to stop drinking before getting intoxicated."[52]

Both of these loss-of-control definitions owe a great deal to Marconi's influential review of the concept of alcoholism that appeared in the *Quarterly Journal* in 1958. In the process of defining alcoholism, Marconi referred to a physical dependence manifested by either the "inability to stop drinking" once started or the "inability to abstain" from drinking in the first place.[53] This notion of an inability to abstain from drinking was a crucial addition to the idea of alcoholism, as Keller pointed out in a summary of the work of many decades. Keller believed that if the loss-of-control phenomenon was restricted to behavior occurring only after the ingestion of alcohol, there were little grounds for labeling alcoholism a disease.[54] Presumably this was because loss of control after drinking does not speak to the question of why the drinking starts again when the alcoholic knows he cannot stop. For Keller, as for Mann many years earlier, the alcoholic had lost the power of choice, of autonomy, over alcohol.

Some of the early scientific formulations of the concept of alcoholism did not put so much emphasis on the loss of autonomy. In 1952, for example, an international scientific committee working under the auspices of the World Health Organization came up with this famous definition of alcoholism:

> Alcoholism is any form of drinking which in its extent goes beyond the traditional and customary "dietary" use, or the ordinary compliance with the social drinking customs of the whole community concerned, irrespective of the etiological factors leading to such behavior and irrespective also of the extent to which such etiological factors are dependent upon heredity, constitution, or acquired physiological and metabolic influences.

The WHO definition goes on to say that alcoholics are those

> excessive drinkers whose dependence upon alcohol has attained such a degree that it shows a noticeable mental disturbance or an interference with their bodily and mental health, their interpersonal relations, and their smooth social and economic functioning; or who show the prodromal signs of such development.[55]

Similarly, Keller's 1958 definition only implies inability or incapacity by referring to the alcoholic's repeated violation of community drinking norms. Keller was clearly following the WHO line:

> Alcoholism is a chronic behavioral disorder manifested by repeated drinking of alcoholic beverages in excess of the dietary and social uses of the community and to an extent that interferes with the drinker's health or his social or economic functioning.[56]

The sociologist John Seeley severely criticized the WHO definition in the *Quarterly Journal*. Noting that the WHO definition ignored the actual intake of alcohol, he argued that such an approach does not permit investigators an opportunity to discover individuals who are exposed to similar and heavy amounts of alcohol and who might share other biological attributes:

> The utility of such a relativistic-sociologic approach is . . . open to grave question. Applied in rigor, it lumps together a member of a teetotaling "community concerned" who takes one drink, and the highest-intake messmate in a regularly free-drinking mess. . . . [It is] vain to speak in this connection of traditional and customary . . . use. The very existence of statute law in a given domain is evidence that custom and tradition have disappeared or become attenuated, and that the "community" of which they were an expression has largely disappeared.[57]

Seeley need not have been concerned. There were already a number of definitions appearing (Marconi, Keller) that ignored the reference to community standards and focused more exclusively on the loss of control of the alcoholics. Even the WHO had shifted more toward this direction by the mid-fifties. The criteria of violation of community norms passed from wide usage, and one's "smooth social and economic functioning" came to mean drinking without problems.

Conclusion

Most scholars have accepted without question that the central goal of the alcoholism movement was to redefine habitual drunkenness as a medical, rather than a moral, problem. A main theme of this book is that this is too limited a view of the movement's specific purpose and import. The movement constructed a theory of alcohol problems that accommodated the rise to dominance of what Gusfield, Bell, and Hofstadter have termed *cultural modernism*. The modernist was basically uninterested in the problems of alcohol; he was interested in the disappearance of alcohol as a central problem in American life.[58] The alcoholism movement accommodated this shift in the dominant cultural outlook with a reductionist explanation for alcohol problems that banished all talk about the danger of the substance and based the problem on the victim. (We take up this theme of the movement in more detail in the next two chapters.)

It is also a thesis of this book that the concept of alcoholism is under increasing pressure to change. The stereotypes of the alcoholic and normal drinker are beginning to fade. There is new and serious effort to reintroduce alcohol to alcoholism policy. This shift is not a return to traditional modes of thought about alcohol ("neo-Prohibition") simply because it restores alcohol to the paradigm. The victory of modernism in achieving liberation of the individual from close social control in matters of personal conduct seems secure. But what does seem to be occurring is a broad recognition that our explanation for alcohol problems must include legal, economic, and social influences on the rates of problems and total consumption. A major element in this change may well be our entry into the "Age of Less." A shift seems to be occurring that challenges the dream of a limitless vista for the unbounded self and the unlimited promise of leisure, consumption, and personal gratification.

II. The Alcohol Alibi

With the discovery of the notion that drinking is not a problem for most people, the belief that alcohol is a social problem was forgotten. One is hard pressed to find any discussion of alcohol policy as a problem in the literature of the alcoholism movement, or anywhere else for that matter.[1]

The changes overtaking American society even before the end of Prohibition were making alcohol less visible as a social problem. Among these changes, Norman Clark notes the disappearance of the saloon as the symbol of alcohol as a major social issue.[2] Replacing the saloon in American thinking was *social drinking*, or the idea that for most people drinking was not a problem. Almost all forms of public drinking behavior and the entire paraphernalia of drinking became legitimated. The presence of alcohol in society, its sale and purchase for use by individual members, drinking in a wide variety of public places, intoxication, becoming ill, hangovers—none of these acts or their occasions were evidence of alcohol as a public problem nor a sign that drinking could not be controlled. Alcohol was unique among pharmacological agents in that its use for self-administered intoxication was almost universally accepted. There were approximately 100,000,000 users of alcohol in the United States by the end of the 1970s and the consumer expenditure for alcoholic beverages was over $35 billion. The alcohol industry, which had been the object of sustained and unrelenting attack during the Prohibition years, quietly slipped out of public attention.

By contrast, in the late 1960s drugs became one of the truly salient issues of American life and indeed, along with the Vietnam

War, dominated much of American politics. The difference in the public's perception and definition of these two problems is revealing. On the one hand, drug abuse was visualized as something like an invading epidemic, coming from outside the community. The experience was viewed as beyond that of "normal" community members, and its substance (the needle, the weed) and users (long hairs, hippies) were strange and alien.

On the other hand, the issue of alcoholism remained buried in the community. This invisibility seems related to the way in which alcoholism became defined as an inner failure of a minority of drinkers, and to the simultaneous removal of drinking and alcohol as a major social problem. The materials of the drinking experience were not at all alien; they were common to the community, legitimated and domesticated.

In retrospect there is an eerie sense of unreality to cover stories on the "Heroin Plague" and the deafening silence regarding alcohol. When the issue of alcohol did surface, it was either to make the point that, although alcohol problems were far more serious than drug problems, alcohol was nonetheless legal, or to make such invidious comparisons as the title of John Kaplan's book, *Marijuana —The New Prohibition*.[3] In fact, the first major call for an investigation of the society's alcohol control laws came from the National Commission on Marihuana and Drug Abuse in 1972.[4]

The alcoholism movement devoted itself for the most part to establishing local, mainly outpatient, clinics; to setting up state alcoholism commissions, which served mostly as sources of information and publicity for the disease concept; to establishing small state alcoholism treatment programs during the 1950s; and, in such locales as Washington, D.C., and St. Louis, to debating the issue of public drunkenness,[5] which came to light during the riots in the cities because of complaints of crime commissions about the burden it placed on local police and courts.[6] But as for alcohol policy, there was almost no interest.

The alcoholism movement itself cannot be credited with this massive inattention to alcohol policy, but it certainly devoted substantial energy to legitimating the view that, since personal control over drinking was a fact of life for most drinkers, alcohol was not a social problem. In Chapter IV, we will look more closely at the consequences of taking a behavioral view of alcohol consumption. This chapter will examine how it was that this disappearance of a social problem was actually accomplished, how by blaming the alcoholic for society's alcohol problems we alibied the new status quo for alcohol.

Alcohol and Cultural Change

The relatively recent disappearance of alcohol as an issue on the national agenda must be placed in the context of a century and a half of frenzied attention to alcohol. The literature on the Temperance movement has been largely unsympathetic, treating the entire period as a great aberration in the American experience. But a more balanced literature exists, and it is growing. There is James H. Timberlake's *Prohibition and the Progressive Movement*, Joseph Gusfield's *Symbolic Crusade*, Norman Clark's more recent *Deliver Us from Evil*, and John C. Burnham's "New Perspective on the Prohibition 'Experiment' of the 1920s." There is also the work of Richard Hofstadter and Daniel Bell, who discuss Prohibition in their writings on status politics and the rise of modernity in American society.[7] Temperance is more and more seen as a very complex and protean movement, not easy to fit into one category.

Understanding the rise and purposes of Temperance is not the purpose of this book, but it is important to place the alcoholism movement within the context of cultural change and cultural politics that has occurred in American society. The Temperance movement seems to have arisen during a period when two major changes began to accelerate. The first was the beginning of the decline of Colonial America as a pre-industrial, agrarian society, an upheaval of a magnitude perhaps not appreciated until recent years. Coupled with this great transformation was the intensification of the drinking customs of the agrarian order, where the use of alcohol seems to have reached truly astonishing levels when compared to modern standards.[8]

In Colonial America, alcohol was a widely accepted and important part of everyday life, central to the family, community, and work. Alcohol was considered the "good creature of God," and drunkenness, except within the gaze of the Puritan leaders of New England, was seen as a natural and thoroughly pleasant part of drinking. The seventeenth and eighteenth centuries in England and the United States saw sharp increases in public drunkenness, perhaps due to the increasing use and importance of distilled beverages, principally rum and whiskey in the United States, and there were strong sermons against drunkenness in New England, and fines and punishment elsewhere, though with little success. All the turbulence, however, did not seem to occasion the belief that the social order was threatened. As Clark observes,

> This lack of any urgent and general social concern suggests that among the truly benign luxuries of the agrarian, preindustrial world, at least beyond New England, were alcohol, and an established church and a traditional technology. . . . The traditional, preindustrial arts of medicine did not doom a man to worry about the color of his liver, and the techniques of work and play specified not more than a very few chores or pleasures which required an icy sobriety.[9]

Widely used as a medicine and as an alternative to a sometimes dangerous water supply, in a culture where the cycle of daily work was often interrupted for grog time and where the tavern promised warmth and hearty conviviality, alcohol was common, and more often than not unremarkable, in Colonial America. The established customs of drinking were intensified by several short-term factors after the Revolutionary War. Farmers found it more profitable to distill their grain as whiskey and transport it westward than to sell it for food. Furthermore, the importation of rum increased sharply during the period 1790–1800, and domestic production increased as well, contributing to a sharp increase in consumption. While accurate statistics are difficult to come by, Clark has estimated that at the opening of the nineteenth century, Americans were drinking ten gallons of absolute alcohol per capita. Others set it nearer six.[10] (The present U.S. level is nearly 2.7 gallons, while France's is 5.75 gallons.)

The breakup of the Colonial order was accompanied by a new surge in immigration, the westward movement of the population, and the beginnings of industrialization. The nineteenth century was a time of cheap land, the cotton gin, the textile mills of New England, the rise of the industrial north, and the factory. As Clark puts it, it was a period when people began to accept the fact that women went to work in factories and children worked in mines.[11] Temperance was a force of protest against these vast changes in American society, an attempt to blame alcohol for a lost stability and social order. Over the next one hundred years (until the end of Prohibition in 1933), Temperance has variously been linked with Abolition and other reform movements, with the Progressive movement, with the reformist attacks upon the costs of industrialism, with the Populists, and finally and most memorably with the voices of cultural retrenchment and fundamentalism.

During the Temperance and Prohibition eras, according to Daniel Bell, the saloon was the dominant symbol of American politics. To the Anti-Saloon League, the saloon signified the urban immigrants and their drinking habits; to the Progressives it represented the corruptions of the urban political machines; to the Populist it stood for the debilitating effects of urban life. The cultural fundamentalists finally prevailed, espousing the point of view of a small-town, rural, and largely Protestant America, fearful of yet another major social revolution.[12]

In turn, the fundamentalists were overruled by the cultural modernists, representing the point of view of sophisticated, cosmopolitan urbanites dedicated not to compulsive production but to compulsive consumption. Gusfield defines these two central types, modernists and fundamentalists, as follows:

> The cultural fundamentalist is the defender of tradition. Although he is identified with rural doctrines, he is found in both city and country. The fundamentalist is attuned to the traditional patterns as they are transmitted within family, neighborhood, and local organizations. His stance is inward, toward his immediate environment. The cultural modernist looks outward, to the media of mass communications, the national organizations, the colleges and universities, and the influences which originate outside the local community. Each see the other as a contrast. The modernist reveres the future and change as good. The fundamentalist reveres the past and sees change as damaging and upsetting.[13]

The social changes and the prosperity of the twenties, added to the growing political power of the urban, immigrant, and largely Democratic voters, only sharpened the tensions between the fundamentalists and the modernists. For one thing, as Bell notes, 1920 was the first year in American history when a majority of persons lived in "urban territory."[14] The urban modernists rejected restrictions in the areas of pleasure, especially drinking, dress, smoking, and codes of sexual conduct. These concerns were not simply valued in themselves; they became the very symbols of the revolt against small-town life and its hypocrisy. Indulgence and pleasure meshed easily with rising incomes, increased prosperity, and the limited but real emancipation of women. The Great Depression failed to stop this movement; it only administered the *coup de grace* to the fundamentalists' vision of self-reliance, and solidified the political power of the new urban majorities. What was required was a theory of alcohol problems that fit this new cultural era, one that was consistent with its rejection of a village morality and that stressed a "non-moral" and "scientific" approach to alcohol problems.

Redefining Problems

In his important article challenging the established belief that the concept of loss of control and addiction was not a familiar idea to those in the Temperance movement, Harry Gene Levine argues that the concept of addiction began to emerge near the end of the eighteenth century in this country and that, in fact, the Temperance movement repeatedly resorted to the idea.[15]

In this regard, Temperance stands in sharp contrast to the previous period, when those individuals, mainly Protestant ministers, who railed against alcohol specifically argued that habitual drunkenness was in fact "desired" by the drunkard. (As Rorabaugh points out, eighteenth-century America, for the most part, was not troubled by habitual drunkenness, since it saw drunkenness as a normal concomitant of drinking.)[16] For example, Jonathan Edwards, in his *Freedom of the Will*, denied emphatically the idea that a distinction could be made between "desire" and "will": "A man never, in any instance, wills anything contrary to his desires, or desires anything contrary to his will. . . . His will and desire do not run counter at all: the thing which he wills, the very same he desires."[17] As Levine points out, Edwards specifically illustrated his points with the drunkard, arguing in effect that the drunkard chooses to behave the way he does and denying the possibility that some persons could be irresistibly compelled to drink:

> Thus, when a drunkard has his liquor before him, and he has to choose whether to drink or no. . . . If he wills to drink, then drinking is the proper object of the act of his Will; and drinking, on some account or other, now appears most agreeable to him, and suits him best. If he chooses to refrain, then refraining is the immediate object of his Will and is most pleasing to him.[18]

Levine suggests that Temperance was more concerned with the habitual drunkard and the dangers of addiction than the historians have previously reported. Can it be that Temperance, Prohibition, and the logic of alcoholism are not so very different after all? This may be true, but it does not help explain why so much emphasis was focused on the impact of alcohol on the family, the workplace, and finally the liquor "trusts" and the saloon.[19]

The Loss-of-Control Issue

Examined superficially, the emphasis in the alcoholism movement upon loss of control appears strikingly similar to the Temperance notion of addiction. Levine quotes Dr. Benjamin Rush on this point:

> When strongly urged, by one of his friends, to leave off drinking [an habitual drunkard] said, "Were a keg of rum in one corner of a room, and were a cannon constantly discharging balls between me and it, I could not refrain from passing before that cannon, in order to get at the rum."[20]

As Levine rightly argues, this is strikingly parallel to the modern view. For example, Mark Keller says:

> Therefore one can say that the essential loss of control is that an alcoholic cannot consistently choose whether he shall drink or not. There comes an occasion when he is powerless, when

he cannot help drinking. For that is the essence or nature of a drug addiction.[21]

It is the virtue of Levine's analysis that it permits a closer scrutiny of just where Temperance thinking and alcoholism as a concept run parallel, and where they diverge sharply. He compares the work of the Temperance movement to those who "discovered" the asylum:

Like asylum advocates, temperance supporters were interested in helping people develop and maintain control over their behavior and actions. Temperance supporters, however, believed they had located, in liquor, the source of most social problems. The Temperance Movement, it should be remembered, was the largest enduring mass movement in 19th-century America. And it was an eminently mainstream middle-class affair. The Temperance Movement appealed to so many people, in part, because it had become a "fact of life" that one could lose control of one's behavior. Even the use of the word "temperance" for a total abstinence movement is understandable when we realize that the chief concern of temperance advocates, and of the middle class in general, was self-restraint. Liquor was evil, a demon, because its short- and long-run effect was to prevent drinkers from living moderate, restrained, temperate lives. In A.A.'s terms, it made their lives "unmanageable."

In the 19th century, the concept of addiction was interpreted by people in light of their struggles with their own desires. The idea of addiction "made sense" not only to drunkards, who came to understand themselves as individuals with overwhelming desires they could not control, but also to great numbers of middle-class people who were struggling to keep their desires in check—desires which at times seemed "irresistible." Given the structural requirements of daily life for self-reliant, self-making entrepreneurs and their families, and the assumptions of the individualistic middle-class world view, *it seemed a completely reasonable idea that liquor, a substance believed to weaken inhibitions when consumed (intoxication), could also deprive people of the ability to control their behavior over the long run (addiction)*[22] [my emphasis].

This passage is remarkable for its insights into Temperance and the nineteenth-century situation. It is also remarkable for its failure to emphasize the crucial distinction between Temperance and contemporary thought about alcoholism. Levine notes the parallels between Temperance writers, who argued that even moderate drinking (sometimes even one drink) would lead inevitably to intemperance, and A.A. members, who argue the same point. But this similarity masks a profound difference. The A.A. philosophy of abstinence in no way constitutes a general stance on alcohol but only on its effects on a small group of individuals. The Temperance writers advocated temperance because they believed that drinking could not be controlled in principle, that addiction was a problem for nearly everyone. In Levine's words, Temperance writers "believed they had located, in liquor, the source of most social problems."[23] It was a "fact of life" that liquor could deprive most people of "the ability to control their behavior over the long run."[24]

This is a strikingly different view from contemporary notions about alcoholism. In the contemporary or modern idea of alcoholism, it is a "fact of life" that most people have personal control of their drinking. Loss of control, addiction, and so on are problems only for a minority of drinkers. Thus, both the modern alcoholism movement and Temperance freely employed such terms as "compulsion," "loss of control," "addiction," in their talk about alcohol problems; but it is only with the concept of alcoholism that the central locus of explanation became seated within the make-up of individuals and not in alcohol as a substance.

Yet another way to appreciate the difference between Temperance views of alcohol and the modern view is to look at the contrast between our view of heroin addiction and our view of alcoholism. Heroin addiction is viewed as a substance problem; most persons are seen as liable for addiction if exposed to the drug. When we say that heroin produces "loss of control" in its victims, we seldom define that as a loss of control over heroin, because heroin is not a substance that everyday logic sees as controllable. When used in the Temperance or heroin context, then, "loss of control" refers to loss of control over behavior generally; in the alcoholism context, it refers to loss of control over a specific substance, alcohol, an idea that only has meaning when it has become a "fact of life" that most people can control their use of alcohol.

Kinds-of-People Explanations

The alcoholism movement's shift in emphasis was, in actuality, a resort to a different form of explanation for alcohol problems—what Albert Cohen calls *kinds-of-people explanations*.[25] The movement required an explanation that protected normal drinking from unwanted restrictions on the individual's use of alcohol, while excusing the alcoholic's behavior. This apparently tricky task was solved rather simply by the use of the form of explanation we normally employ in explaining illness.

It is by now a commonplace that illness is a social concept.[26] As members of a common culture we have constructed an everyday logic aimed at understanding the phenomena of being "ill" or "incapacitated." One of the central criteria for labeling behavior "illness" is that it not be motivated. The ill, unlike the criminal, must not be seen as striving for a value.[27]

Typically we see this disability as temporary in nature and as occurring because of some factor in the environment. The individual in question is less likely to be stigmatized, since his disability is neither permanent nor self-inflicted. What is more, those individuals who are not sick (not disabled) are seen as, in some general sense, capable of fulfilling their normal role expectations.

A rough distinction, at least in terms of everyday logic, can be drawn between disease and illness. Typically, disease is what in everyday logic produces illness. The opposite of disease is, in most cases (but not all), the mere absence of disease. In the case of illness, however, the situation is somewhat more complicated, at least usually. Those who are not disabled are "abled," and this does not simply mean freedom from some condition but the positive presence of some general capacity or ability to meet their role obligations as members of society. This is because, in the case of disease, what is being contrasted is the presence or absence of some condition; in the case of illness, what is being contrasted is the presence or absence of some capacity, ability, or faculty that is central to the functioning of the individual as a moral agent.

This difference is marked by the very different way we think of those who are ill and the way we normally think of actors in the everyday world with rights, duties, and so forth. Again, the distinction can be made by comparing the criminal and the sick. Sickness, unlike criminality, is a condition that occupies space and time.[28] We talk about illness in much the same way we talk about physical objects, granting it an entity status. The defining characteristics of the criminal have location in neither space nor time. The criminal is discussed, at least usually, in terms of actions, choices, and events, not in terms of some enduring attributes built upon the model of physical objects (unless, of course, we mean to speak of the criminal as if he were sick). As Aubert and Messinger have put it, when we come to illness, we depart from our usual way of describing actors and actions and talk about "being ill" in naturalistic, entity-like terms.[29]

We employ this language of objectification to describe the phenomena of alcoholism. The early attempts to define alcoholism as the mere violation of community norms was replaced for the most part with language that treated alcoholism as a condition, a condition usually described in terms of traits or attributes of the alcoholic. If these were not treated as actually physical in nature (biochemical, hereditary, etc.), they still were described as psychological states that persisted in space and time. In other words, we have developed over the years a naturalistic language to talk about alcoholics, much as we have for most other types of illness.

But the equally important point is that we have largely succeeded in talking about social drinking in the same naturalistic way. Thus the social drinker and the alcoholic are described as two fundamental types possessing rather fixed and permanent characteristics. Normal or social drinkers possess a personal capacity to control their drinking, and it is this stable characteristic that makes them more or less invulnerable to problems. These individuals may have been born with the ability or have learned how to control their drinking as members of a drinking culture. Alcoholics and social drinkers, therefore, do not differ simply because they are two types of individuals, one type observing the rules or norms for drinking for the most part and the other type repetitively and chronically violating the rules. These two individual types differ in *kind*; they are two different "kinds of people."

Modernity and Personal Competence

It is no accident that we commonly speak of persons being "able" to control their drinking: Abilities, skills, and capacities have entity-like status and can be roughly assimilated to the idiom of physical reality. Despite Levine's arguments that the Temperance movement discovered "addiction," one wonders whether it is wise to compare this mode of thinking to the modern point of view. It is possible to believe that one can lose control of one's behavior, without accepting the specifically modern mode of thought that leans so heavily on metaphors of illness and incapacity and on loose analogies with physical or natural objects. The Temperance era, while not totally ignorant of this mode of thought, was likely to see norm compliance as the result of diligence, self-restraint, and will—not skill or competence. The modern view is more likely to see achievements as a result of natural assets and attribute them to faculties, skills, competences, or abilities. When modern man says that behavior can be controlled, he often means that something (in our case alcohol) that is, or was, perceived as problematic is now perceived as controllable. Particularly with the rise of modernity and the impulse to release the self from the idea of either external or internal fetters (at least in many matters), the idea of will became much less dominant and was increasingly replaced with the idea of capacity, ability. It is probably not possible to enumerate with any precision all the specific reasons for this shift, but they surely include reasons like the rise of psychoanalysis and psychiatric modes of thought, modern ideas of disease causation, and the continuing and enduring emphasis in American culture on individualistic modes of thought. The point is that the emphasis on will as a central feature of explanation declined with the drive to free the individual from restraints on personal life and to excuse those who violated rules or norms from blame. What arose was an emphasis on differences between individuals based in terms of their natures and physical traits rather than their character.

The concept of alcoholism helped shift attention away from the substance of alcohol, serving the ideological function of supporting the new status quo for alcohol by "blaming the alcoholic" for society's alcohol problems (but excusing their behavior). This was never a very conscious process. Indeed, the idea that most people could personally control their drinking seemed obvious. But behind this "veil of obviousness" lay the ideological functions of alcoholism: to endorse the new order for alcohol by locating the source of America's alcohol problems within the skin of the alcoholic.

Contemporary Ideas of Disease Causation

This emphasis on individual ability or inability suggests that if we are to understand the concept of alcoholism we should look, not to the emergence of the concept of addiction, but rather to such concepts as "accident proneness," "immunity," "vulnerability," and "susceptibility." As Vickers has pointed out, modern medicine has shifted more and more toward looking for the individual basis of disease:

> The study of psychosomatic disease leads medicine to view an increasing field of illness as highly individual behavior, the response of a particular person to a situation to which he is vulnerable. Even having an accident is coming to be regarded as a form of such behavior. The concept of accident proneness plays an important part in industrial medicine, and its exploration provides ever more material to answer the question, "Why me?"[30]

Immunity

One of the most profound changes in our ways of thinking about disease began to occur after the appearance of innoculation technology in the eighteenth and nineteenth centuries. This new technology can be seen as the beginning of change in the relationship between the categories of *agent*, *host*, and *environment*. Previously, the agent or outside influence was seen as a general hazard. Great emphasis was placed upon securing protection from these dangerous influences through separation, sanitation, or other physical barriers. All individuals were believed potentially vulnerable; the emphasis was upon constructing barriers outside them.

Gradually, as the mechanism of immunity began to be more clearly understood, we came to appreciate two significant facts.

When exposed to harmful agents, the body can, in special circumstances, develop protective mechanisms (antibodies, for example) against these agents. They can, in a word, acquire *immunity*, where this means some sort of specific individual, biological protection.

We also learned that human beings are frequently exposed to agents of many serious diseases without becoming symptomatic. Of those exposed to tuberculosis, for example, only a minority develop disease. This knowledge, added to the growing advances in immunization technology, produced a shift away from emphasis on controlling the agent or pathogen and toward a better understanding of why a minority of those exposed to infectious agents became infected.[31]

As the science of immunology has progressed, more and more of our ideas of disease have accommodated this notion. In his delightful *Lives of the Cell*, Lewis Thomas pokes fun at our great fear of "germs," a fear that is generously exploited on television by deodorant and disinfectant manufacturers.[32] Thomas sees these "paranoid" delusions as due to our "need for outside enemies" as well as our memory of how things used to be with "lobar pneumonia, meningococcal meningitis, streptococcal infections, diphtheria, endocarditis, . . . syphilis, and, always, everywhere, tuberculosis. Most of these have now left most of us, thanks to antibiotics, plumbing, civilization, and money, but we remember."[33]

Thomas goes on to point out that during epidemics, meningococci for the most part cause few problems for the host population of humans. It is "only in the *unaccountable minority*, the 'cases,' that the line is crossed, and then there is the devil to pay."[34] Later, in discussing the public misconception of the power of modern medicine, Thomas argues that, for most problems, things get better of their own accord, without the intervention of some outside chemical agent or other therapy. We thus "are paying too little attention, and respect, to the built-in durability and sheer power of the human organism."

René Dubos, who has best captured the shifts in our thinking about disease, has the following to say about the transformations in ideas of causation:

> The sciences concerned with microbial diseases have developed almost exclusively from the study of acute or semi-acute

infectious processes caused by virulent microorganisms acquired through exposure to an exogenous source of infection. In contrast, the microbial diseases most common in our communities today arise from the activities of microorganisms that are ubiquitous in the environment, persist in the body without causing any obvious harm under ordinary circumstances, and exert pathological effects only when the infected person is under conditions of physiological stress. In such a type of microbial disease, the event of infection is of less importance than the hidden manifestations of the smouldering infectious process and than the physiological disturbances that convert latent infection into overt symptoms and pathology. This is the reason why the orthodox methods based on the classical doctrines of epidemiology, immunology, and chemotherapy are not sufficient to deal with the problem of endogenous diseases. The need is to develop procedures for reestablishing the state of equilibrium between host and parasite.[35]

The increased emphasis on disease as produced by errors in the human organism, which normally functions to resist disease, while a relatively recent one, has led to increased appreciation for the significance of the body's powers to withstand infection or to recover from infection—and the ubiquity of infectious agents. As Dubos indicates, our attention has shifted from the agent to processes occurring inside the human body, and to the differential capacities of individuals to withstand disease. Both in the past and now, only a minority of us succumbed. The point Thomas and Dubos seem to be making is that that minority has become very much smaller. But this is due to a number of things, only one of which is the miracle of the human body (a point Thomas especially tends to blur).

It is easy to see how the idea of the vulnerable minority would prove attractive, almost irresistible, to those thinking about broader social problems, especially alcoholism. For a movement that arose at a period when cultural modernism was newly ascendant, the shift in thinking about disease causation from an exclusive focus on the agent to questions of host vulnerability and susceptibility must have seemed a striking parallel to the modern way of thinking about alcohol problems. Thus it is no surprise to find analogies to contagious disease rather frequently in discussions of alcoholism, particularly when the point is somehow to discuss the role of alcohol as a necessary but clearly not sufficient explanation for why some people became alcoholic.

The Domesticated Drug and Immune Users

Reliance on metaphors of vulnerability and immunity can be found repeatedly in the alcoholism literature, and for some authors is quite explicit. John Gordon, a prominent epidemiologist and public health professional, in 1958 in the *New York State Journal of Medicine*, expressly compares the problem of alcoholism to that of tuberculosis.[36] Gordon notes that in both cases the vast majority of the population is exposed to the agent (alcohol and the bacillus), and in both cases this exposure produces an "infection," perhaps conferring a kind of immunity. The central issue is why a minority of those who are infected unaccountably become alcoholics or tubercular. Relying on the analogy, Gordon does not see the utility of measures to control the agent (of alcohol) itself, since this is so difficult and because only a few become acutely ill, and a 1969 publication from the branch of the National Institute of Mental Health that preceded the National Institute on Alcohol Abuse and Alcoholism reaffirms this theme: "Although alcoholism would be impossible without alcohol, alcohol can no more be considered its sole cause than marriage can be considered the sole cause of divorce, or the tubercle bacillus the sole cause of tuberculosis."[37]

Perhaps the fullest analogy to infectious disease, and specifically tuberculosis, has been made by Morris Chafetz. In his book *Why Drinking Can Be Good for You*, Chafetz has the following to say about alcohol as the cause of alcoholism:

> For centuries, the focus was on the substance—alcohol. The belief that alcohol caused alcoholism was reinforced when specific organisms (for example, the tubercle bacillus in tuberculosis) were found to be related to the cause of some diseases. Since in Western societies the prevailing belief has been that human beings are basically weak-willed, it followed that exposure to the temptation of alcohol would inevitably

lead to alcoholism. And the reverse, of course, was true: Without alcohol there would be no alcoholism. Equally true: Without a tubercle bacillus, there would be no tuberculosis. And yet in both conditions (alcoholism and tuberculosis), exposure is unrelated to illness.

Most people have the tubercle bacillus within them, have not developed active tuberculosis. Most people drink and do not become alcoholic. This obvious fact shifted the focus, in a large way, to the person. What makes a person vulnerable? There are all kinds of theories—entire books have been written about the causes.

I believe that if you mix the pharmacologic action of alcohol, a person in physical, psychological, or social pain, and a society that is ambivalent, conflicted, and guilty about its use of alcohol, you have a working answer.

We know alcohol is a readily available anesthetic agent effective in temporarily relieving all types of pain, and that pain (from whatever origin) cries out for relief. We know a society's confusion over a substance often results in over-emphasizing its value. But we might ask: In America we're all exposed to the unhealthy focus on drinking, we all have alcohol, we all have pain—why do some people become alcoholics, while the vast majority do not?

Usually the added ingredient is being influenced by someone, often during the formative years, who set the model for solving problems with alcohol. Among two-thirds of all alcoholics, the model was someone very close.

Again, in this as other general observations, there are exceptions. And with some alcoholics it's hard to pinpoint the cause or causes of the problem.[38]

An Unaccountable Minority

For most authorities, the reference to ideas of immunity is not so explicit. However, the emphasis is still on an unaccountable minority who are vulnerable to problems. One of the early HEW reports places the same emphasis on the dichotomy of an immune majority and a small, vulnerable minority.

The overwhelming majority of drinkers in the United States—an estimated 90 percent of them—have apparently learned to consume alcoholic beverages without significant hazard to themselves, their families or society. Yet the problems caused by the relatively few who have chosen neither abstinence nor moderation, but have become excessive or problem drinkers, affect the entire American society. Although the ratio of problem drinkers to the total population is relatively small, their numbers are large. The misery they cause themselves and others is enormous.[39]

In Thomas Plaut's 1968 report for the Cooperative Commission on the Study of Alcoholism, *Alcohol Problems—A Report to the Nation*, the same litany is found. After a review of the significant differences in rates of alcoholism and problem drinking among groups who use alcohol, and the admission that attitudes and drinking practices may influence rates, the report states:

Clearly, people would not become problem drinkers in an alcohol-free society. In this sense the alcohol is a necessary condition for the development of problem drinking. On the other hand, since the vast majority of alcohol users do not become problem drinkers, other factors—biological, psychological, and sociological—must be involved in the development of the disorder.[40]

In an article entitled "The Process of Addiction to Alcohol," under the section "The Problem of Explanation," Selden Bacon has this to say: "The action-of-alcohol plus a-user-of-alcohol, although forming a necessary precondition to alcoholism, does not provide a sufficient explanation; for example, only 1 of 15, or 20, or 25 users becomes an alcoholic."[41] Bacon notes that the most effective predictors are social categories: Irish and Anglo-Americans show higher rates of alcoholism than American Jews and Italian-Americans. But "even this approach is little more than a first step":

It may be true, granted a national average among males in the U.S.A. of 6 or 7 alcoholics among 100 alcohol users, that Anglo-Americans and Irish-Americans for decades provide 9 or 10 alcoholics per 100 male drinkers while Jewish Americans provide only 1 or 2 per 300; but the explanatory power is not very great. There are Jewish male alcoholics and, perhaps more significantly, 90 out of 100 male Irish-American and Anglo-American drinkers do not become alcoholics. [42]

This way of conceptualizing the problem of explanation in the field of alcoholism is well-nigh universal. Bacon ignores the intriguing distinctions between different groups and their rates of problems as sources of theory on alcohol abuse, and instead puts the emphasis on the fact that most persons do not become alcoholics. The impression generated is that despite differences between groups, the important difference lies between a majority that apparently suffers no harm and a vulnerable minority that accounts for most of the problems.

For Bacon, this unaccountable and vulnerable minority of alcoholics were not even drinkers. In an article with the provocative title "Alcoholics Do Not Drink" (1958), Bacon elaborated on this theme: "He is no more a drinker than a kleptomaniac is a customer or a pyromaniac is a campfire girl. Alcoholics may consume alcohol. They do not drink." [43] Bacon suggested that alcoholics share none of the "normal" or "healthy" motives of the vast majority of social drinkers. The drinker (read social drinker) indulges in a social practice that, with few exceptions, involves two or more participants. In order to be socially functional the drinking habits of one of the participants must be satisfying to the others. The essential social meaning or significance of drinking lies in the reciprocal set of satisfactions derived by the participants. Furthermore, as Bacon pointed out, the social exchanges involved in drinking usually occur on legitimated occasions and in legitimated settings, with familiar and legitimate paraphernalia—such as mugs, glasses, kegs, and signs—and accompanying behaviors—such as singing, sociability, and good fellowship. [44] Besides the social meanings and functions of drinking, there are individual (nonsocial) rewards such as mild tranquilization and relaxation. Essentially, however, social drinking is shaped by a concrete set of rules, paraphernalia, settings, and so forth that Bacon called the "drinking charter." [45] By contrast, the alcoholic consistently (repetitively, habitually) violates the drinking charter. The alcoholic, according to Bacon, lives in a different symbol universe, his drinking being an altogether different experience, so different, in fact, that the term drinking is not at all appropriate. [46]

This way of thinking about alcohol problems has been encouraged by the fact that the availability of alcohol in society must be taken into account. Differences in rates of problems among groups seem less significant than the fact that most drinkers do not experience problems. This conclusion might not have occurred so easily with such problems as suicide or crime (here we tend to find rate explanations). But for alcoholism, the infection metaphor as a mode of explanation seems intuitively correct: alcohol is the agent; the drinker is the host; and since only a small fraction of those exposed to the agent experience problems, the source of the problem must lie in the differential vulnerability of some hosts.

The Integration Hypothesis

Using such frameworks, in time the alcoholism movement began to develop a set of ideas about how the majority of drinkers remained free of problems. The result was to further domesticate alcohol and render it less problematic. This set of ideas—usually called the *integration hypothesis*—also sought to shed light on how a minority of individual drinkers still developed serious alcohol problems, that is, alcoholism.

As Bruce Johnson has pointed out, a small group of researchers, state alcoholism directors, clergy, and others who were unhappy with the exclusive focus on the disease aspects of alcoholism and treatment were chiefly responsible for the development of the integration hypothesis, or what is also known as the *ambivalence* theory of alcohol problems.[47] This group secured a grant for what ultimately became the Cooperative Commission on the Study of Alcohol Problems and its study, published in 1968 as *Alcohol Problems*. Ultimately, the group's ideas formed the foundation for both the prevention theories of Morris Chafetz (and his policy of "responsible drinking") and the call for a consensus on drinking and a national educational campaign by the Education Commission of the States.[48]

In part, these ideas and groups were something of a break with the "orthodox" alcoholism movement. The belief was that, in addition to the problem of alcoholism, research should focus on the categories of "problem drinking" and "social drinking." This early development within the movement was already a sign of impatience with the rigidity inherent in the concept of alcoholism, a rigidity that policymakers especially would find restricting. The important point, however, is that at the outset the focus was on both the integration of alcohol into American culture and our ambivalent attitudes toward it.

The Idea of Ambivalence

Actually, the differences between the "orthodox" alcoholism position and the integration hypothesis are too easily overemphasized. It is true that those focusing on the idea of ambivalence were not as concerned with clear-cut distinctions between the phenomenon of addiction (alcoholism) and "problem drinking"—a rather loose term suggesting problems with alcohol but not necessarily classical "loss of control"—as the "orthodox" voices were. In addition, they did not emphasize ambivalence for the purpose of creating an identifiable entity called alcoholism. Nevertheless, most of those looking at the broader issues of drinking and culture still called for treating alcoholism as a disease for which treatment services should be provided.

The integration hypothesis was constructed from some rather durable ideas that have been with the alcoholism literature since the founding of the movement. The idea of ambivalence is just such an example. In 1940, Abraham Myerson wrote that a primary source of alcohol problems was our cultural heritage of ambivalent attitudes toward alcohol.[49] On the one hand we had the "ascetic" tradition, which was reflected in Temperance and Prohibition; this tradition taught the denial and fear of pleasure and specifically abstinence from alcohol. On the other hand, our culture (as most others) has also had a strong hedonistic tradition, a tradition that encourages the use of alcohol for pleasure and intoxication. Both of these trends or values have formed a sort of witch's brew in our cultural milieu, creating conflicting attitudes toward the substance—encouraging unrestrained intoxication in some settings and strict abstinence in others. The result has been confusion, uncertainty, guilt, and a host of other problems. Myerson argued for a third way, a Hegelian synthesis of asceticism and hedonism that would be temperance.

In 1945, Robert Bales wrote an influential paper in which ambivalence also plays a part; the restrained use of alcohol in Jewish culture is favorably contrasted to the "utilitarian" or hedonistic drinking (drinking for intoxication) found in English, Irish, and American culture. Bales also explicitly rejected the idea that the amount a society drank was related to rates of alcoholism: "High rates of alcohol use do not necessarily mean high rates of alcoholism."[50]

A number of subsequent studies of drinking among Italians, Orthodox Jews, and the Irish repeated these themes: the important feature of alcohol use in a culture was not how much alcohol the society used, but rather the ways in which it used alcohol.[51] For example, the social scientist Albert Ullman, in an issue of the *Annals of the American Academy of Political and Social Science*, claimed that a culture will tend to have lower rates of alcohol problems when the rules governing the use of alcohol are clear, uniform, and not prohibitive; when members of the culture are exposed to alcohol at an early age and observe adults using alcohol in moderate amounts in settings that discourage the use of alcohol as an intoxicant (such as at meals or during religious ceremonies); and when the excessive use of alcohol including drunkenness is uniformly discouraged and proscribed.[52] Ullman's normative model came to be referred to as the "integration hypothesis." In this way, the new orthodoxy about the causes of alcoholism was codified.

Alcoholism and Cultural Norms

This set of ideas was not just a reaction against the narrow disease focus of the alcoholism movement; it was almost more a reaction against the legacy of Prohibition and against policies of alcohol control through law and regulation. These ideas began to take on a programmatic focus: alcohol and its use are not well integrated into American culture; attitudes toward the use of alcohol are ambivalent and inconsistent; where alcohol is well integrated into a culture (say, for the Italians or the Orthodox Jews), alcohol is widely used but there are few problems. In this paradigm, what seems to matter is not so much whether a culture uses alcohol or how much it uses, but how it uses it, where "how" means the functions, attitudes, motives, and consequences of that use.

To many, the problem was that there was in fact no clear consensus on drinking in this country (this was a principal point of the
Cooperative Commission in *Alcohol Problems*).[53] The ambivalence
theme writers tended to see the lack of consensus as largely the result of the excesses of the Prohibitionists and Temperance enthusi-
asts, whose attitudes toward alcohol had created guilt and anxiety
among drinkers. Jerome Skolnick's research, for example, emphasized the role of negative attitudes toward alcohol among parents
and subsequent alcohol problems among offspring.[54] The several
Yale studies of the drinking styles of Italians and Jews noted their
strict conformity to a drinking charter, and a corresponding lack of
conformity among Anglo-Saxon Protestants.[55] For the Orthodox
Jews, on the one hand,

> the social functions of drinking are strikingly clear. Drinking
> is to draw the family together, to cement the bonds of larger
> group membership, to activate the relationship between man
> and deity. This is understood by the participants. The rules
> and procedures of drinking are about as ritualized as those of
> a university football game or a church service. Violations of
> the rules, or violations of propriety while drinking, are
> quickly and severely penalized.
>
> The custom is learned from infancy; it is instilled at the
> time that basic moral attitudes are learned and is taught by
> prestigeful members of the group (parents, rabbis, elders).
> The custom is closely entwined with family and religious con-
> stellations. No great emotional feeling about drinking as such
> is particularly noticeable; there have never been experiences
> with prohibition; there are no abstinence movements; there
> is no Dionysiac cult or worship in drinking. Members of this
> group sneer at other groups that exhibit drunkenness. . . . All
> members of this society drink, they do so hundreds of times
> every year, they use beer, wine and distilled spirits. . . .
> Alcoholism is practically unknown.

For the Anglo-Saxon Protestant group, on the other hand,

> the social functions of drinking are rather vaguely and some-
> what defensively described; they concern drawing people—
> both family members and also complete strangers—together,

often for purposes of "fun," often to allow relaxation from (rather than, as in the preceding case, closer adherence to) moral norms. The rules and procedures are on occasion rather specific, but also show enormous variability so that a given individual may follow one set of rules with his family, another with business or professional associates, and a third on holiday occasions, and show even different patterns when away from the home town. Sanctions for violations are extremely irregular, ranging from accepting laughter to violent physical attack. . . . The custom is generally learned between the ages of 15 and 20. Sometimes the learning stems not from parents, ministers, physicians, elders and teachers, but from other adolescents. There is great emotional feeling about the problem on the mass level as well as by individuals. Activating the custom, especially by the young, is often attended with feelings of guilt, hostility, and exhibitionism, and may occur as a secretive practice insofar as parents or employers are concerned. . . . Perhaps three-quarters of the males over 15 years of age and perhaps over one-half of the females over 15 years of age use alcoholic beverages, there being not too much use of wine, relatively greater use of beer by men, and use of distilled spirits. . . . Alcoholism is not rare in this group. Perhaps 3 to 7 of every 100 users of alcohol are alcoholics.[56]

Similarly, Chafetz's 1965 *Liquor: Servant of Man* advances this theme.[57] One of the book's principal points is the long and constructive use of alcohol in cultures throughout the world, the positive functions of alcohol throughout history, and the controlled use of alcohol among Jews and Italians. If anything, later advocates of the integration hypothesis had become more and more pro-alcohol in their stance.

Responsible Drinking

Elsewhere, Chafetz offered a plea for developing a consensus on drinking in the United States, including teaching young people in school "how to drink," just as we teach them "how to drive," and abolishing age restrictions for the use of alcohol. Responsible drinking for Chafetz meant a number of things. The main emphasis was on the individual's responsibility to himself and others and on the development of responsible decision-making. This would lead away from irresponsible drinking, including intoxication, and driving and drinking.[58] While the suggestion that youngsters could be taught in school to drink responsibly (he suggested sherry) is a little fantastic, it must be acknowledged that Chafetz raised the issue of social controls over drinking, albeit in a timid way and always explicitly rejecting public controls. But the major emphasis in this movement, especially after it was instituted in the NIAAA, was upon developing the capacities of individuals—for instance, strengthening personal controls rather than social controls.

The integration hypothesis and its successor, *responsible drinking*, can be seen as an attempt to develop a more sophisticated set of ideas regarding the development of problem drinking and alcoholism by incorporating into the theory the ways in which cultural factors can encourage or discourage alcohol problems. As Chafetz put it: "By providing educational information and experience with their peers in group settings at school, and by integrating their drinking experience with family use as well, immunization against unhealthy, irresponsible drinking behavior can be provided as a bulwark against alcoholism."[59] The integration hypothesis begins with the assumption that controlling alcohol not only will not work but will make matters worse. Attempts to control the substance directly stem from our tradition of asceticism and Prohibition and can only lead to fear, ambivalence, and in many cases, higher rates of alcoholism.

In more recent years, when the theme became "responsible drinking," the notion of alcohol's integration was usually expressed as "alcohol is here to stay." Thus, as with the treatment of infectious diseases, the emphasis shifted from viewing alcohol as an exogenous and dangerous agent to an endogenous and mostly benign ("domesticated") agent. By emphasizing prevention and elaborating the rules of the drinking game, the integration hypothesis and the responsible drinking campaign of the NIAAA under Chafetz's leadership did permit the reintroduction of alcohol as a topic for critical scrutiny and, in a sense, ended the silence of the alcoholism movement on this subject. On the other hand, the reintroduction of the topic of alcohol was never a retreat from the position that alcohol was not the problem. In fact, it constituted a more sophisticated expression of this central idea of the alcoholism movement.

Alibiing Alcohol

Both the integration hypothesis and "responsible drinking" have received formidable criticism, especially from researchers who have examined the seemingly well-established fact that countries like Italy have few alcohol problems (it turns out that they enjoy some of the highest cirrhosis rates in the world). The current policy of the NIAAA no longer is to endorse responsible drinking. But for our purposes, this episode presents yet more evidence that the concept of alcoholism has been influenced by a theory of personal immunity and attempts not just to locate and define the phenomenon of addiction but also to proclaim that addiction is a problem of certain incapable persons and a culture that refuses to "integrate" alcohol fully.

The conclusion seems obvious that a main feature of the responsible drinking campaign and the integration hypothesis was the attempt to provide a sophisticated argument in support of the idea that alcohol was normative for modern American culture and that society should help people, especially young people, to adapt to the world of drinking. The central problem was to clear away the guilt and ambivalence of a confused past and to accept the changed situation brought about by the new order that existed after Prohibition.

These ideas were espoused by the modernists, people who saw themselves as rational and cosmopolitan. Furthermore, they helped broaden a "simplistic" view of alcoholism based on disease models that ignored the role of prevention. Prevention became part of the task of liberating society from the burdens of the past. Replacing the thicket of prohibitions about alcohol would be ideas stressing the fact-of-life aspects of alcohol: the ordinariness of drinking and the need to provide some form of cultural immunity against alcohol problems for larger numbers of people than in the past. Paradoxically, immunity was to be achieved not by insulating individuals further from alcohol, but rather by integrating alcohol more fully into the culture. The term *alibi* signifies that alcohol was removed

from the harsh light of blame, and was, for the time being, vindi-
cated.[60] Alcoholism was simply described in terms that fit a new era,
one that was anxious to put small-town limits on behavior behind it.

The central ideas of the alcohol movement were developed to
conform to this basic turning away from cultural fundamentalism.
This embrace of modernist views is the very heart of the alcohol
alibi. And with the alibiing of alcohol came a new "culprit," the alcoholic: alcoholism alibied the new status quo for alcohol by "blaming" the alcoholic for America's problems with alcohol.

III. The Hidden Alcoholic

A basic function of the idea of alcoholism is to alibi and hide the role of alcohol in society's alcohol problems, locating the source of the problems in a small minority who unaccountably cannot control their drinking. The irony is that this idea of alcoholism not only hides the role of alcohol but also helps drive the alcoholic further from view.

The *hidden alcoholic* is a central image of the alcoholism movement. To the movement, this term means that the alcoholic denies his problem and conceals himself because society stigmatizes his condition. The structures of secrecy are not only found among suffering alcoholics; they are widespread even among "recovering alcoholics." In fact, the more one unravels the idea of alcoholism, the more one discovers a relationship between secrecy, the hidden alcoholic, and anonymity, on the one hand, and modern ideas about alcohol, social drinking, and alcoholism, on the other.

The potency of the idea of secrecy is strikingly revealed by Alcoholics Anonymous's policy of anonymity. It is odd that, with all the scholarly literature on A.A. (or the Fellowship, as it is also called), there is so little written about this policy.[1] Anonymity within the Fellowship means far more than *individual anonymity* for the recovering alcoholic. In fact, A.A.'s policy of anonymity is primarily a policy of *organizational anonymity*.[2]

The Fellowship's policy of anonymity might only be an interesting oddity except for the fact that it bears on a cornerstone of the alcoholism movement's philosophy—the dream of lifting the stigma associated with alcoholism. The alcoholism movement's leaders believe that it is this stigma that causes so much "hidden alcoholism" and denial on the part of alcoholics. Marty Mann made this point in one of her earliest discussions about the goals of the National Council of Alcoholism; and twenty-five years later she repeated it before the Senate subcommittee that led to the legislation creating the NIAAA.[3]

What seems not to have occurred to many, however, is that it is the concept of alcoholism itself that may be the major contributing factor to the persistent stigma associated with alcoholism. As we have seen, the disease concept connotes a special kind of disability, one that is much like mental illness. In the concept of alcoholism, the disability is a defect that makes one vulnerable to behavioral and emotional problems when one is exposed to conditions that others can withstand. This susceptibility is more or less permanent; as A.A. puts it, the alcoholics are "like men who have lost their legs. They can never hope to grow new ones."[4]

The organization and policy of the Fellowship is designed to take this permanent handicap and to bestow on it something of a special status, using the mechanisms of secrecy and the bond of community. What is troubling, however, is the possibility that this practice of secrecy only reinforces and perpetuates the idea that alcoholics are categorically different, defective, and hence deserving objects of stigma and rejection.

The Anonymous Army

Among the kinds of evidence that can be brought to bear on the question of whether a condition in society should be defined as a public problem, the public especially values the knowledge and expertise of the recovered victim. Whether it is because of our curiosity about the alien character of the deviant experience, or because the deviant honors us in his repentant return to normalcy and respectability, or because the professionals seem to have so little competence in these matters, is not entirely clear. Nonetheless, the recovered and repentant alcoholic, drug addict, or criminal enjoys special status as an expert witness. His or her very presence is both testimony to the existence of a serious problem and a sign of the possibility of change.

No doubt the helpless position of the professional and scientist in the face of many problems of deviance accounts for much of the mystery surrounding the recovered victim. It is reasonable to assume that if for some reason alcoholism were suddenly revealed to be successfully treatable within the traditional medical model, the recovered alcoholic might well lose much of his notoriety.

Until that time, however, part of the mystique stems from the "otherworldly" experience that surrounds many of these social problems. It is no accident that we often refer to recovery from alcohol or drug problems as the "journey back" or the "way out."[5] With these labels we confess a cultural view of deviant experiences as alien, beyond the pale of everyday experience. Deviance in all societies is not only an object of stigma and isolation but also a source of endless fascination. The world of the drug addict, the alcoholic, the homosexual, is the world of the alien, the lost, the damned, or the cursed. Is it only a coincidence that recovered alcoholics in Alcoholics Anonymous often refer to nonalcoholics as "civilians" or "earth people"?[6]

Deviance and Anonymity

There seems to be a mutual recognition by both the "normal" and deviant members of society of the powerful societal mechanisms working not only to label deviance as strange and different from normality, but also to hide and shield the deviant performance.[7] Increasingly, however, the victims choose to challenge the label of deviant and to demand a change in society's response and reaction to their condition. In some cases this has amounted to a demand for the "right to be different";[8] in other cases the demand is that society accept, at least in part, responsibility for their plight. From the mentally ill to the homosexual, deviants are challenging the notion that they should be regarded as categorically different as persons.[9]

Curiously, the Fellowship has refused to consider this course of action. Indeed, it sometimes seems as if A.A. is reluctant to surrender the advantages and notoriety it enjoys as a result of its secrecy and unique status. Thus, the major self-help organization working in the field of alcoholism—Alcoholics Anonymous—has converted the individual desire for anonymity into an organizational imperative. Selden Bacon sympathetically commented on this posture of Alcoholics Anonymous in this way:

> In the case of alcoholism, no great single hero stands out as the prophet of new ways in facing the problems of alcoholism.

Instead of a Dorthea Dix or Clifford Beers, instead of a Joan of Arc or a William Lloyd Garrison, there appeared an organization of anonymous sufferers from alcoholism who had found a way out.[10]

Looking at a similar phenomenon from another point of view, Hannah Arendt has suggested that addiction as a process can be likened to a gradual withdrawal from public view and an orientation to an exclusively private world.[11] Arendt was speaking of the process of the individual's gradual withdrawal into the world of other addicts and addiction; but this process of withdrawal and isolation can be found among some organizations designed to help the deviant, especially those of the self-help variety. Nowhere has this process become more advanced and well articulated than with Alcoholics Anonymous.

As we shall see, the growth and attention of the policy of anonymity is an important part of the story of A.A. and especially of one of A.A.'s co-founders, Bill Wilson—or Bill W., as he was known over the years to members of A.A. But its more significant aspect is not A.A.'s policy of concealing the identity of the individual members who have recovered from alcoholic or damaging drinking. In fact, in recent years anonymity among recovered alcoholics has begun to show signs of erosion. With increasing frequency a number of well-known persons—Harold Hughes, Dick Van Dyke, Mercedes McCambridge, Billy Carter, Joan Kennedy, Betty Ford, Wilbur Mills, to name a few—have stepped forward and identified themselves as recovered alcoholics.[12]

The more fascinating story, however, is how the policy of anonymity has worked to shape the entire posture of A.A. toward the outside world. Indeed, A.A. is an interesting case of that small class of organizations that utilize mechanisms of secrecy and concealment. These are organizations that for one reason or another have adopted an official policy of withdrawal from the larger society—such organizations as secret societies, monastic orders, and underground or resistance organizations. For example, members of the Fellowship are not permitted, as a matter of policy, to reveal their public identity to the media. Bill Wilson, in fact, reportedly refused a cover story in *Time*, even though the magazine offered to photograph only the rear view of his head.[13]

The purpose of comparing A.A. to an underground organization—or for that matter to a secret society—is to highlight the impact of this practice of secrecy on our beliefs about what the alcoholic is and especially on the issue of stigma. Such a comparison also helps us to appreciate the benefits and burdens of secrecy for an organization like A.A. There is no better place to turn for this than an essay by Vilhelm Aubert on secrecy and the Norwegian underground during World War II.[14]

Secrecy and the Underground

Applying the insights of Georg Simmel's "Secrecy and the Secret Society,"[15] Aubert illuminates the underground as a countermodel to public organizations, which operate in full public view with complex paraphernalia and hierarchy. It also helps raise many questions about the practice of anonymity within Alcoholics Anonymous. While the Fellowship lies between the underground and a normal public organization, it has many curious and striking features that place it oddly close to the model of the underground: its view of itself as a special (even privileged) remnant, set apart from the rest of society and given an important mission; the excitement of working behind the scenes and "passing" in the everyday world; the radically decentralized organization consisting of thousands of autonomous "meetings" where last names are rarely used; the deliberate denial of formal, charismatic leadership; the vow of poverty by "living off the land"; the refusal to accept outside support—these are strange characteristics to meet in a time when so many other groups take up advocacy and demand changes in the larger society.

Like the Norwegian underground described by Aubert, A.A. has no formal leadership, no visible hierarchy, virtually no permanent facilities, and no membership lists. It refuses to make formal alliances or common cause with other organizations, to take a stand on the issue of alcohol, and to call attention to the toll alcohol problems exact from society and the public. In the Fellowship's view, such openings to the outside world would only weaken its unique character. This policy of anonymity and withdrawal from the public issues surrounding alcohol and alcohol problems derives from acceptance of the idea that alcoholism is the problem of a unique minority, not a public problem or issue. The Fellowship's major purpose and mission is to assemble and organize that unique minority and to help it achieve self-sufficiency and mutual support.

Anonymity and Modernity

As a modern and unique self-help movement, A.A. is also similar in some instances to the fraternal societies with Temperance orientations that sprang up in the United States and elsewhere during the nineteenth century to cope with the disorder and isolation created by the forces of industrialism.[16] It has one unique feature, however, that sets it apart from these kinds of Temperance societies based on mutual aid. A.A. came into being at the juncture of the ascendancy of cultural modernism and the collapse of Prohibition and the fundamentalist perspective on alcohol. A.A. was, and is, unequivocally on the modern side in this dispute. As a result, even though it dealt with alcohol problems, it paradoxically had to make sure that it was not seen as in any way negative toward alcohol or anti-modern in its view.

A.A. feared that its view of alcoholism as a personal problem was a rather new and still precarious idea—one that could easily be misunderstood as an anti-modernist attack on alcohol. Thus, A.A. went underground, at least in part, in order to escape the possibility of being betrayed into association with a Temperance past. A.A. did not hide in the urban society, nor does it now. Rather it makes itself unobtrusive, blending into the established order for alcohol and drinking and avoiding being confused with the small-town revival's confessions and its rebuke of alcohol.

A.A.'s attitude toward alcohol is not simply neutral; it is quite patently affirmative. This fact was beautifully captured, at least for me, in a statement made at an A.A. meeting by a member leading the meeting: "If it weren't for the fact that I am an alcoholic, I would get "fried" [drunk] every night." Those unlucky few who were unable to enjoy emancipation from alcohol restrictions did not wish to appear to challenge the new fact of life of alcohol in modern society. The modernist orientation of A.A. is often missed by those who see A.A. as anti-professional and religious in nature. While there is indeed an anti-professional attitude among many who are in

A.A., and while there is a strong spiritual component, neither aspect challenges the distinctively modern features of A.A.'s views toward alcohol and alcoholism.

This thesis about anonymity, the Fellowship, and modernity is at odds with Ernest Kurtz's recent interpretation of A.A. as distinctively anti-modern (or perhaps post-modern). Kurtz argues that A.A. developed a philosophy of the alcoholic as permanently limited, as "not-God."[17] This is, in his opinion, a clear challenge to the modern idea of the autonomous and capable self. Kurtz' thesis would be more persuasive if A.A. made more universal its philosophy of the self as limited, using it to comment on the modern vision of the self. As it is, in a culture where the self is seen as autonomous and capable, and where limits to the self are seen as repressive, A.A.'s philosophy of individual limits for a small minority sounds less like criticism than like cultural endorsement. Indeed, the policy of anonymity as it serves to communicate the idea of the alcoholic as a limited being explicitly endorses the larger context, in which, at least in regard to alcohol, most people are not personally limited.

The Fellowship

The elaborate privacy stratagem of Alcoholics Anonymous was the result of a gradual process that began with a chance meeting of two alcoholics in Akron, Ohio in 1935. One was a New York stockbroker by the name of Bill Wilson, who, after years of struggling with alcoholism, had recently had a spiritual experience that decisively altered his struggle against the bottle, thanks to the influence of an old school friend who had sobered up after joining the Oxford Group movement (the organization now known as Moral Re-armament).[18] The other was Dr. Bob Smith, an Akron physician who for years had tried unsuccessfully to stop drinking. Smith seemed helped by talking with Wilson, someone who had actually conquered the bottle and who espoused few of the moralizing platitudes that had never helped in the past. Smith took his last drink on June 10, 1935, and the origins of A.A. are traced to that date.

Wilson and Smith began to search for other alcoholics in need of help. Soon the duo became a trio of recovered alcoholics. From

1935 to 1938, A.A. grew in just this way, with the group in Akron led by Dr. Bob Smith and the handful of members in New York led by Bill Wilson.

The policy of anonymity they gradually devised is based on three official principles: protection of the organization, protection of the identity of the recovering alcoholic, and, finally, the spiritual discipline of doing good in secret. Each of these principles is based squarely on a radical elaboration of the notion that alcoholism is almost exclusively an individual problem. Alcoholics are people who have failed as drinkers. Alcoholics ought not, either individually or as members of A.A., expect help from the public in their recovery. Indeed, the early experiences shaping the policy of anonymity within A.A. convinced co-founder Wilson that A.A. could not expect help from the public on behalf of a "bunch of drunks."

Organizational Protection

Following Prohibition, it was not precisely clear what stance should be taken by an organization devoted to helping alcoholics sober up. One thing was clear, however; all efforts should be made to dissociate the group from Prohibition sentiments.[19] It was in 1937–1938 that A.A. began to separate itself from the Oxford Group and its activism and publicity-seeking.[20] A.A. stressed instead a withdrawal from the world and from political and social struggles. The tradition of anonymity began to take hold slowly, however, and was probably not complete until after World War II.

Today, the organization claims an active membership of 1,000,000 in 20,000 groups scattered throughout the world, and 350,000 members in 14,000 groups in the United States and Canada. But its leadership remains anonymous. The identities of Bill Wilson and Bob Smith were revealed only upon their deaths. Alcoholism—unlike many other social problems—is being attacked by an "anonymous army" that does good "in secret."

From its founding until the early 1940s, the organization was small, confined principally to the groups in Akron and New York. As Robert Thomsen's biography, *Bill W.*, recounts, these early years were filled with great frustration.[21] Wilson constantly dreamed of establishing A.A. on a national scale, of attracting generous phi-

lanthropic support from wealthy patrons, of media articles, of a network of A.A. hospitals. Time and again these hopes were dashed.
For example, a promising meeting with a spokesman for John D.
Rockefeller, Jr.—a meeting that Wilson hoped would result in a
generous check for the fledgling organization—resulted instead in
bitter disappointment; Rockefeller believed that charity would ruin
the struggling young organization. A promised feature article in the
Reader's Digest that might have attracted nationwide publicity
fizzled out at the last moment because the editorial board feared its
controversial theme. The lengthy project of compiling the stories of
the founding of A.A. and of the early members of the organization,
which became the "bible" of A.A., *Alcoholics Anonymous*, was undertaken not only to serve as an inspiration to the hundreds of thousands of readers who needed a sign of hope that recovery was possible but also in the hope that it might bring badly needed funds and
public attention to the struggling organization. In the early years,
however, the book received little attention.

A crucial episode seems to have taken place in 1940, when Wilson
successfully worked with members of Rockefeller's staff to organize
a banquet for some of the richest businessmen in New York. Because his father was ill, the banquet was chaired by young Nelson
Rockefeller. The success stories of A.A. were told in plain, simple
fashion. Dr. Foster Kennedy, who had written about A.A. in the
Journal of the American Medical Association, spoke.[22] The potential
of A.A. for addressing the tremendous problem of alcoholism
seemed to Wilson self-evident. He prayed that the banquet would
result in a flood of generous financial support. At the end of the
meeting Wilson sat in stunned disbelief as the businessmen filed
politely out without donating a penny. This episode seems to have
been critical for the Fellowship. Many members became convinced
of the futility of winning generous outside assistance for the
organization.

It was a 1941 article in the *Saturday Evening Post* by Jack Alexander that finally gave the organization some financial security and
publicity.[23] The growth and expansion of the Fellowship can perhaps
be traced to this publicity more than to anything else. Thomsen reports that in 1941 membership in the Fellowship jumped from fifteen hundred to eight thousand.[24] New groups began to spring up
all over the country.

This success likely formed new dreams of publicity and public support. Prominent A.A. members became involved in developing new and public groups advocating a community approach for alcoholism. Mrs. Marty Mann was one of these. Soon after the founding of the Yale group and the Summer School, Mann became publicly associated with the Yale program, and founded the National Committee for Education on Alcoholism in 1944. Wilson was prominently listed in the curriculum of the Yale Summer School of Alcohol Studies as the director of A.A. According to A.A.'s official history, other members who enjoyed some prominence freely publicized their connection with A.A. This seems to be a thinly veiled reference to Mann's work (and indeed to Wilson's publicity-seeking); in the early years of her work in alcohol education Mann freely acknowledged her connections with A.A.

The continual publicity for Wilson, Mann, and others created turmoil within the organization. Wilson and Mann were reminded of the spiritual discipline of anonymity and of the need to avoid the sin of pride. The old fear that some figure publicly identified with A.A. might get drunk and disgrace the organization was advanced. There also was fear that other members might embroil the Fellowship in a controversy. For example, one member seems to have advertised A.A.'s affiliation with Prohibition sentiments, which was a misrepresentation. In addition, Mann seemed to imply that her efforts to build the National Committee for Education on Alcoholism in 1946 had been endorsed by A.A.[25] Wilson himself had been confronted by members of the Akron wing in 1941 with charges of exploiting the Fellowship. Succumbing to pressure, both Wilson and Mann gradually withdrew from a visible A.A. role.

Wilson finally came to suppress his obvious charisma and other assets as a public figure. When he testified before Senator Harold Hughes' Senate Special Subcommittee on Alcoholism and Narcotics in 1969, television cameras were not allowed and photographs were permitted only from the rear. Indeed, Wilson's anonymity, after its resumption in the 1940s, was only broken with his death in 1971. The same agreement was enforced with the other founder, Dr. Bob Smith, who died in 1950.

As a result of these early difficulties, the tradition of anonymity at the public level gradually became the ironclad way of protecting the Fellowship and ensuring its survival. This policy meant that, while close friends might be told of one's membership in A.A. and while civic groups might be addressed so long as last names were not used, personal anonymity at the level of the press, radio, and television was strictly observed. Photos of A.A. members addressing organizations and identification of A.A. members by name in news stories disappeared as the Fellowship went underground.

In 1950, Alcoholics Anonymous officially codified the tradition of anonymity and defined its relation to the outside world in a set of basic organizational principles known as the Twelve Traditions:

1. Our common welfare should come first; personal recovery depends upon A.A. unity.
2. For our group purpose there is but one ultimate authority—a loving God as He may express Himself in our group conscience. Our leaders are but trusted servants; they do not govern.
3. The only requirement for A.A. membership is a desire to stop drinking.
4. Each group should be autonomous except in matters affecting other groups or A.A. as a whole.
5. Each group has but one primary purpose—to carry its message to the alcoholic who still suffers.
6. An A.A. group ought never to endorse, finance, or lend the A.A. name to any related facility or outside enterprise, lest problems of money, property, and prestige divert us from our primary purpose.
7. Every A.A. group ought to be fully self-supporting, declining outside contributions.
8. Alcoholics Anonymous should remain forever non-professional, but our service center may employ special workers.
9. A.A., as such, ought never to be organized; but we may create service boards or committees directly responsible to those they serve.
10. Alcoholics Anonymous has no opinion on outside issues; hence the A.A. name ought never be drawn into public controversy.
11. Our public relations policy is based on attraction rather than promotion; we need always maintain personal anonymity at the level of press, radio and films.
12. Anonymity is the spiritual foundation of our traditions,

ever reminding us to place principles before person-
alities.[26]

The argument for the Fellowship policy of anonymity was force-
fully stated in Wilson's essay, "Why Alcoholics Anonymous Is Anonymous."[27] Anonymity was required as a sacrifice "for the common
welfare" of the Fellowship. A.A. found that "it had to give up many
of its own rights for the protection and welfare of each member, and
for A.A. as a whole."[28] These sacrifices had to be made or the Fellowship could not continue to exist:

> In our Twelve Traditions we have set our faces against nearly
> every trend in the outside world. We have denied ourselves
> personal government, professionalism, and the right to say
> who our members shall be. We have abandoned dogoodism,
> reform, and paternalism. We refuse outside charitable money
> and have decided to pay our own way. We will cooperate with
> practically everybody yet we decline to marry our society to
> anyone. We abstain from public controversy and will not
> quarrel among ourselves about those things that so rip society
> asunder: religion, politics and reform. We have but one pur-
> pose, to carry the A.A. message to the sick alcoholic who
> wants it.[29]

Wilson's various failed enterprises in the early years of the Fellowship were probably a key factor in the emergence of this policy.
The failure to obtain support from Rockefeller, the collapse of the
dream of a special network of A.A. hospitals, and the years of struggling with almost no funds seem finally to have persuaded Wilson of
the futility of a large-scale popular movement. This, and the constant opposition of other members who did not share Wilson's ambi-
tion, resulted in the formal codification of the Fellowship's policy of
anonymity. To this day A.A. refuses outside contributions, even
from deceased benefactors.

A.A. is headed by a governing board of trustees, called the General Service Board, two-thirds of whom are alcoholics. The chairman has traditionally been nonalcoholic. The alcoholic members of
the board are never referred to by their last names.

The trustees oversee the organizational finances, the operation of
a small permanent staff in New York City (called the General Ser-

vice Office), and all public relations activity. Like most other voluntary organizations, this control is largely formal, with much day-to-day decision-making power in the hands of the staff. The General Service Office has few opportunities to make policy, however, since it has no control over the local groups. The permanent staff deals basically with the outside world, handling inquiries from professionals, hospitals, and religious organizations. It aids in the starting of new groups, and one of its major jobs is the publication of an international directory containing the meeting times and places of groups throughout the world, for the use of members who travel.

Another major function of the General Service Office is the dissemination of official literature. Distributed mainly through A.A. groups, this literature seldom reaches the general public. The organization newsletter, called *The Grapevine*, can be obtained by members for a small fee and is usually mailed in a sealed, plain envelope.

The link between the local group and the General Services Office is the annual General Service Conference. The Conference is made up of delegates from state assemblies, which in turn are composed of elected members from the local groups. Several thousand members usually attend. The Conference debates policy questions (the tradition of anonymity has been discussed in recent years), but basic policy changes have not been undertaken. In fact, the Conference has no formal legal status, and it is not known how it could formally influence the Board.

In its surrounding community, the Fellowship attracts very little attention. Of course, the policy of organizational poverty and "living off the land"—Tradition Seven states that "every A.A. group ought to be fully self-supporting, declining outside contributions"— is a big factor in the Fellowship's low visibility. Small voluntary contributions are taken at each meeting for such items as rent, coffee, and the purchase of literature for newcomers. The decision to rely upon voluntary contributions from the members has meant that the groups must meet in austere, simple surroundings, usually used for other purposes, and cannot secure permanent facilities that might attract community attention.

In most major cities meetings begin and end at a set time throughout the city. By and large, the meetings are held in church facilities at times when they are not being used. The meetings usually take place in the evening and receive a minimum of publicity in the local media. In large cities, to contact an A.A. group, one can call a central telephone number and obtain directions to the nearest meeting place.

Protection of Identity

As he gradually began to conform to the rules of anonymity, Wilson spoke increasingly of the Fellowship as a "life raft." Save for anonymity the members—individually and collectively—would be lost. The founders of Alcoholics Anonymous believed that anonymity and the protection of the identity of the alcoholic were a basic appeal of their new organization, since they believed, rightly, that because of the stigma attached to the condition most alcoholics wanted to remain anonymous. Thus, anonymity served the second important function of concealing an individual's presumed special vulnerability to alcohol.[30]

There are no formal criteria for membership in the Fellowship, the only requirement being a desire to stop drinking. People enter the organization from a wide variety of callings and stations, and there are no clear ways to infer membership from some other group, since alcoholics do not occur as a natural group; they are "collectivities" dispersed (even if not randomly) throughout society.[31]

The structure of the Fellowship at the local community level (and at all levels for that matter) gives maximum protection against the exposure of its members' identities. Throughout all of A.A. there are no records of membership. In many areas members identify themselves in meetings only by their first names; it is quite possible to attend a group for a number of years and not know the last name or outside identity of many of the group's members. This is often strange and difficult for the new member, since the advertising of status and accomplishment is such a widespread and accepted part of social interaction. One of the earliest and strictest norms, however, introduced to the fledgling member (commonly called a "pigeon") is the rule of anonymity—especially the anonymity of the other members.

Even if the member is acquainted with the outside identity of another member, there is a strong taboo against revealing this identity to other members or to nonalcoholics outside the Fellowship. This creates some special problems. Since members are drawn from such diverse callings, it is not unusual for two members to meet while in the company of a nonmember, who may wonder how the two know each other. The protection-of-identity taboo requires the A.A. members to invent elaborate if vague references to previous acquaintanceship. Likewise, in refusing a drink, a member usually devises excuses that do not expose his organizational affiliation. And, of course, the rule against breaking one's anonymity at the level of press, radio, and television is almost never violated by A.A. members.

There are basically two types of A.A. meetings. One is the open meeting that anyone—including nonalcoholics—can attend. These meetings often begin with the admonition that nonmembers must pledge not to reveal the identity of anyone at the meeting whom they might recognize. Usually a team of three members relate their personal experiences. No last names are used and the narratives are censored so as not to betray the speakers' identities.

The second type is the closed meeting, reserved for members of the Fellowship. This meeting is usually devoted to discussion of the Twelve Steps, and members often go into detailed discussions of their past or current difficulties.[32] An atmosphere of trust and protection is ensured by excluding nonmembers.

The strategies of secrecy and protection practiced by members of the Fellowship are simply elaborations of techniques that secret organizations have long practiced. They also exploit the widespread anonymity of urban existence. Even before joining the Fellowship, the deviant drinker has in all likelihood developed a repertoire of concealment strategies. Just as the drinking alcoholic is concerned with the strategies of "passing" in normal society, so is the member of the Fellowship (the sober alcoholic) concerned with "passing" as a nondrinking but otherwise normal member of society. But the use of presentational strategies—as well as taking advantage of the natural social cover of everyday life—is not just a strategy of those who must lead a sort of double life; the modern urbanite is anonymous to most he meets.[33]

Thus, the Fellowship serves the prospective sober alcoholic as a sort of school for survival, as a post-graduate course in learning the strategies of avoidance and concealment so necessary for a new career of nondrinking in a world that views drinking as "normal" and expected behavior.

Doing Good in Secret

The Fellowship goes beyond the protection of the organization and the identity of the individual alcoholic in justifying its policy of anonymity. Ultimately it justifies the policy in spiritual terms. The spiritual argument is traced directly to the Christian Gospels and perhaps most explicitly to the Gospel of Matthew: "Take heed that you do not your alms before men, to be seen of them: otherwise ye have no reward of your Father which is in heaven."[34] Purity of goodness can only be assured when there are no worldly rewards for its expression, such as public approval and notoriety. So long as A.A. remains anonymous in its mission of assisting the recovering alcoholic, it will have taken a giant step in protecting its members from the corrupting influences of power, recognition, and public approval found in the world of politics.

It is a cardinal tenet of the Fellowship that the lust for recognition and power is a primary cause of the alcoholic's drinking. (Here, not a little of Bill Wilson's self-acknowledged "publicity-seeking" seems to have left its mark on the Fellowship's ideology.) A.A. literature describes the alcoholic prowling the taverns and bars searching for easy approval and attention. According to A.A., recovery is only possible by suppressing and eliminating such approval-seeking activities. The Fellowship must be content with doing its good works in secret; secrecy is its own reward.

It is remarkable how A.A. came gradually to see the tradition of anonymity as Christian, especially since A.A. was born directly from the Oxford movement, which emphasized massive publicity, including the use of celebrity converts who chose not to hide their lamps under a basket. While many Christians would likely side with the Oxford Group—at least in part—and argue that Christ's admonitions against such acts as fasting in public were never meant to create a church that did not actively and aggressively promote its mission, A.A. appreciated the value of private charitable acts as potent Christian gestures.

The Washingtonians

The Fellowship argues that its policies of anonymity and withdrawal from public controversy are in fact the very secrets of its survival. It points to the experience of another organization similar to A.A. but born almost a century ago—the Washington Temperance Society—because the Society's experience offers a fascinating contrast to the Fellowship.[35]

The story begins in 1840, when a group of six friends drinking in a Baltimore tavern debated in jest whether to send part of the group to attend a local temperance organization. On impulse, the six went through with the idea. They drafted a temperance pledge, named themselves the Washington Temperance Society, after George Washington, elected officers, assigned dues, and agreed to meet weekly and to bring new members. The idea was not quixotic—temperance societies were sweeping the country, and, as de Tocqueville pointed out, Americans needed little excuse to form associations.[36]

The group continued to convene in the same tavern for several weeks until the owner evicted them for ruining his trade. The society then rented a meeting place and began a series of testimonials about members' experiences with alcohol. The idea was instantly successful and the meetings soon became crowded with interested listeners. Many came forward to sign the pledge.

In November of the same year the new society decided to hold an open meeting in the Masonic Hall, and invited the public. Having drawn a large crowd, the Washingtonians decided to continue public meetings on a monthly basis. The format of the meetings was quite simple. Members were encouraged to attend as many meetings as possible during the week (by then there were several groups meeting throughout the city of Baltimore), to bring a new member, and to relate their experiences.

Some men of great speaking and leadership ability were attracted to the movement. One was John W. Hawkins. Hawkins had a plain speaking style of great force, and physically dominated any meeting. The growth of the movement was partly due to the wide use of newspaper publicity by such skilled orators as Hawkins who toured the country and obtained signatures for the pledge. For example, when Hawkins and several other members were invited to address Temperance audiences in New York, their meetings there were successful and given great publicity in the daily press and the Temperance journals. An open-air meeting of four thousand was held in a New York City park, a New York branch of the Washington Temperance Society was formed, and over two thousand reformed drunkards had signed the temperance pledge within a few weeks.

The campaign for the next three years enjoyed spectacular growth. The American Temperance Union estimated that over five million persons had signed the pledge by 1843, and that over ten thousand local societies had been formed. In 1844, the Washingtonians sponsored the largest Temperance meeting held to that date. Over thirty thousand members of Temperance organizations throughout the country attended.

Then, just as suddenly as it rose, the movement passed out of view. The peak of growth seems to have been reached in 1843–1844. The wave of public interest in the plight of the drunkard passed on to the need for prevention through abstinence and Prohibition. What little effort remained for the rehabilitation of the suffering drunkard passed to the new Temperance lodges, such as the Sons of Temperance, formed in part by Washingtonian members.

To the founders of A.A., the reason for the failure of the Washingtonians is clear. The movement "did not have a chance from the moment it determined to reform all America's drinking habits. Some of the Washingtonians became Temperance crusaders. Within a very few years they had completely lost their effectiveness in helping alcoholics, and the Society collapsed."[37] However, there is another, more plausible reason for the decline of the Washingtonians. The Washingtonians were lost not so much in a hostile environment as in an overly receptive one. Temperance was a highly popular cause. There is little reason to believe that, if the Washingtonians had stayed out of public controversy, they might have survived. To the contrary, this brief history suggests that they only flourished so long as they could keep a minimal identity as part of the Temperance groundswell. Eventually, they were absorbed by the larger and more powerful Temperance Movement. The Temperance Movement overwhelmed the interest in the reformed drunkard, and went on to the larger issue of drinking and abstinence per se.

The Costs of Secrecy

Whatever the drawbacks of the public route taken by the Washingtonians, the Fellowship's own policy of secrecy has its shortcomings. Perhaps the major danger lies in the attractions of secrecy for its own sake. Simmel suggested that secrecy can become *the* primary reward of organizations where once it only served as protection.[38] Just as with federal agencies who use secrecy for security reasons and find themselves elevating the practice for its own sake, A.A. runs the risk of encouraging attraction for a "way of life" in a secret society.

It may be that this secrecy has become a major attraction of membership within the Fellowship. For example, some A.A. members suggest that, if a "cure" for alcoholism were found, they would continue coming to meetings, despite opportunity to return to "normal" drinking. This feeling must partially stem from the rewards of fellowship that are the benefits of all organizational life. On the other hand, there is likely some feeling of attraction for membership in a secret society—in this case, of those who have made the "journey back"—in which all the appeals of special knowledge and ceremonies can be enjoyed. Unfortunately, such rewards can only be enjoyed at the cost of reinforcing the stigma inherent in our ideas about alcoholism.

In our culture, with its emphasis on the liberation of the self from community restraints and limits, those who experience problems with alcohol are placed in an excruciating dilemma. On the one hand, they wish to acknowledge that they are not morally weak or lacking in character; on the other hand, they are forced to witness that society is not responsible for their condition and that alcohol is not a public problem. Thus the alcoholic is caught in a double bind and forced to act something like a double agent who works on his own behalf, defining himself as personally not responsible for his condition, but also works for society, signaling that the larger society is not responsible for his condition either. Anonymity, at least in the view here, is not simply or only a protective measure against the stigma arising from ideas about alcohol problems. Anonymity is part and parcel of the ideological function of the idea of the alcoholic, which portrays alcoholics themselves as largely responsible for society's alcohol problems. The elaborate and striking emphasis in A.A. on withdrawal from the community could only make sense to a culture supremely confident that alcohol and alcohol policy are not an issue in alcoholism. If and when that confidence is undermined (and the signs point in that direction), the position of A.A.'s anonymity will be seriously threatened.

While the alcoholism movement devised a theory of alcohol problems that did not blame the alcoholic for his or her condition, the idea of alcoholism still locates the cause of most of society's alcohol problems in a vulnerable minority. Were it not for the personal vulnerability of alcoholics to alcohol, many of society's alcohol problems would be nonexistent. Anonymity is both a policy that shields the alcoholic from blame and yet paradoxically professes the alcoholic to be the location of society's alcohol problems. It is a piece of double-talk that will only disappear when the role of cultural norms in alcohol problems is fully appreciated. As Jesse Pitts has said of the entire stratagem of medicalizing deviance, the deviant is no longer guilty of his crimes, but he is not innocent of his illnesses either.[39] The policy of anonymity rests squarely on this paradox: the alcoholic seeks to escape from the stigma of moral failure by confessing the stigma of incapacity or disability. And the policy of anonymity is designed to protect not only the alcoholic but also the larger society from the risk of seeing itself as implicated in the problem of alcoholism. To put it another way, the manifest functions of the policy of anonymity are indeed to protect the Fellowship and to affirm that the alcoholic is powerless—in Kurtz' words "not-God." But the ideological functions of that policy are to protect and affirm a new moral order for alcohol and the values of a culture that defines social drinking as a personal achievement. Like the entire idea of alcoholism, anonymity functions to alibi the new status quo for alcohol and to protect the larger society from change. To see that this is so, we have only to imagine what would happen to the doctrine of anonymity if a time were to come when alcohol problems were seen as involving more than failed individuals, and society's role in determining rates of problems were fully acknowledged. If a post-modern view of alcohol and alcohol problems were to emerge, one that discarded the idea of the alcoholic as uniquely vulnerable to alcohol, what would be the point of continuing rituals of secrecy and anonymity? Even today we must ask: from whom are the alcoholics hiding?

IV. The Myth of Social Drinking

While there have been questions raised about the concept of alcoholism almost since the beginning of the alcoholism movement, within the past decade the number of counterclaims and alternative perspectives has become more numerous and insistent. It is no accident that the emergence of a new perspective on alcohol problems came almost simultaneously with the creation of the National Institute on Alcohol Abuse and Alcoholism. In the seventies and the eighties the policy imperatives of national bureaucracies devoted to dealing with public health problems, such as alcoholism, drug abuse, pollution control, or consumer protection, seem to dictate a rather special set of explanations or perspectives for these problems—perspectives that inevitably clash with a concept like alcoholism.

In the case of alcoholism policy, the new perspectives are, so it seems, the precursors of what can be very loosely referred to as a post-alcoholism paradigm for alcohol problems.[1] While these perspectives do not in any sense mean that a clear consensus exists for an alternative to the alcoholism paradigm, there are signs that such an alternative is gradually taking shape, one that differs markedly from the alcoholism model.

The stereotypes of alcoholism and social drinking have been used to shift attention away from alcohol and the body of cultural, social, and legal norms sanctioning its use. They have created the idea that there are two fundamental types who use alcohol, and that alcohol policy is relatively impotent in the face of these two realities (especially alcoholism). As we shall see in this chapter and Chapters V and VI, this is not the case. The fact is, these stereotypes have been collapsing of their own weight during the last decade. We are here simply hastening the process so that we can begin to think of alcohol problems, not simply, or only, in terms of individual attributes, but also in terms of the larger environment of law and societal context.

Defining the Normal and the Deviant

Behind a veil of obviousness lurks the absolutely fundamental fact that *every* society is predicated upon the unquestioned assumption that its members, in their overwhelming majority, are not only competent to conduct their everyday affairs in accordance with whatsoever their society counts as correct forms of conduct, but where a choice is possible . . . will freely *elect* to do so. Put differently, every society assumes that its members, in their overwhelming majority, are responsible for their doings, which is to say that they are *moral* agents. I say, "in their overwhelming majority," because it is also everywhere recognized that in no society is the socialization process so wholly efficacious as to produce members who, without exception, do all the things they are supposed to do and refrain from doing all the things they are supposed not to do. Every society, that is, recognizes that it has its deviants.[2]

Using such commonsense or everyday logic as this, we describe and explain deviance through a process of typification.[3] We define deviance in terms of two fundamental and opposed individual types (the normal and the deviant), seeing each class as composed of individuals who share some defining trait, and seeing the two classes as fundamentally different. Theories of deviance, especially the labeling perspective, however, almost universally focus on the fallacy behind our commonsense categories of deviance. Despite the fact that "typification, ways of perceiving the world by means of categorical types, is the essence of social communication and interaction,"[4] labeling theorists and sociology in general have sought to challenge the reductionism inherent in our everyday logic and stereotypes as inadequate explanations for deviance. Labeling theory, with roots in symbolic interactionism, challenges the view that de-

viance is a property that inheres in the deviant act or the deviant
person, and also the view that deviance and normality are two fundamental and opposed types that are categorically different.

According to Becker, this effort has been a central concern of the
labeling theorists.[5] It underlies, for example, the well-known formulation by Kai Erikson:

> Deviation is not a property *inherent* in certain forms of behavior; it is a property *conferred upon* these forms by the
> audiences which directly or indirectly witness them. Sociologically, then, the critical variable is the social *audience* . . .
> since it is the audience which eventually decides whether or
> not any given action or actions will become a visible case of
> deviation.[6]

This and similar definitions of deviance tend to generate many
questions. Perhaps the most common are whether deviance occurs
when it is unlabeled, and whether unlabeled deviance (such as alcoholism) occurs randomly in the population. The latter question
typically arises because many believe that, despite the presence of
social factors, there are still important individual correlates of deviance. While it may be true that the labeling school sometimes
goes too far in seeing labeling as merely a social process, thereby
ignoring individual factors, the central achievement of this perspective remains unchallenged. When we see normality and deviance as
opposite types, and when we reify deviance by treating it as a property that inheres in certain forms of behavior, we proliferate a reductionism that both ignores or distorts crucial processes of direct
social formation and obscures the very real heterogeneity of the two
types. Nevertheless, even when the importance of social and cultural processes are recognized, one is not committed to the view
that there are no psychological or physiological correlates of deviance, and that unlabeled deviance occurs randomly in society.
The aim is not to eliminate the role of individual factors but to challenge the process of defining deviance in terms of discrete types. It
is this viewing of the world of alcohol problems through the lens of
simple types that obscures the influence of the social environment
and makes too much of differences between the alcoholic and the
normal, "social" drinker.

As we noted in Chapter II, Albert Cohen refers to this form of explanation as a kinds-of-people explanation. This is the quintessential form of typification found in deviance explanations. It is central to the process of analogizing deviance to illness (medicalizing deviance), a process that treats the deviant behavior in naturalistic terms, assuming that an underlying condition gives rise to that behavior.

Ability Explanations

It has been the claim of the alcoholism movement that their view of alcoholism represents a shift away from moral categories, such as weakness of will or willful misconduct, and toward the scientific categories of illness and disability. This claim must be judged as more assertion than accomplishment, if it means that the claim was based on the discovery of alcoholism as a disease.

The alcoholism movement has since this shift been caught in numerous logical and empirical tangles, and we can better understand these difficulties if we examine more closely what is entailed in ability explanations. *Ability explanations* are members of a broad class of explanations called *dispositional explanations*.[7] If we strike a glass with a knife and it breaks, we can refer to the blow as breaking the glass; or we can say the glass broke because it was brittle. The latter explanation is dispositional because it refers to properties possessed by the broken object itself that caused it to break.

Similarly, if an individual falls from a boat into a lake and drowns, we can offer at least two kinds of explanations for the drowning. We can assert that the individual drowned because the water interfered with his oxygen supply, causing him to suffocate. This is the ordinary form of "cause-effect" explanation. We could also say that the individual drowned because he or she was unable to swim. This is a dispositional explanation and, more specifically, an ability explanation. Ability explanations are comparative in nature; the individual drowned because of an internal property that some possess (the ability to swim) but the victim did not. This lack of ability explains the drowning. Ability explanations may be forthcoming when two or more people fall from the same boat and some of the group drown while others swim to shore, or when many in the society or community have the ability to swim and could have swum to shore.

It is the form of explanation we typically use when we describe the success and failure of differing individuals in performing a physical skill or activity that possesses some degree of difficulty or complexity. Finally, and most importantly for our purposes, it is the kind of explanation that is often forthcoming when some people in a society suffer a harm like alcoholism, and when we wish to say that they could not have helped it.

Ability and Will

The consequences of this shift in the way we describe alcoholism have been profound and are revealed if we contrast dispositional terms based on "weakness of will" and "inability" or "loss of control." There is a vast literature in philosophy regarding the use of such terms as *will*, *ability*, and *capacity* that is largely ignored by most social scientists.[8] What is fascinating about this literature is that it gives us insight into what was achieved when we actually began to talk about alcoholism and social drinking in a new way, and this in turn helps clarify what we mean when we speak of alcoholism as a disease.

Some of the insight has to do with the process of change in language, the difference between what we mean when we say that someone fails at some activity because he is "weak-willed" and what we mean when we say someone is "unable" to perform some activity.[9] Weak-willed usually means that the person who fails (say, in stopping smoking) could succeed if he or she tried harder. Furthermore, this attempt is an effort not connected to some fixed structure of the person; it is rather seen as something of a characterological trait, where this term means a moral and nonphysical aspect of the person. Also, when we use the term "will," we usually are referring to resisting the force of temptation coming from within the person or without, but again there is no hint that this force or strength possessed by the person has some physical or permanent foundation (although it is true that we see these as "summary dispositions," that is, that we tend to speak of someone with "willpower" when we mean that that person predictably has a great deal of self-control).

What is interesting is how rare it is to find topics such as "will" or "willpower" in the alcoholism literature when the subject is alcoholism, or even excessive drinking and drinking without problems. The fact is that people who lack willpower are still viewed, again in terms of our commonsense categories of everyday logic, as being able to do a thing if only they were to try hard enough. This way of thinking about alcoholism and drinking, however, is alien to our modern views. Very early in the days of the alcoholism movement, for example, E. M. Jellinek argued for a very limited use of the term *disease* (in our terms inability or loss of control) because this way of talking would spill over into our way of thinking about all excessive drinking. For "sooner or later," he said, such a misapplication would "reflect on the legitimate use too and, more important, will tend to weaken the ethical basis of social sanctions against drunkenness."[10] This is truly a prophetic insight into what has come to pass. We are now in a position where the entire range of social sanctions for drinking and drinking problems have been undermined by the forms of language we use to view the entire experience of drinking.

When we use such terms as ability or capacity (also the term control because it is a variant of ability) we do, in fact, roughly think of a physical or structural foundation for that capacity. The point is that, as Arnold Kaufman, J. L. Austin, and others have argued, when ordinary men and women use terms such as ability or capacity, they usually are referring to conditions that exist beneath the skin of the person to whom they refer, and assume that these internal conditions represent causally relevant properties for the successful performance of a given task.[11] It is not necessary that we specify exactly what is inside individual drinkers, only that we appreciate that when we talk this way about drinking we shift our gaze from the will, or moral nature, of drinking, and look upon the activity as resting on some (albeit vague) physical foundation. As Aubert and Messinger have noted, we resort to language we commonly use when we talk about the physical world, seeing abilities and control as properties that persist in space and time.[12]

Ability explanations are at the heart of our widespread tendency to blame alcoholics for society's alcohol problems. Knowing this about our everyday logic and commonsense categories will help us see the magnitude of the fundamental mistakes we have made with this simple shift in language. It will not be easy to move away from this language, but we can point to some promising direction. Our hope lies in establishing that the absence of alcohol problems is never a purely personal accomplishment, but is a direct consequence of social as well as individual factors.

Is Alcoholism a Disease?

In looking at the flourishing literature on the question of alcoholism as a disease, instead of a comprehensive review we shall focus on how the leading critics have sensed the puzzles in our thinking about alcoholism, but fail, finally, to return to consider the issue of alcohol and alcohol policy. One who pinpointed a major contradiction is Thomas Szasz, who in a long series of publications has challenged the notion of mental illness as a disease, proclaiming that his central task is to "expose the false substantives and entities that lie behind our view of mental illness."[13] He has also applied the same logic to the field of alcoholism, arguing that we should view alcohol use, even heavy use, more like a habit rather than like a dispositional property of the user. In some areas, the argument of Szasz regarding the question of false entities and substantives, and the typifications that arise from these entities, parallels the argument set out here. Of course, there are sharp differences between the present author's views of how we then should look at alcoholism and drinking generally after the misleading idioms are replaced. Szasz opposes attempts to control the use of substances as paternalistic and wrong categorically while I would say that controls are a necessary and justified part of our overall policy to reduce alcoholism. But Szasz begins at the right place, by examining the language we use to describe the phenomenon of alcoholism.

Claude Steiner, like Szasz, rejects the disease view, arguing that the claim that alcoholism is a disease "seems to imply that it is 'an interruption or perversion of function of any of the organs, an acquired morbid change in any tissue of an organism, or throughout an organism, with characteristic symptoms caused by specific micro-organismal alterations.'"[14] Steiner suggests that this does not seem to be descriptive of a large number of "bona fide" alcoholics. He wonders if, after the day of the alcoholic's last drink and until his next binge, there is any perversion or interruption of function of any organ?[15] Steiner argues for a game framework (transactional analysis) as a way to view alcoholism, leaving the alcoholic a realm of choice in which to change his or her behavior. He also clearly supports the thesis that many alcoholics could return to controlled, or normal, drinking.

William Rohan also questions the logic of the disease concept and our tendency to rely on physical analogies. He claims that "the observed behavior is thought to be caused by a more important internal disposition beyond what is seen."[16] According to Rohan, "the term 'alcoholism,' connotes a special internal disposition to account for persistent drinking associated with physical and social harm."[17] Although its exact nature is unspecified, it allegedly acts as a governing source of drinking behavior. Rohan sees this reference to internal properties as misleading and urges that we consider the activity or behavior of the drinking act itself, instead of looking for internal causes. He also suggests that we look to the context for heavy or alcoholic drinking in order to gain a more adequate depiction.

Similarly, David Robinson notes that our concepts of disease are so varying and these are so loosely applied to a broad range of alcohol-related problems that the danger of confusion and ambiguity is unavoidable.[18] For example, it matters a great deal whether we make an analogy between alcoholism and a disease like diabetes or one like small pox. In the case of the latter, a judicious bout of alcoholic behavior might serve to "innoculate" the victim to further problems.[19] As Robinson notes, the conventional notion of a disease or illness is such that, even when a person acts negligently and breaks his leg, he cannot mend his leg by the exercise of "will power." But this aspect of our idea of illness does not pertain to alcoholics; when the health professional remonstrates with them to attempt to stop drinking, he is asking, in a sense, for the exercise of will. One might object that alcoholism is a condition more like heart disease or diabetes; in this case, the patient must strive to avoid certain foods and keep a regimen if his condition is to improve. But again, we have at the outset—and by definition—referred to the alcoholic as one who cannot control his behavior over alcohol. This leads, as Claude Steiner notes, to a "joyless" attitude on the part of therapists who treat alcoholics.[20]

The difficulties with the idea of alcoholism have, as Robin Room has noted, been discussed for many decades now.[21] This is surely the case, but the puzzles remain: Does some discrete clinical entity called alcoholism exist? Are there in actuality varieties of alcoholisms? Is the alcoholic responsible not for his illness, but for trying to get well? Can the alcoholic "try" on his or her own, or do we mean that he or she can only do so with outside intervention? What about the growing number of reports that alcoholics control their drinking at least to some extent, or have even returned to normal drinking? Does this mean that something is wrong with at least some of our ideas about alcoholism, or are these reports about persons who were not truly alcoholic? In the next two sections some of these reports about the differences between alcoholics, and the alcoholic's control, or lack of control, over drinking will be reviewed.

It will help to remember that much, if not most, of this confusion comes not just from the way we think about alcoholism, but from the way we think about drinking altogether. We have created two major types of drinkers—those with personal ability to control their drinking and those without. As long as our description of the problem is so vastly over-simplified there will remain confusion in all realms.

The Myth of Alcoholism

Most reviews of the literature have rejected a common set of personality factors predisposing individuals to alcoholism. Thus, Nancy Mello, in her authoritative review of the literature, finds no evidence supporting the notion that alcoholics share some common psychological, biological, or physiological trait. She states that, beyond the "pharmacological commonality of tolerance for and dependence upon alcohol, alcoholics are a heterogeneous group."[22] Even Mark Keller concludes on a humorous note that "alcoholics are so different in so many ways that it makes no difference." Keller goes on to formulate Keller's Law: "The investigation of any trait in alcoholics will show that they have either more or less of it."[23] Mansell Pattison and Mark and Linda Sobell, for their part, conclude that except for sharing alcohol problems, all alcoholics are not the same.[24]

Attempting to show this central fallacy behind the concept of alcoholism is the same as trying to prove that a way of thinking based on the alcoholic as a fundamental type is systematically misleading. This is always difficult to do. We can attempt to cast doubt on the likelihood of the argument with empirical evidence. The accumulating evidence that alcoholics have more control over their drinking than our ideas about alcoholism would suggest bears on this point. Also, research that shows that alcoholics can in some instances return to a lower intake of alcohol challenges our ideas about alcoholism. In other cases, we have to resort to *reductio ad absurdum* arguments, and show how references to alcohol problems in an idiom of personal control lead to absurd or logical paradox, or are inconsistent with our other ways of using language, or are not good scientific procedure. But we cannot once and for all show that these inner traits do not exist, since they are always hidden from us, and can only be assumed. This is one principal reason that this form of argument is so enduring. But evidence is accumulating that suggests that our ideas about alcoholism are misleading because they focus exclusively on "control" as an attribute of the individual only, and ignore the contexts that make the term "control" sensible.

The Alcoholic's Control

The first strand of research, that the alcoholic exhibits substantial control over his drinking, has been reviewed in several places. Nancy Mello's overview perhaps is the best.[25] She concludes that a number of experiments tend to show that alcoholics can manipulate or control their drinking to a rather surprising extent. Typically this research is conducted on persons in institutional settings who are diagnosed as alcoholic and who are promised valued rewards (money, for example) for drinking on a controlled basis.

Mello challenges the stereotype that the alcoholic has a predictable and invariant style of drinking—that is, to drink as much as possible. She argues that "the lack of experimental data about drinking patterns has led to an implicit reification of concepts like 'need' and 'craving' which are defined by the behavior that they are invoked to explain."[26]

Similarly, Pattison and the Sobells cite over fifty published reports of studies, conducted mostly since 1965, that support the notion "that chronic alcoholics can and do engage in limited, nonproblem drinking without encountering deleterious consequences."[27] They point out that in "the past 15 years an impressive number of studies have robustly demonstrated that even the drinking of chronic, skid-row alcoholics is subject to their precise control under appropriate environmental circumstances."[28] They argue that these findings on the ability of alcoholics to control their drinking "demonstrate that within a hospital or laboratory environment, the drinking of chronic alcoholics is explicitly a function of environmental contingencies."[29] They suggest that we need to reformulate our ideas about loss of control:

> In summary, then, the degree of control that one demonstrates with respect to drinking behavior is likely to be situation-dependent and individual-specific, even if that individual has had drinking problems in the past. If "loss of control" is retained as a concept at all, it should not be regarded as a mysterious phenomenon. It is simply a concise way of summarizing the prediction that if an individual engages in drinking within a context similar to the one in which drinking has previously resulted in undesirable consequences, such a pattern is likely to be repeated in the future unless substantial changes occur in either the environment or the individual's manner of interacting with that environment.[30]

Pattison and the Sobells make a crucial point that bears directly on the central issue raised by this book. Our idea of alcoholics as fundamental types formed at some earlier point in time and acting in a certain way irrespective of the social environment or cultural context is constantly being eroded by careful research. The idea of "personal control" over alcohol is fatally ambiguous because it trains our gaze at the kinds of individuals standing behind drinking behavior and away from social, environmental, and cultural contexts that directly shape behavior. As Pattison and the Sobells argue, "It would be valuable to consider anyone in the general population as having the potential to develop alcohol problems defined simply as adverse consequences resulting from the use of alcohol—with various individuals having differing degrees of susceptibility."[31]And clearly these degrees of susceptibility are not only a function of individual attributes, but also of environmental contingencies.

The Return to Normal Drinking

The evidence suggests, then, that some alcoholics exhibit surprising control over heavy or at-risk drinking. In recent years another and related controversy has arisen over whether the diagnosed alcoholic can ever return to moderate or limited drinking. This is a sensitive subject, especially with those who adhere to the Alcoholics Anonymous position that alcoholics can never drink again. One of the few critical books on A.A., A. H. Cain's *The Cured Alcoholic*, was furiously denounced by A.A. sympathizers, mostly because it announced that the "cured alcoholic" could learn, under careful supervision, to return to "controlled" drinking.[32]

Over the years, there have been scattered reports in the literature of alcoholics who have returned to limited or more moderate drinking.[33] These reports have usually been opposed either on the grounds of poor research design or because it is claimed that the subjects were not truly "alcoholic" in the first place. The controversy reached front-page dimensions, however, with the widespread publicity generated by a large Rand Corporation study, which suggested that many alcoholics successfully returned to moderate or limited drinking after treatment.[34] The study also suggested that abstinence might not be the only appropriate outcome for treatment, a point of view that Pattison and the Sobells, Mello, and many others already shared:

> The key finding of the relapse analysis is that relapse rates for normal drinkers are no higher than those for longer-term abstainers, even when the analysis is confined to clients who are definitely alcoholic at intake. While the sample is small and the follow-up periods are relatively short, this finding suggests the possibility that for some alcoholics moderate drinking is not necessarily a prelude to full relapse, and that some alcoholics can return to moderate drinking with no greater chance of relapse than if they abstained. This finding, especially if

verified for larger samples and for longer follow-up periods, could have major implications for theories of alcoholism. In particular, it calls into question the conception that alcoholism is caused exclusively by a physiological predisposition to addiction.[35]

The report was furiously attacked in the media by representatives of the National Council on Alcoholism, and spokesmen for the National Institute on Alcohol Abuse and Alcoholism reaffirmed their support for abstinence as the principal treatment objective.[36]

The Rand group has recently reversed itself on the question of whether alcoholics in treatment can return to limited or moderate use of alcohol. A four-year follow-up of alcoholics in treatment indicates that only 8 percent of those in treatment can sustain moderate drinking.[37] This may seem to many as something of a victory not only for abstinence as a treatment goal but also for the traditional notions of the alcoholic as categorically different and predisposed to addiction. But the idea of addiction should be kept separate from the idea of alcoholism (susceptibility). Persons who become addicted to a substance may find it easier to stop altogether than to reduce their use drastically. But this in no way justifies the conclusion that alcoholics are persons who have some innate inability to drink moderately and who are predisposed to addiction; it may merely mean that for some who are exposed to large amounts of alcohol over long periods of time, the likelihood that many will be able to reduce this heavy intake substantially is slight.

The emerging consensus, while not yet an alternative movement, is that alcoholism is a "myth," in the sense that it claims that alcoholism constitutes some unique and definable clinical entity. Instead, alcoholics are quite diverse as a group. Nor is there evidence that alcoholics are distinctly different from nonalcoholics in terms of some predisposing biological or personality trait; alcoholics differ from nonalcoholics mainly in the amount of alcohol they consume.

Waxing and Waning Problem Drinkers

In the sixties, several studies were sponsored by the National Institute of Mental Health to measure drinking patterns and "prob-

lem drinking." Earlier we noted the efforts of some in the alcoholism movement to seek a less vague definition of alcohol problems,
one that was less wedded to fixed ideas about disease and loss of
control, and the Institute-sponsored studies are an example of this
effort. The Cooperative Commission Report, *Alcohol Problems*,
stressed the need for a new problem drinking focus. Paradoxically
this change in focus has only helped to further undermine the
movement's tendency to think of alcohol problems in terms of two
fundamental types. By "problem drinking" the NIMH-sponsored
research meant such self-reported problems as frequent intoxication, binge drinking, psychological dependence, problems with
spouse or friends, job or financial problems, and problems with the
police or accidents. A sample survey conducted in 1967 interviewed
1,359 adults representative of the total population of the United
States, and attempted to measure the extent and seriousness of
these problems among American adults.

The survey reported surprising findings[38] (see Table 1). As many
as 43 percent of the men and 21 percent of the women had moderate
or severe alcohol-related problems.[39] It is risky to call these figures
prevalence rates, since drinking problems seem to come and go.
Nonetheless, in this survey Don Cahalan is satisfied that 9 percent,
or approximately nine million adults, are problem drinkers.[40] According to Cahalan, however, "an additional 9 percent of the total
sample (16 percent of men and 3 percent of women) said they had
had such problems in the past."[41]

There is considerable evidence that alcohol problems come and
go, or "wax and wane," as Josephine Williams puts it. The highest
rates of problems are among young males, and there is strong evidence that as they grow older they "mature out." The situation regarding drinking problems is subject to such change that individual
measures underestimate the prevalence of problems at a given
point in time, and among some groups the "turn over" over a three-
year period approaches 50 percent for some problems.[42] This means
that as many as half of those individuals reporting frequent, heavy
drinking as a problem will indicate, three years later, that this is no
longer a problem, while at the same time their places will be taken
by other individuals reporting the same problems. As Room puts it,
it is as if there were only so many barstools in the United States, and
when anyone falls off one, someone else climbs on.[43]

Table 1

Moderate and Severe Drinking Problems among
American Men and Women

ALCOHOL PROBLEMS	% MEN	% WOMEN
Moderate	(N = 751)	(N = 608)
Psychological dependence	31	12
Frequent intoxication	3	1
Marital problems	8	3
Health problems	6	4
Financial problems	6	2
Total (for 11 specific problems)	28	17
Severe	(N = 751)	(N = 608)
Psychological dependence	8	3
Frequent intoxication	14	2
Marital problems	8	1
Binge drinking	3	—
Police problems, accidents	1	1
Total (for 11 specific problems)	15	4

Source: Don Cahalan, *Problem Drinkers* (San Francisco: Jossey-Bass, 1970), p. 37.

More recent survey research into problem drinking is reflected by Table 2. Such surveys indicate that 10 percent of all drinkers can be classified as problem drinkers, and another 26 percent as persons having potential problems with alcohol. The highest rates of problem drinking occur among the 18- to 20-year-old age group—21 percent. There are substantial and steady declines in problem drinking in older groups.

These surveys, with their portrait of a very volatile problem drinking population, challenge our idea of alcohol problems and social drinking as two rather fixed realities. The evidence that problems come and go, that younger problem drinkers frequently mature out, helps erode the remaining stereotypes and myths surrounding drinking.

The findings of survey research regarding the volatility of problem drinking, plus the experimental findings regarding the alcoholic's "control," have seriously challenged the idea that alcoholism

Table 2

Rates of Problem Drinking among American Drinkers,
by Drinking Population, 1973–1975

	% FOR EACH SURVEY			
DRINKING POPULATION	Mar. 1973	Jan. 1974	Jan. 1975	June 1975
All drinkers				
No problems	64	70	65	63
Potential problems*	26	24	24	26
Problem drinkers†	11	6	10	10
Men				
No problems	57	66	62	57
Potential problems*	29	27	23	31
Problem drinkers†	14	8	15	13
Women				
No problems	74	77	70	73
Potential problems*	21	19	27	21
Problem drinkers†	5	4	3	6

*A potential problem drinker experienced two or three of sixteen problem drinking symptoms frequently or four to seven symptoms sometimes.

†A problem drinker experienced four or more of sixteen problem drinking symptoms frequently or eight or more symptoms sometimes.

Source: HEW and NIAAA, *Third Special Report to the U.S. Congress on Alcohol and Health* (Washington, D.C.: G.P.O., 1978), p. 11. Based on Paula Johnson, David Armor, Susan Polich, and Harriet Stambul, "U.S. Adult Drinking Practices: Time Trends, Social Correlates, and Sex Roles" (draft report for the National Institute on Alcohol Abuse and Alcoholism under contract no. ADM 281-76-0020, July 1977).

is a fixed attribute of special people. This has led critics like Craig MacAndrew and Joseph Schneider to refer to the disease concept of alcoholism as a social achievement rather than as a discovery of a scientific nature.[44] MacAndrew asks the question that still remains, like the Cheshire cat, even after we learn that alcoholism is a myth, or at least not a disease in the literal sense: "How are we to make sense of the fact that there are people in the world who, while seemingly like us in other respects, engage in a project that is so patently pernicious?"[45]

The answer would seem to lie in challenging, at least in part, the commonsense categories on which our ideas of drinking are based. We cannot escape our customary way of looking at the world entirely; central to that world is a process of typification that both describes and explains (makes sense of) the world, especially in terms of the actions of individuals as moral agents.

Again, the solution would seem to lie in challenging the idea that control over alcohol is solely or principally a personal achievement. If we learn that control over alcohol is a direct social achievement as well as a self-achievement, then both the alcoholic and the normal drinker do not seem such different types. This stratagem also requires a challenge to our modern ideas about self- or personal control over "normal" drinking, or what we shall call "the myth of social drinking."

The Myth of Social Drinking

The myth of alcoholism is the shadow of the far more pervasive myth: this is the myth of the social drinker as a type that is a product of mysterious abilities or capacities that are possessed by most members of society. Our goal is not to reject the idea that alcoholics or social drinkers exist; it is rather to challenge our seeing the reality of drinking in terms of two dichotomous personal types. It is not the reality of the problem that is denied, but the reality of our description and explanation of the problem.

The interesting point is that no one seems to have asked whether the majority of drinkers actually possess the personal ability to control their drinking. The question sounds almost absurd. There is, however, a subtle ambiguity in the use of the word "control." In some instances when it is said that most persons are able to control their drinking, all that is meant is that most people do not have problems with alcohol. The idea of personal control over alcohol remains in the background. Thus, when the argument is made that "most people cannot control their drinking," this sounds like a neoprohibitionist claim that most people either have, or sooner or later will have, problems with alcohol. This argument flies in the face of what everybody knows, and the scientific evidence as well: most people, most of the time, do not experience problems with alcohol.

The ambiguity can be cleared up by distinguishing between two terms: personal control and social control. *Social control*, as Morris Janowitz uses the term, refers not only to conforming behavior but also to the capacity of a society to regulate itself regarding key values such as minimizing alcohol problems.[46] Thus alcohol problems (rates) might be seen as a weakening, at least in part, of society's social controls for alcohol use. These failures may be attributed to many factors beyond merely personal or individual characteristics: changing laws for the control of alcohol; cultural forces encouraging alcohol use; economic activities of the alcohol industry; the fortunes of the economy; or the differential social norms for alcohol use in force for women, men, the young, the old. *Personal control*, on the other hand, may be said to be the individual's psychological and physical mastery of his or her personal environment and is likely a factor—but only one factor—in the overall rates of problems.

Thus, when we claim that most people are able to control their drinking, we confuse the two terms, social control and personal control, making the achievement (or failure) of social control seem principally the consequence of personal factors. The use of "control" to refer to a mainly personal achievement is the central fallacy behind the idea of alcoholism. Before we can claim that most drinkers have some personal ability to control their drinking, we would need evidence that, if they were exposed to almost any environment that heightened the risk of problems, they would still be able to avoid them. For example, we would need evidence that the vast majority of drinkers drank frequently and substantially, and still exercised personal control over their drinking, avoiding problems because of personal abilities they possess. Otherwise, the absence of problems may simply be due to a low intake of alcohol (due to widespread and enduring social controls over alcohol use?) and a lack of opportunity for problems.

How can we infer whether it is personal control or the influence of the environment that shapes American drinking practices? How can we discern whether it is personal choice and personal control that determines American drinking practices, or whether the individual's choices about alcohol are constrained and channeled by the social environment? The evidence, I think, turns on how one interprets the distribution of drinking patterns in American culture. This evidence suggests very powerful constraints and channels for individual drinking.

The "individual choice" model suggests that the great majority of drinkers operate in an environment relatively free of limits, constraints, or channeling forces. It suggests that, by and large, persons determine for themselves how much they will drink, and seek to derive maximum benefits from drinking while restricting problems. The atmosphere is relatively permissive and affirmative for alcohol. This culture has as its modal (most frequent) drinker an individual who drinks regularly, yet seeks to avoid serious problems. On the other hand, a culture of constraint would serve to channel an individual's choices regarding alcohol, limiting its importance in everyday life. In this culture, the modal ideal would be an individual who drank on the average far less than what was safe for him individually.

To evaluate the United States we would need a standard that would permit both the regular, frequent use of alcohol and the avoidance of future problems, a standard that would be useful in testing a drinker's personal control over alcohol. This standard would, in effect, be a response to the question often asked about alcohol: What is a safe individual limit for the use of alcohol? What amount can I safely use on a daily basis and still avoid future problems?

One historical standard that has been suggested is Anstie's Limit, devised by a nineteenth-century English physician who studied the mortality rate of drinkers. Anstie argued that if a person were to drink one and one half ounces of pure alcohol daily (roughly three drinks), he would avoid problems.[47] (Curiously, there is a popular test of one's control over drinking that is based on the same level of consumption: two drinks daily—no more, no less—for six months. If one drinks this amount exactly despite the turbulence of daily life, one can assume personal control over drinking.) What is the evidence from survey research regarding American drinking practices? How many Americans do in fact come close to such a standard of "maximum safe use?"

The *American Drinking Practices* survey conducted in the mid-1960s by Cahalan, Cisin, and Crossley reveals that up to 60 percent of all drinkers fall into the infrequent or light categories, and up to 75 percent of all adults are either abstainers or are infrequent to light drinkers.[48] As the following figures show, at any given point in time, an overwhelming majority of the adult population has minimal or no involvement with alcohol:

Abstainers	32%
Infrequent	15%
Light	28%
Moderate	13%
Heavy	12%

Subsequent survey research reveals similar trends in consumption. The overwhelming majority of all drinkers drink far less than a maximum or upper safe limit for alcohol use. Of course, there is very strong evidence that survey research seriously understates (perhaps 40 to 60 percent) the total consumption for drinkers.[49] Dean Gerstein of the National Academy of Sciences has attempted to allocate the current per capita consumption (2.7 gallons of absolute alcohol) among ten drinkers, assuming the relative proportions set out in *American Drinking Practices*. The twenty-seven gallons of absolute alcohol would be distributed among the ten as follows: three drinkers would not drink at all during the year; three more would drink one and one half gallons between them; and the remaining four would drink one and one half gallons, three gallons, six gallons and fifteen gallons, respectively.[50]

This calculation gives a reasonably accurate picture of the distribution of total consumption by American adults. What is striking is that only the drinkers drinking six or fifteen gallons consume as much as Anstie's Limit, or one and one half ounces of absolute alcohol per day (three drinks). A person consuming three gallons of absolute alcohol annually will consume 192 ounces of absolute alcohol per year, or less than one ounce per day. Thus, the curious anomaly: Americans who drink two ounces of absolute alcohol every day would be classified by the NIAAA as "heavy drinkers." Put another way, 85 percent of all adults either do not drink at all or drink less than an amount that might be a safe individual limit. Table 3 indicates trends in alcohol consumption from 1971 to 1976. Notice that individuals who drink one ounce of ethanol every day, on the average, are classified as heavy drinkers. Eighty-nine percent of all adults sampled from 1971 to 1976 fell short of this upper safe limit.

Table 3
Trends in Alcohol Consumption, 1971–1976

TYPE OF DRINKER	1971	1972	1973 (Spring)	1973 (Fall)	1974	1975	1976	6-YEAR AVERAGE	OUNCES OF ETHANOL CONSUMED IN 1 DAY*	AMOUNT CONSUMED†
			% IN EACH DRINKING CATEGORY							
Abstainer	36	36	34	37	33	36	33	35	0	Drinks less than once a year or never
Lighter	34	32	29	30	28	31	38	32	0.01–0.21	One drink a year up to 3 drinks/week or 12 drinks/month
Moderate	20	23	23	21	28	21	19	22	0.22–0.99	4 to 13 drinks/week or 13 to 58 drinks/month
Heavier	10	10	14	11	11	12	10	11	1.0 or more	2 or more drinks/day or 14 or more drinks/week
(N)	(2,195)	(1,544)	(1,588)	(1,603)	(1,578)	(1,071)	(2,510)	(12,090)		

*The measure is derived from the frequency of drinking each type of beverage (beer, wine, and distilled spirits) expressed in number of occasions per day, multiplied by the amount of ethanol consumed on a typical drinking day (assuming ethanol proportions of 0.04 for beer, 0.15 for wine, and 0.45 for distilled spirits).

† A drink is the equivalent of one 12-oz. can of beer, one 4-oz. glass of wine, or one 1-oz. shot of distilled spirits, each of which contains approximately ½ oz. of ethanol.

Source: HEW, NIAAA, Third Special Report to the U.S. Congress on Alcohol and Health. (Washington, D.C.: G.P.O., 1978), p. 7. Based on Paula Johnson, David Armor, Susan Polich, and Harriet Stambul, "U.S. Adult Drinking Practices: Time Trends, Social Correlates, and Sex Roles" (draft report prepared for the National Institute on Alcohol Abuse and Alcoholism under contract no. ADM 281-76-0020, July 1977).

Table 4

Consumption Trends for American Men and Women, 1971–1976

TYPE OF DRINKER	1971	1972	1973 (Spring)	1973 (Fall)	1974	1975	1976	6-YEAR AVERAGE
% IN EACH DRINKING CATEGORY								
Men								
Abstainer	30	28	25	26	24	27	26	27
Lighter	29	29	24	29	24	27	33	28
Moderate	26	28	29	26	34	26	24	27
Heavier*	15	15	22	19	18	20	18	18
Women								
Abstainer	42	44	42	47	42	45	39	43
Lighter	40	34	35	32	32	35	44	37
Moderate	13	18	17	17	21	15	15	16
Heavier	5	4	6	4	5	4	3	4

*Statistically significant linear trend $p < 0.05$, indicating an increase.
Source: HEW, NIAAA, *Third Special Report to the U.S. Congress on Alcohol and Health* (Technical Support Document; Washington, D.C.: G.P.O., 1978), p. 11. Based on Paula Johnson, David Armor, Susan Polich, and Harriet Stambul, "U.S. Adult Drinking Practices: Time Trends, Social Correlates, and Sex Roles" (draft report prepared for the National Institute on Alcohol Abuse and Alcoholism under contract no. ADM 281-76-0020, July 1977).

Table 4 breaks down consumption trends for the same period among males and females. Females are even less likely to approach the upper safe limit for drinking, with an average of 4 percent of all drinkers reaching the maximum. This compares to an average of 18 percent for all males.

What do these figures add up to? First, it would seem that if the maximum safe limit were a plausible test of a widespread ability for most persons personally to control their drinking, very few individuals would meet the test. They would either fall far short of this standard, or drink substantially more. In fact, if per capita levels of drinking in the U.S. shifted upward to approach Anstie's Limit, our per capita figure would triple, far exceeding the level prevailing in France (second only to Portugal in per capita consumption); and the evidence presented in the next chapter suggests that we would inherit many of France's alcohol-related health problems. One is struck by how far below this level the great majority of American drinkers falls. The point of safety is either surpassed—considerably—by a small minority of drinkers, or it is substantially avoided by the great majority of drinkers.

This fact suggests that the cultural norm for drinking in the United States is neither permissiveness nor personal safety. It is instead a norm of constraint, encouraging minimal or infrequent use. While decades of indifference to alcohol policy have contributed to sharp increases in total consumption, the norm still seems not to be that level of safe use consistent with personal safety but rather that use that limits the numbers who exceed the safe limit. Both norms permit use (at least potentially), but the limit is social, not personal.

Still, we tend to think of ourselves and our alcohol problems in terms of personal controls rather than social controls. Our preference for personal choice over social controls is reflected in the commonsense individualism that so dominates our way of thinking about the world—a way of thinking that has subtly shaped our social sciences and our theories of alcoholism. As Eliot Freidson notes:

> Our civilization emphasizes choice over constraint, the individual over the group, and the actor over the environment. . . . Essentially, our instinct is to analyze the human world by reference to individual motives, values, and knowledge rather than by reference to the organization of the human world itself. Thus, in attacking what is wrong in the world our inclination is to emphasize what is wrong in the individual and pour our efforts into ways of changing the individual rather than his environment.[51]

Freidson goes on to underline two central flaws in this common-sense individualism:

> Such common-sense individualism characteristically makes two flawed assumptions. The first is that since the human world is made up of individuals there is no such thing as a relatively stable, structured, social environment that constrains, limits, and channels an individual's behavior regardless of his personal qualities. . . . The second flawed assumption of common-sense individualism is that the individual's characteristics are definitely formed at some point of time into a stable and fixed bundle of knowledge, motives,

and values, and that therefore he will act, from that time of formation and subsequently, more or less the same way no matter what the environment he acts in may be.[52]

Freidson concludes that both assumptions are simply untrue:

> Granted that in the last analysis groups are indeed composed of individuals and therefore exist only through individuals . . . [b]oth the social and the physical environments limit the resources and opportunities for choice available to [the individual] quite independently of his own individual desires and capacities.[53]

Clearly, the myth of social drinking is based on a simple, and in some contexts, quite legitimate notion: people possess powers, abilities, skills, capacities, or resources that account for their success or failure in performing specific actions involving difficulties or hazards. Furthermore, people differ in their abilities. These ideas are valid, when used in limited contexts. Flying an airplane, skiing on a steep slope, riding a wave, or performing difficult surgery permits a commentator to use the language of skills and capacities because he can test his statements. The trouble begins when the notion of abilities is used as an unverifiable analogy that distorts the phenomena to which it refers.

Typifying alcohol problems through ability analogies seems natural because of the simple but misleading fact that most individual drinkers do not experience problems with alcohol. We can avoid this central difficulty by a simple change of focus. We should cease using such terms as "control" and "ability" to speak about drinking behavior unless we include reference to the environmental contingencies and idiosyncratic factors that make the terms meaningful. Our explanation for alcohol problems must become more detailed and complex by including reference to such factors as: cultural and legal restraints, economic variables, and the social contexts that directly shape drinking behavior. This shift in emphasis will still permit us to speak of the individual consequences of heavy alcohol consumption, including addiction and other disabilities. It will avoid, however, the endless search for the "stuff" that alcoholics and social drinkers are made of.

Category Mistake

The central confusion generated by the fallacy inherent in our ideas about drinking and alcoholics rests on what the philosophers call a *category mistake*. Category mistakes occur when we misclassify a set of phenomena, usually by falsely granting them the status of entities or substances. In Gilbert Ryle's famous example, a visitor to Oxford who asks to see the "university" after being shown the several colleges is guilty of a category mistake.[54] The visitor mistakenly assumes that the term "university" stands for some separate entity.

The same kind of confusion has arisen around what we commonly refer to as alcoholism or alcohol problems. The terms *alcoholism* and *alcohol problems* are essentially descriptive terms meaning harmful drinking or drinking "at risk." While the harm of drinking is the result of specific actions and events, the category mistake occurs when a commentator then moves beyond description by inferring that people drink this way principally because of the stuff they are made of.

Language analysis may seem unnecessary in view of the large volume of evidence that already discredits the notion of control in so many other ways. But if the root of our myths surrounding alcoholism and social drinking is our tendency to talk and think about these phenomena in an idiom of individual abilities, capacities, and control, then we will likely never eradicate these mistakes and myths until we abandon systematically misleading language. Asking "why" a minority of drinkers are unable to control their drinking may make perfect sense grammatically, but the view of reality that is created by this way of talking about alcohol problems is based on a category mistake and leads to confusion in all realms.

Blaming the Victim

It is clear that similar ways of thinking are also common in wide areas of social policy. William Ryan has detailed the ways in which we attribute a wide variety of social problems to the behavioral failures of the victims of these problems.[55] For example, Daniel Moynihan defined black poverty as the result of a behavioral inability, as if blacks are unable to strive for long-term goals, such as education and stable employment. Moynihan pointed to the weakness of the black family—the absent father, the dominant mother—as the root of this inability. As Ryan suggests, the implication is that if it were not for this incapacity, the black would find his place in society.[56] But, as Ryan says, this conclusion is unacceptable to those with insight into the pervasive mechanisms of racism and social inequality. It is likely that collective measures against these inequalities—measures that could affect all members of society—will be needed.[57]

Ryan describes the various steps in "blaming the victim" in this way: "First, identify a social problem. Second, study those affected by the problem and discover in what ways they are different from the rest of us as a consequence of deprivation and injustice. Third, define the difference as the cause of the social problem itself."[58] He later elaborates on the second step, suggesting that we identify the problem group as essentially different from the larger population. In his words, "the Different Ones are seen as less competent, less skilled, less knowing—in short, less human." Ryan clearly sees this redefinition as focusing in a judgmental way on the behavioral differences between the two groups, and, thus, this redefinition is at the heart of the problem.

The myth of social drinking functions as a powerful and pervasive ideology that legitimates and alibis the new situation for alcohol consumption that emerged with the collapse of Prohibition and the decline of traditional or fundamentalist perspectives. This ideology located the source of society's alcohol problems solely within the skin of the alcoholic, forcing the moral gaze of society away from the larger issues surrounding alcohol and the conditions of its availability in society. In the next two chapters we will examine the empirical evidence supporting the view that alcohol control policies do indeed make an important difference in determining the rates of many of society's serious alcohol problems.

V. The Alcohol Connection

If there has been one area of strong consensus among the various factions gathered within what has been loosely called the alcoholism movement, it has been that a connection between alcohol—and especially alcohol control policy—and alcoholism has been simply unthinkable. For example, one distinguished group of commentators has said:

> The view that normal drinkers and alcoholics comprise two quite separate groups within the population, which this concept has meant for many workers, has rendered meaningless or at least of low priority the contemplation of measures intended to affect the prevalence of alcoholism through the general regulation of alcohol consumption. The drinking of the alcoholic came to be seen as independent of other drinking: a symptom of pathological factors peculiar to him, and these not amenable to change by measures that would affect the normal drinker. As a consequence, scientists understandably concentrated their attention mainly on the alcoholic per se in an effort to discover the distinctive causal factors.[1]

Whenever suggestions were made to the contrary, to wit, that alcohol control policy might have something to do at least with rates of alcoholism, the reaction was swift and predictable. In a recent paper, for example, Robin Room recounts the disheartening experience of Milton Terris, the well-known epidemiologist and past president of the American Public Health Association (1966–1967), who broke from the herd and examined the relationship between various governmental restrictions on the availability of alcohol and cirrhosis mortality rates during the twentieth century.[2] Terris looked at, among other things, the impact of Prohibition on cirrhosis rates in the United States, Canada, and England and Wales; the impact of wine rationing on cirrhosis in Paris during the German Occupation of World War II; and varying rates in cirrhosis mortality among occupational groups.[3] Terris' findings strongly suggest that there is indeed a strong temporal relationship between restrictions on the availability of alcohol and sharp declines in cirrhosis mortality. For example, Terris found that the cirrhosis rates in the United States, Canada, England and Wales, and Paris all fell precipitiously during World War I. In the United States, this rate fell from somewhere between 13 and 15 per 100,000 population to a low of 7 in 1920, where it remained until 1933. In Paris, however, where there was no Prohibition, the rate rose rapidly. In England and Wales it rose slightly during the period after Wartime Prohibition and then declined during the thirties.[4]

Terris argued that these trends can be explained by two key factors: drastic restrictions on the availability of alcohol and the use of taxation techniques (especially in England) to discourage the consumption of spirits. He further gathered evidence to show that disposable income, as this is roughly indicated by class, accounted for differential rates of alcoholism mortality among various occupational groups (rather than exposure to occupational hazards as others had argued).[5] Consequently, Terris concluded that "governmental fiscal and regulatory measures to reduce per capita alcohol consumption can markedly lower mortality from cirrhosis of the liver."[6]

Whatever the strengths and weaknesses of this kind of retrospective and exploratory epidemiology, of crucial interest to the politics of alcohol policy was the way in which Terris' work was received by some in the public health community. Terris read his paper at the 1966 meeting of the American Public Health Association. The published discussion of the paper (by Jack Elinson) reveals "considerable unease" about the paper's "provocative analysis."[7] The discussant cites various pieces of counterevidence, jokes about "having a drink or two" at lunchtime "before some impulsive local government is led by Dr. Terris' skillful presentation" to alter control laws, and then suggests that, as with the possible association of cervical cancer with frequency of intercourse, there might be some matters better left unknown: "the implications for prevention—if this were a factor—[might be] just too horrible to endure. I think most of us have a similar feeling about alcohol."[8] Elinson put his finger on the temper of the times, however. Even as late as the 1960s, we not only did not want to think about the relationship of alcohol availability and alcoholism; the relationship was simply too horrible to endure.

The Legacy of Prohibition

In large part, the mass refusal even to think about the connection of alcohol policy and alcohol problems can be traced to the Prohibition experience. Whatever else might be true about the problem of alcoholism, attempting to restrict drastically the availability of the substance in order to curb alcoholism is widely believed to have been a colossal mistake.

Prohibition has provided us with a convenient metaphor with which to condemn unpopular policies. For example, in the 1960s, when we were faced with the striking paradox of widespread alarm over the nation's drug problems (heroin, marijuana, methadone, speed) while nearly every expert knew that the nation's leading drug was alcohol, many in the drug field pointed directly to the bitter experience of Prohibition as a model of the wrong way to deal with drug issues. One author referred to our policy of making marijuana possession illegal as the New Prohibition.[9] Now, ten years later, those who argue the connection between total consumption and heavy consumption are quickly branded as "neoprohibitionists."

But there is something of a quiet revolution occurring in our understanding of Prohibition. A small group of researchers has re-examined the Prohibition period and arrived at some rather startling insights. John C. Burnham, Norman Clark, and Joseph Gusfield are adding to the earlier (and largely ignored) work of Warburton and Joliffe and Jellinek.[10] What seems to be emerging (or in many instances re-emerging, since these scholars so often have discovered the work of others whose careful research preceded theirs) is the destruction of several key myths about this period.

One of the most frequently repeated nostrums about Prohibition is that the period achieved almost the opposite of what it set out to do: it caused people to drink more than ever. Even national leaders in the field of alcoholism cling to this view. Morris Chafetz, for example, claims that we tried Prohibition and wound up with people drinking more than ever.[11] But the facts simply do not support this myth, as Table 5 shows.

The per capita consumption of alcohol (in gallons of absolute alcohol) from 1850 to the present indicates that, up to 1910, consumption stood in excess of 2.50 gallons per citizen. After Prohibition the figure for alcohol consumption was 0.97 (1934), a tremendous decline in consumption. These estimates of consumption during Prohibition, of course, are subject to many questions since the estimates of consumption are based on illegally acquired alcohol. All the studies of this period (Gusfield, Joliffe and Jellinek, Jellinek, Warburton, and Burnham), however, agree that the decline during the period of Prohibition was dramatic, especially up until the midtwenties.[12] Comparing the 1911–1915 rate (2.56) with the 1935 rate (1.20) suggests that Prohibition may have reduced consumption by one-half (see Table 5). The evidence for the impact of control measures on alcoholism, alcohol-related diseases such as cirrhosis, and psychiatric diagnosis is just as substantial. Drastically curtailing the availability of alcohol did, in fact, reduce these problems, just as Terris claimed.[13]

There is evidence that, as the twenties progressed, widespread evasion of the law, as the bootlegging trade became organized and established, undermined Prohibition. But some of the forces undermining Prohibition were likely to have occurred anyway. There seems to have been during the 1920s a "youth" explosion like that of the 1960s, a phenomenon that also occurred throughout much of Europe. Café society, "rebellious youth," smoking, dancing, and the rise of the media (especially movies) all contributed to creating a set of attitudes that stood opposed to the values of the dominant "dry" forces.[14] (As Clark points out, however, when the 1928 Congress returned, the drys were perhaps more powerful than at any other time.)[15]

There are many other elements to the legend of Prohibition: the rise of crime, the mafia, disrespect for the law. Some of this is true (though Burnham believes that the rise in crime is largely exaggerated).[16] But despite reports that Prohibition strictures were being

Table 5

Apparent Per Capita Consumption of Alcoholic Beverages, in U.S. Gallons, of the American Drinking-Age Population, 1850–1976

YEAR	DISTILLED SPIRITS Beverage Volume	Ethanol Volume	WINE Beverage Volume	Ethanol Volume	BEER Beverage Volume	Ethanol Volume	TOTAL ETHANOL VOLUME
1850	4.17	1.88	0.46	0.03	2.70	0.14	2.10
1860	4.79	2.16	0.57	0.10	5.39	0.27	2.53
1870	3.40	1.53	0.53	0.10	8.73	0.44	2.07
1871–1880	2.27	1.02	0.77	0.14	11.26	0.56	1.72
1881–1890	2.12	0.95	0.76	0.14	17.94	0.90	1.99
1891–1895	2.12	0.95	0.60	0.11	23.42	1.17	2.23
1896–1900	1.72	0.77	0.55	0.10	23.72	1.19	2.06
1901–1905	2.11	0.95	0.71	0.13	26.20	1.31	2.39
1906–1910	2.14	0.96	0.92	0.17	29.27	1.47	2.60
1911–1915	2.09	0.94	0.79	0.14	29.53	1.48	2.56
1916–1919	1.68	0.76	0.69	0.12	21.63	1.08	1.96
1920–1933: Prohibition							
1934	0.64	0.29	0.36	0.07	13.58	0.61	0.97
1935	0.96	0.43	0.50	0.09	15.13	0.68	1.20
1936	1.20	0.59	0.64	0.12	17.53	0.79	1.50
1937	1.43	0.64	0.71	0.13	18.21	0.82	1.59
1938	1.32	0.59	0.70	0.13	16.58	0.75	1.47
1939	1.38	0.62	0.79	0.14	16.77	0.75	1.51
1940	1.43	0.67	0.01	0.16	16.29	0.73	1.56
1941	1.58	0.71	1.02	0.18	17.97	0.81	1.70
1942	1.89	0.85	1.11	0.20	20.00	0.90	1.95
1943	1.46	0.66	0.94	0.17	22.26	1.00	1.83
1944	1.00	0.76	0.02	0.17	25.22	1.13	2.06
1945	1.95	0.88	1.13	0.20	25.97	1.17	2.25
1946	2.20	0.99	1.34	0.24	23.75	1.07	2.30
1947	1.69	0.76	0.90	0.16	24.56	1.11	2.03
1948	1.56	0.70	1.11	0.20	23.77	1.07	1.97
1949	1.55	0.70	1.21	0.22	23.48	1.06	1.98
1950	1.72	0.77	1.27	0.23	23.21	1.04	2.04
1951	1.73	0.78	1.13	0.20	22.92	1.03	2.01
1952	1.63	0.73	1.22	0.21	23.20	1.04	1.98
1953	1.70	0.77	1.19	0.20	23.04	1.04	2.01
1954	1.66	0.74	1.21	0.21	22.41	1.01	1.96
1955	1.71	0.77	1.25	0.22	22.39	1.01	2.00
1956	1.31	0.81	1.27	0.22	22.18	1.00	2.03
1957	1.77	0.80	1.26	0.22	21.44	0.97	1.99
1958	1.77	0.80	1.27	0.22	21.35	0.96	1.98
1959	1.86	0.84	1.28	0.22	22.15	1.00	2.06
1960	1.90	0.86	1.32	0.22	21.95	0.99	2.07

Table 5 (cont.)

YEAR	DISTILLED SPIRITS Beverage Volume	Ethanol Volume	WINE Beverage Volume	Ethanol Volume	BEER Beverage Volume	Ethanol Volume	TOTAL ETHANOL VOLUME
1961	1.91	0.86	1.36	0.23	21.47	0.97	2.06
1962	1.99	0.90	1.32	0.22	21.98	0.99	2.11
1963	2.02	0.91	1.37	0.23	22.51	1.01	2.15
1964	2.01	0.95	1.41	0.24	23.08	1.04	2.23
1965	2.21	0.99	1.42	0.24	23.07	1.04	2.27
1966	2.26	1.02	1.40	0.24	23.52	1.06	2.32
1967	2.34	1.05	1.46	0.25	23.81	1.07	2.37
1968	2.44	1.10	1.51	0.26	24.33	1.09	2.45
1969	2.51	1.13	1.62	0.26	24.90	1.12	2.51
1970	2.56	1.15	1.84	0.29	26.95	1.17	2.61
1971	2.62	1.18	2.08	0.33	25.90	1.17	2.68
1972	2.60	1.12	2.16	0.31	26.62	1.20	2.63
1973	2.61	1.12	2.25	0.33	27.49	1.24	2.69
1974	2.57	1.10	2.13	0.31	27.76	1.25	2.66
1975	2.58	1.11	2.24	0.32	28.08	1.26	2.69
1976	2.54	1.09	2.26	0.33	28.09	1.26	2.68

Note: Figures are for comparative purposes only; amounts are calculated according to tax-paid withdrawals. Data through 1973 are based on a drinking-age population 15 years old and over; data since 1973 are based on a drinking-age population 14 years old and over.
Source: HEW and NIAAA, *Third Special Report to the U.S. Congress on Alcohol and Health* (Washington, D.C.: G.P.O., 1978), p. 6. Based on Mark Keller and Carol Gurioli, *Statistics on Consumption of Alcohol and on Alcoholism* (New Brunswick, N.J.: Rutgers Center of Alcohol Studies, 1976).

observed by many in the working class, the unpopularity of the measure among many who wrote for the media and the mockery of the legislation in the movies created a legend that is hard to put aside. Whatever the partial successes of Prohibition, it is likely that this period will remain as *the* national symbol of paternalistic interference with personal liberty. In the final analysis, Prohibition was really less about alcohol than cultural change and conflict. Society's alcohol problems are, and were, serious indeed, but not so serious as to justify Prohibition, for reasons we will explore in Chapter 7.

The Per Capita Consumption Thesis

In 1968, an article by Jan deLint and Wolfgang Schmidt, two Canadian researchers at the Addiction Research Foundation in Ontario, Canada, appeared in the *Quarterly Journal of Studies on Alcohol*. The study began with this sentence: "An important question in the study of alcohol use is the statistical distribution of consumption in a population."[17] As a matter of fact, almost no one working in the area of alcoholism research or even survey research into the drinking behavior of national populations regarded the study of the statistical distribution of consumption in a population as an "important question." For the Canadians, however, this was indeed an important issue. The article published in the *Quarterly Journal* reported the results of an early 1960s survey investigating the purchasing practices of those buying distilled beverages and wine from retail stores in Ontario Province.[18] Since purchasers were required to fill out forms giving their names and addresses and the amounts ordered, the researchers had a convenient source of data on the pattern of sales.

The results of this research demonstrated that purchases were neither normally nor bimodally distributed, but rather log-normally distributed. (A logarithmic normal curve is a curve with one mode or peak, positively skewed, which descends smoothly with mathematical [logarithmic] precision.) The distribution of purchases showed the largest number of purchasers buying small quantities, a very much smaller group buying somewhat larger (or what might be called moderate) amounts, and a very small group purchasing quite a bit. The researchers also analyzed the frequency of purchases and the amounts purchased by the heavy buyers and the evidence revealed that this group was not buying in large quantities for others, but more frequently in large quantities for their own consumption.[19]

These data in themselves would probably not have created much of a stir among alcoholism researchers. What did arouse controversy was the researchers' interpretations. DeLint and Schmidt argued that this consumption confirmed the findings of the French alcohol researcher Sully Ledermann, who had argued that the distribution of alcohol consumption in all Western societies was "log-normal." Using the Ledermann "equation," the Canadians calculated the distribution of purchases that might be predicted and found a very close approximation with their empirical study. The actual distribution of purchases of alcohol closely approximated the pattern anticipated by the Ledermann model.

Implications of the Ledermann Model

Sully Ledermann was a French demographer who, during the 1950s, published a study of the distribution of consumption among various Western nations. Ledermann noted that "alcohol consumption cannot be normally distributed since this would imply that the dispersion around the mean could only range from zero to about twice the mean. In all the countries from which alcohol consumption data are available, however, drinking well in excess of twice the national average occurs."[20] Ledermann proposed the logarithmic normal curve as the best fit to the distribution of alcohol use. He documented his thesis on the basis of nine diverse surveys of drinking:

> (1) The distribution of the consumption of wine and alcohol by 274 men aged 45 to 65 of whom 136 were patients in a general medical ward and 138 were cancer patients; (2) A study (1951–1952) dealing with the consumption of alcoholic beverages of Italians residing in the United States and of Americans of Italian origin; (3) A study, based on field work conducted by the Doxa Institute, of the consumption of wine in Italy; (4) Distribution of the alcohol consumption of 1750 motorists in Chicago in 1935–1937; (5) Distribution of the blood alcohol level of 624 persons who came for treatment of "professional sickness" to a center of the Social Security Department of Health and Welfare (France 1951–1953); (6) The distribution of the quantity of wine and spirits bought in 1948 by 6492 Finns; (8) The distribution of the quantity of spirits bought in 1948 by 28,000 Swedes; (9) A study undertaken by the French National Institute of Hygiene on the wine consumption of 181 tuberculosis patients before their illness.[21]

Ledermann argued that these studies all supported his thesis: consumption in most societies is distributed log-normally. The results of the Canadians' research tended to confirm Ledermann's original hypothesis. Further work by Ledermann, Skog, Bruun and his colleagues, Cartwright and his colleagues, and the varied research of Schmidt, deLint, Robert Popham, and Reginald Smart in Canada has tended to support the broad outlines of Ledermann's thesis, at least to the extent that alcohol consumption is not normally or bimodally distributed in the population, and that the level of general consumption is related to the prevalence of problems.[22]

Ledermann's work was practically unknown to English and American scholars, and, if the Canadian group did nothing else, it introduced, at least to a minority of American alcoholism researchers, the work of this French scholar, who only rarely wrote in English. Because Ledermann and the Canadians, deLint and Schmidt, emphasized the distribution of consumption across a population, and because of the emphasis given by these writers to the rather stable and predictable form this frequency distribution assumes, this line of research has become widely known as the "distribution of consumption" thesis.

There are a number of critical implications—and some varying interpretations—of the Ledermann model, most directly relevant to alcohol policy. The first is that consumption in the general population is neither distributed normally nor bimodally. A bimodal distribution would seem intuitively to be most consistent with the alcoholism model, with a very large group of so-called moderate drinkers distributed around some norm for moderate drinking, and a separate and smaller group of alcoholics distributed around the mode for heavy or alcoholic drinking. But the empirical evidence does not square with this commonsense view. A central point of the Ledermann thesis that is confirmed in general population surveys of drinking is that consumption is distributed among a very large group that drinks very little and seldom, a much smaller group that drinks regularly but not at risk, and a very small group that drinks heavily and "alcoholically." The progression from each category is relatively smooth, and among the more frequent drinkers each successive group composes a smaller proportion of the drinking population. There is no "bump" or shift in the curve for heavy, alcoholic drinkers. One implication of this general point is that drawing a line between nonalcoholic and alcoholic consumption is difficult and ultimately arbitrary.

Second, a change in the mean is accompanied by a change in the same direction in the rates of prevalence for such alcohol problems as cirrhosis. For Ledermann, this was because the model is a special one-parameter case of the log-normal distribution, in which the range is fixed on the right and left bounds and with the dispersion relatively invariant among populations with the same mean. Ledermann reasoned that since it is not possible to drink less than zero, the left bound must be fixed. Ledermann fixed the right bound by the biological limit of consumption after which death is likely to result. He posited this limit to be one liter of absolute alcohol per day (365 liters of absolute alcohol per year).[23] Furthermore, to Ledermann and the Canadians there is no major variation in the shape or form of the curve among populations with comparable limits of average consumption. These special conditions add up to a one-parametric distribution of consumption, in which average consumption and heavy consumption covary.[24]

Figure 1 illustrates the various shapes of the curve, and the conditions under which the dispersion shifts when the mean consumption of alcohol has increased. When this happens, the mass of the curve shifts rather smoothly to the right, increasing the numbers of those who drink at higher rates, including the very highest levels of consumption.

Some of the articles critical of the Ledermann thesis focus on the simple correlation between levels of consumption and rates of such alcohol problems as cirrhosis, noting that these findings are not novel, and that they are, moreover, aggregate, retrospective, and subject to the dangers of spurious correlation.[25]

Another line of attack questions the basis on which the distribution was inferred, the ways in which the data were gathered, or the special properties of the curve. For example, Gary Miller and Neil Agnew devote considerable space in their review to arguing that the Ledermann thesis does not stand if Ledermann was wrong about the right bound being fixed at 365 liters of absolute alcohol per year. They claim that this would mean that the distribution may not be a special one-parameter case of the log-normal curve; there may be two parameters. If this is so, Ledermann's entire thesis is undermined since there are a number of dispersions that can be imagined for a given average consumption if the right bound is not determined. Miller and Agnew go on to suggest that "alcoholics"

Figure 1

The Ledermann Consumption Model: Distribution Curves of Alcohol Use in Norway, Canada, and France in 1968 by Average Daily Consumption (Ounces of Spirits)*

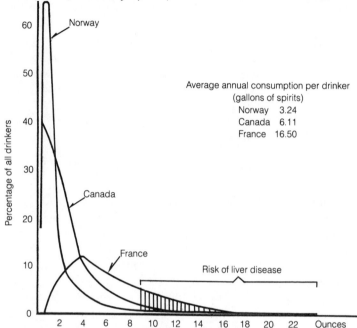

*The average annual consumption is in imperial gallons. The higher the average per capita intake, the more the distribution curve shifts toward the high-intake end of the scale. The hatched area indicates the levels of intake associated with a proven risk of liver disease.

Source: Reproduced with permission from Harold Kalant and Oriana J. Kalant, *Drugs, Society, and Personal Choice,* published by the Addiction Research Foundation, Canada.

might in fact be a distinct population buried within the statistics of "heavy drinking," especially in countries with a high average level of consumption (such as France).[26]

Douglas Parker and Marsha Harman similarly suggest that Ledermann's constant (the limit of one liter of absolute alcohol per day) is open to serious question, and again, if this constant is disturbed, the entire thesis is challenged. The survey evidence gathered by Ledermann to support the log-normal thesis is also challenged on a number of other points by Parker and Harman, as well as by N. M. H. Smith.[27] For example, the validity of using clinical populations seems questionable to them, as do the small numbers in many of the samples.[28]

In the Canadians' view, while there are deficiencies in Ledermann's original study, Ledermann supplemented his study with new data that further confirmed his thesis, and the subsequent confirmation of these findings by their own work and that of others is persuasive.[29] For example, the Norwegian scholar O-J. Skog, perhaps the most sophisticated critic of the log-normal thesis, has made much the same point. He notes that a simple one-parametric distribution (such as the Ledermann distribution, in which only the mean varies) is likely to give a fairly good approximation of the distribution of consumption in a general population. Skog has also stated that "Ledermann's theory of the distribution of alcohol consumption is a remarkable example of scientific intuition. From a very modest data base, he reached conclusions which later studies have supported as essentially sound."[30]

Evidence for this point can be gleaned from the rather large number of empirical findings of survey researchers among a wide variety of populations revealing that "differences as to dispersion between populations with similar levels of consumption are quite small."[31] This is an important empirical finding because a principal objection brought against the distribution thesis (as we have seen) is that countries with the same average or mean consumption of alcohol can have quite different dispersions. If this were true, then at least logically there would be nothing to prevent populations of the same average consumption from exhibiting quite different patterns of consumption within that mean. As Bruun and his colleagues have commented:

> to acknowledge the possibility of differences with respect to dispersion is simply another way of saying that a given amount of alcohol can be distributed among individuals in many different ways. And this, it will be remembered, was precisely the opinion of those who objected to seeing the problem in terms of total consumption.[32]

The source concludes:

> the apparent stability in dispersions seems to indicate a certain invariance in the distribution pattern. The *prima facie* possibility of substantial differences between different cultures does not, according to the available evidence, manifest itself in real life. The reasons for this invariance are largely unknown; little research has been done on this subject and given our present state of knowledge no plausible explanation can yet be offered, other than that the level of consumption of each individual may be presumed to reflect his social milieu. One might well say, to paraphrase Euripides, "tell me the company you keep, and I'll tell you how much you drink."[33]

The Canadians argue that, in the final analysis, three key propositions flow from their and Ledermann's work:

> 1. A change in the average consumption of alcohol in a population is likely to be accompanied by a change in the same direction in the proportion of heavy consumers.
> 2. Since heavy use of alcohol generally increases the probability of physical and social damage, the average consumption should be closely related to the prevalence of such damage in any population.
> 3. Any measures, such as those regulating the availability of alcohol, which may be expected to affect overall consumption, are likely also to affect the prevalence of alcohol problems, and hence should be a central consideration in any program of prevention.[34]

Room has suggested that the debate over whether or not the distribution of consumption is log-normal and whether the connection between average consumption and heavy consumption exhibits "quasi-mathematical" properties is somewhat beside the point. One need only say that if a "strong temporal relationship between the overall consumption level and cirrhosis mortality can be shown, whether the consumption is distributed log-normally or otherwise is largely immaterial to policy considerations. From this perspective, the whole argument over the Ledermann curve has been a diversion from the policy issues of the interrelations of prices and other controls, consumption levels and cirrhosis mortality."[35]

A Sociological View of the Ledermann Thesis

The response to the Ledermann model of alcohol consumption has been interesting and revealing. The preoccupation with the special properties of the curve risks another form of reductionism, and parallels the alcoholism movement's preoccupation with entity explanations for alcohol problems. The solution to the riddle of the Ledermann model does not lie in reifying the properties of the curve, seeing the curve as a cause rather than as a descriptive model. Instead, we should inquire as to what sociological factors might help explain this pattern of consumption. The most plausible explanation for the distribution of alcohol consumption lies along the lines of Floyd Allport's model of "conforming behavior" developed in the early thirties. (Room first noted Allport's work.)

Allport reported a number of studies that were conducted by himself and others on the nature of conforming behavior.[36] He had in mind such goal-oriented and rule-guided behavior as arriving at church on time, stopping at a stop sign, kneeling at church, arriving at work on time. He observed that a wide range of empirical studies indicate that the distribution of conformity with the rule or norm was unimodal and heavily skewed toward conformance. That is to say, the great majority of individuals conformed rather closely to the rule; a smaller group committed minor deviations; a much smaller group broke the rule noticeably and barely conformed; and, finally, a very small group flagrantly ignored the rule. Allport noted that when compliance was monitored (such as when a policeman is stationed at the intersection where the stop sign was located) the rate of conformity increased, with the rate of nonconformity and violation declining.

Allport's work is strikingly parallel to Ledermann's findings. Allport suggested that four factors played a role in conforming behavior: the rule or norm itself (or in Allport's terms conformity-producing agencies), biological tendencies, personality factors, and chance. We do not have to follow Allport's scheme to outline an explanation for the distribution of alcohol consumption based on four variables: norms restricting drinking; their "restrictiveness," or their location relative to a defined point described as harmful drinking; norm sanctions; and systematic forces for norm alteration, change, or evasion.

In this view, then, the distribution of alcohol consumption is a member of a large class of social behaviors commonly referred to as "conforming behavior." The pattern or distribution is unimodal (referred to technically as leptokurtic), and positively skewed, with the right slope of the curve smoothly descending; each successive interval in the curve contains a smaller proportion of the population.[37] The form or shape of the curve of consumption is dominated primarily by the norms and sanctions restricting or regulating the use of alcohol. A primary consideration in determining the shape or dispersion of the curve is the position or location of the norm that dominates the distribution. *The closer the norm to the point determined to be a rate of alcohol consumption that places most users at risk for problems, the higher will be the numbers who drink at risk.*

Another important factor in determining the dispersion of the curve are systematic forces for either liberalizing or evading alcohol norms. The two most likely forces for liberalizing existing alcohol norms would be cultural modernism and commercial interests such as the liquor and advertising industries. Factors such as prices and controls that are supposed to sanction and support the norm can also become systematically weakened over time (through inflation or rising disposable incomes), leading to further departures from established norms.

The role of personality or individual characteristics cannot be dismissed; certain personality traits may be differentially found in conformity, defiance, or innovation. But the issue is whether the prevalence of these traits or characteristics in one society is such that it is an additive factor, skewing the distribution of consumption further to the right more than for other societies. It seems plausible that personality characteristics determine the incidence of problems (where incidence means who specifically is located at a given position on the distribution). It also seems plausible that the prevalence rates for alcohol problems in every system are increased because of personality or other individual characteristics leading to an increased dispersion of the distribution of consumption. It does not seem likely, however, that this would be an important factor in explaining rates *between* systems nor short-term fluctuations in consumption. It is very unlikely that the disparity between rates of heavy consumption in Mississippi and California, and between Norway and France, is determined to any great extent by differences in the prevalence rates of certain personality characteristics. Rather the differences in aggregate consumption are predominantly due to the operation of norms for alcohol use, and their restrictiveness, in effect in differing areas, groups, or nations—as well as the supporting sanctions—plus the added factors of social movements for innovation and change.

Of course, there is no single set of norms regarding alcohol use; there is wide variation between the sexes, ages, regions, ethnic groups, and strong urban-rural differences. Despite this variation, however, the overall structure of drinking norms is still supportive of the social order—the dominant norms restrict alcohol use; heavy or alcoholic drinking is not the norm for any group of consequence.

This suggests something of an explanation as to why empirically we do not find a bimodal pattern of consumption in the drinking population. Even in the case of norms of defiance or norms sanctioning or supporting heavy consumption, there is no separate "central tendency" existing apart from the norms for appropriate or approved use. Where the position of drinking norms shifts toward increased use, the overall structure remains the same: the dominant normative pattern restricts or limits alcohol use. The norms for heavier use that are found among specific ages and groups (young males or certain occupational groups) do not exist in a vacuum. The influence of the dominant norms restricting use is never absent—even for the groups in question. These norms constantly constrain patterns of heavy use and encourage conformity. The heavy user or the alcoholic cannot be considered apart from the larger social environment. Even in his own immediate environment, most of the individuals the heavy consumer will encounter use substantially less alcohol than does he. The crucial issue is the structure of norms and sanctions that restrict alcohol use; a rise in consumption is to be taken as indicating a relaxation of existing norms and supporting sanctions (especially prices and control, or broad economic circumstances or cultural forces that have the same effect).

Per Capita Consumption and Cirrhosis Mortality

What is the evidence for the idea that there is a strong temporal relationship between consumption levels and rates of alcohol problems? Researchers who have investigated the temporal relationship between per capita consumption and cirrhosis find a very high correlation. In countries where per capita consumption is low, cirrhosis mortality tends to be low. In countries where per capita consumption is high, cirrhosis mortality is high. Table 6 presents the per capita consumption of alcohol for a large number of mostly Western nations and the associated rates of alcoholism. The correlation between the two variables is extremely high. Table 7 presents temporal and regional correlations between rates of cirrhosis mortality and per capita alcohol consumption for a number of Western nations, as well as for selected provinces, states, and departments. A quick visual examination of the coefficients reflects the high correlations that result in temporal and regional comparisons. The outstanding exception, and one that has puzzled many researchers, is the case of the United Kingdom.[38]

Against the plausible objection that these temporal correlations may not reflect cause-effect relationships, the investigations of Jellinek, Terris, Massé et al., and others into the impact of sharp curtailment of the availability of alcohol during periods of Prohibition in the United States, Canada, and Finland indicate that these restrictive policies were followed by sharp declines in average consumption and cirrhosis rates (see Figures 2 and 3).[39] The same is true for the extreme shortages of wine because of rationing in Paris during both world wars, as Figures 2 and 3 indicate.

The Strike in the Finnish Alcohol Monopoly Stores

There is one other rather striking study in the literature of the impact of sudden restrictions in the availability of alcohol. This is the study conducted by the Social Research Institute of Alcohol Studies of the strike by the State Alcohol Monopoly (ALKO) retail clerks in Finland, causing a closing of the ALKO stores from April 24 to May 31, 1972.[40] Since the news of the impending strike had been available for some time before the actual closing, the Social Research Institute of Alcohol Studies (funded by ALKO) had time to conduct a rather ambitious and remarkably detailed study of the strike's impact. The overall impact of the restrictions caused by the closing of the ALKO stores can best be appreciated in terms of the fact that

Table 6
Annual Consumption of Alcohol and Rates of Death from Liver Cirrhosis

COUNTRY	PER-DRINKER CONSUMPTION (LITERS) (1966 OR 1967)*	ESTIMATED RATES OF DRINKERS IN EXCESS OF A DAILY AVERAGE OF 15 CL OF ABSOLUTE ALCOHOL PER 100,000 POPULATION AGED 15 AND OLDER†	RATE OF DEATH FROM LIVER CIRRHOSIS PER 100,000 POPULATION AGED 15 AND OLDER (1963, 1964, OR 1965)‡
France	25.9	9,405	45.3
Italy	20.0	5,877	27.3
Portugal	19.5	5,652	42.7
Spain	17.1	4,635	24.3
Austria	16.0	4,212	35.0
W. Germany and W. Berlin	16.0	3,978	26.7
Switzerland	15.8	3,901	19.7
Luxembourg	12.5	2,988	34.2
Hungary	12.4	2,952	12.9
U.S.A.	12.0	2,198	18.4
U.S.S.R.	11.4	2,655	13.1
Canada	11.1	2,272	10.0
England and Wales	10.9	1,946	3.7
Rep. of Ireland	10.9	1,946	4.5
Denmark	9.4	1,818	10.2
Belgium	9.3	2,052	12.9
Poland	9.0	1,752	8.6
Sweden	8.4	1,515	7.9
Netherlands	7.7	1,456	4.9
Finland	5.9	945	4.6
Norway	5.9	945	4.7

*Alcohol consumption data were taken from the 1968 Annual Report of the Dutch Distillers' Association.
†The numbers of drinkers in excess of a daily average of 15 cl of absolute alcohol were tabulated on the basis of data provided in J. Hyland and S. Scott, "Alcohol Consumption Tables: An Application of the Ledermann Equation to a Wide Range of Consumption Averages" (Ontario, Canada: Addiction Research Foundation, mimeographed, 1969).
‡United Nations, *Demographic Yearbook of the United Nations, 1966* (New York: Statistical Office of the United Nations, Department of Economic and Social Affairs, 1967).
Source: de Lint and Schmidt, "Consumption Averages and Alcoholism Prevalence," *British Journal of Addiction* 66 (1971): 100.

Table 7

Correlations between the Liver Cirrhosis Mortality Rate and Per Capita Alcohol Consumption

AREA	SERIES	CORRELATION COEFFICIENT	PROBABILITY LESS THAN
Australia	1938–1959	.65	.005
Belgium	1929–1959 (less 1940–1945)	.75	.001
Canada	1927–1960	.88	.001
Alberta	1929–1960	.85	.001
Manitoba	1935–1960	.86	.001
Nova Scotia	1932–1960	.60	.001
Ontario	1930–1960	.89	.001
Quebec	1929–1960	.43	.05
Saskatchewan	1943–1960	.77	.001
Canada	9 provinces 1955	.81	.01
Finland	1933–1957	.78	.001
France	1925–1958	.62	.001
France	23 departments 1950	.76	.001
Holland	1927–1958	.57	.001
Sweden	1926–1956	.45	.05
United Kingdom	1931–1958	−.68	.001
United States	1934–1958	.60	.005
United States	45 states 1939	.61	.001
United States	48 states 1944	.78	.001
United States	46 states 1950	.76	.001
United States	46 states 1957	.86	.001
International	11 countries 1956	.78	.005

Notes: In all instances, liver cirrhosis mortality was expressed as an unstandardized rate: deaths per 100,000 population aged 20 and older; and the measure of alcohol consumption comprised sales of alcoholic beverages expressed as imperial gallons of absolute alcohol per capita of population aged 15 and older. The international series comprised Australia, Belgium, Canada, Denmark, France, Finland, the Netherlands, Sweden, Switzerland, the United Kingdom, and the United States.

Source: Kettil Bruun et al., *Alcohol Control Policies in Public Health Perspective* (Helsinki: Finnish Foundation for Alcohol Studies, 1975), p. 42. Based on R. E. Popham, "Indirect Methods of Alcoholism Prevalence Estimation: A Critical Evaluation," in *Alcohol and Alcoholism*, ed. R. E. Popham (Toronto: University of Toronto Press, 1970), pp. 678–685.

Figure 2

*Death Rates for Liver Cirrhosis, United States, England and
Wales, Canada, and Paris, 1900–1964*

Source: Milton Terris, "Epidemiology of Cirrhosis of the Liver," *American Journal of
Public Health* 57 (1967): 2085.

these stores accounted for almost half of all sales of alcoholic beverages in Finland.

There is not sufficient space to report all the ingenious methods
employed by the Social Research Institute to record the impact of
the strike. Notable among them, however, in addition to surveys of
the Finnish population, were attempts to record the use of illicit
beverages, to scrutinize reports of public drunkenness, and to observe public intoxication in selected sites in Helsinki (for example,
at the centrally located railway station) before, during, and after the
strike. Nurses from thirteen outpatient clinics for alcoholics kept

Figure 3

Death Rates for Liver Cirrhosis and Apparent Per Capita Consumption of Absolute Alcohol from Spirits and Wine, United States, 1900–1964

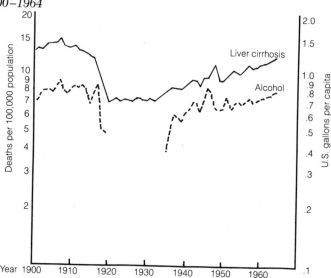

Source: Milton Terris, "Epidemiology of Cirrhosis of the Liver," *American Journal of Public Health* 57 (1967): 2077.

records on the frequency of daily visits for hangover treatment. Results of blood tests undergone by persons suspected of drunken driving were analyzed. In each of these and other measures, attempts were made to control for annual, seasonal, or daily cyclical fluctuations by gathering comparable data for earlier or later periods.

The results reported by the study are striking indeed. There was apparently a marked decrease in arrests for public drunkenness, with the total number of such arrests dropping to half of the normal level. The arrests resulting from excessive drinking of wines decreased the most, whereas the arrests caused by the ingestion of light beer and denatured surrogate alcoholic products increased tenfold. As might be expected, the impact of the strike fell differently on different groups of those arrested for public drunkenness. Among persons living in private homes, arrests decreased 60 percent from the pre-strike rate, while arrests of those lodged in barracks for itinerant persons decreased 54 percent. The homeless group arrest rate decreased by 31 percent.[41]

The effects of the strike on drunk driving were also noticeable, but not very remarkable. The researchers speculated that operating an automobile was likely to be highly correlated with drinking in licensed restaurants. Since these establishments were not affected by the strike, the low impact on this category is perhaps not surprising. Likewise, the decrease in alcohol-related visits to polyclinics and hospitals was noticeable, particularly visits occasioned by injuries from accidents or fights. On the negative side, there was some increase in the procurement of supplies for the illegal distilling of alcoholic beverages, as well as the use of surrogate alcohol beverages by homeless alcoholics.[42]

The survey of Finnish adults was mainly an attitude survey to determine the reactions of the public to the strike itself, rather than an attempt to measure changes in actual drinking behavior. On the whole, most people simply ignored the strike at the personal level, yet saw it as a good thing for the entire society. As Klaus Mäkelä, the director of the study, noted, it became clear during the survey that alcohol inhabited a rather small place in the daily lives of most Finns.[43]

Measures Liberalizing the Availability of Alcohol

The reports of drastic restrictions of the availability of alcohol through governmental measures or "natural experiments" such as the Finnish strike are typically dramatic in their impact either on general consumption or alcohol problems. The usual pattern of change in alcohol legislation since the period of Prohibition, however, has been toward liberalizing alcohol control measures, toward increasing the physical availability of alcohol. These innovations include such changes as relaxing the restrictions on hours of sales or locations of sales outlets or total sales outlets, liberalizing the kinds of beverages that are permitted in general commercial distribution systems (such as permitting beer to be sold outside state monopoly stores), permitting "liquor by the drink" or different kinds of retail bars (such as when Canada permitted "cocktail" lounges), or lowering the age limit for purchasing either distilled beverages or beer and wine.

The problem with these kinds of policy changes is that they are nearly always marginal in their impact, incremental in nature, and very difficult to measure in terms of their effect on overall consumption or on alcohol problems. For example, despite the furious controversy that has persisted in some southern and southwestern states (namely Oklahoma and North Carolina) over the issue of "liquor by the drink," there is very little in the literature to indicate just what effect permitting liquor by the drink brings. C. W. Bryant's study in the early 1950s, for example, did not find any significant impact in the transition to liquor by the drink in the state of Washington.[44]

Drinking and Changing the Age of Majority

In recent years there has been much public attention given to the question of lowering the drinking age. Over the past decade, a number of states (at least half) have lowered the age of majority in order to permit young persons to vote, to enter into contracts, and to purchase alcoholic beverages.[45] These laws have remained relatively uncontroversial except for the lowering of the drinking age. At least initially, opposition to this change came from some church groups and law enforcement officials. The public has, at least before the controversy grew after the change in law, supported the changes, in part because of the belief that teenagers were already drinking, and also because of the constitutional amendment lowering the voting age to eighteen in federal elections. If a person is old enough to be drafted, or so the argument goes, then he is old enough to drink alcoholic beverages.

These changes were implemented in many different ways. Some states lowered the legal drinking age to nineteen, some lowered it to eighteen, and many lowered it to eighteen only for beer and wine. The controversy that has emerged over the legal drinking age has focused on drinking and driving. There is a substantial body of research that suggests that the change in these laws may have contributed to increases in alcohol-related crashes and fatalities. As Paul Whitehead and R. G. Ferrence argue, "The available data conclusively point to an increase in alcohol-related collisions of various types (fatal, personal injury, and property damage) in Massachusetts, Michigan, Illinois, and Ontario."[46]

Many of these studies have focused on the change in Michigan. Richard Douglass was among the original group of researchers who pointed to the increase in alcohol-related crashes in that state as a result of a change in the Michigan law in 1971. Subsequent analysis by Douglass suggests that there was also a significant increase in the availability of alcohol (especially draft beer) in Michigan during the period when the law was taking effect. Douglass' research suggests that the increase in availability combined with lowering the age limit may have contributed to an increase in the alcohol-related crash rate.[47]

Richard Zylman has challenged these conclusions, arguing that a change in police methods of recording crashes created an artificial rise in recorded crashes in Michigan.[48] Zylman suggests that the clamor aroused by opposition to the change caused police to record any instance of alcohol-involvement in crashes, whereas previously alcohol-related crashes would be recorded and noted only in the most flagrant cases. But as Whitehead and Ferrence point out, the data cited by Zylman could just as easily support the idea that the change in the law itself was directly responsible.[49]

Emerging Trends in International Consumption

Pekka Sulkunen, a researcher with the Finnish Social Research Institute for Alcohol, has analyzed the experience in Finland and other industrialized nations, attempting to isolate common patterns.[50] It is important to recognize the similarities among the industrial nations because of the huge proportion of world-wide recorded consumption attributable to the industrial nations. As Sulkunen points out, "Argentina, New Zealand, Chile, Canada, the United States, and Japan, together with the countries of Europe, consumed roughly four-fifths of the alcohol used for drinking purposes throughout the world. The combined population of these countries, on the other hand, amounted in 1968 to about 800 million, or less than a quarter of the world total."[51]

Clearly the industrialized societies can be grouped into three overlapping categories: wine-drinking countries, beer-drinking countries, and spirits-drinking countries. Wine-drinking countries almost invariably have the highest total consumption, largely because wine is taken at meals and is an important source of calories. Spirits-drinking countries are typically the lowest in per capita consumption.

Sulkunen examined the growth in levels of consumption since the 1950s in the countries where data was available, and discovered that there was a marked increase in total consumption for almost every country during the post–World War II period, especially during the sixties. This increase was especially sharp for the spirits-drinking countries. Consumption in beer-drinking countries also increased rapidly. In wine-drinking countries the increase was less rapid. According to Sulkunen, wine is decidedly losing ground as a source of alcohol, in the midst of total increases in alcohol consumption.[52] What seems to be happening is that drinking tastes are converging throughout Europe, North America, and the rest of the industrialized world. For example, places where spirits have long been the dominant form in which alcohol is consumed (such as the Nordic countries) are experiencing great growth in beer consumption.

But what is more, and this is the important point, these upward trends typically do not result in one beverage replacing another, but rather in new beverages and new styles of drinking being added to traditional patterns. Sulkunen is worth quoting on this point:

> The development that has taken place resembles a cumulative process, in which new elements are piled on top of old ones, forming new strata over the total constellation of drinking habits and customs and reinforcing the old traditions in the bargain. The strata of drinking patterns lying underneath absorb ingredients from the new ones without being undermined—at most, they might undergo a change in character.[53]

Sulkunen goes on to remark that his research bears out Klaus Mäkelä's "addition hypothesis," or the idea that new drinking styles and patterns typically are added to, rather than substituted for, established patterns.

(What is just as interesting as Sulkunen's findings is the structure and form of his argument. Drinking and even heavy consumption are described in terms of structural and aggregate language—"layers," "strata," and the like—with almost no attention to individual attributes. This research stands in sharp contrast to typical American studies, including survey research. These modes of description anticipate future conceptions of drinking patterns and even problematic phenomena.)

In the United States, the increase in levels of consumption is similar. Apparent total consumption in 1960 was 2.07 gallons per capita (see Table 5). This rose to 2.68 in 1971, a growth of almost one-third, and remained at that level until 1976. In recent years the level has increased again, rising to 2.82 gallons in 1978. The United States consumes a very large fraction of its total alcohol consumption in the form of distilled beverages (1.09 gallons absolute alcohol—ethanol—in 1976, or roughly 40 percent of the total), yet beer remains the leading beverage (1.26 gallons absolute alcohol in 1976); Americans consumed only 0.33 gallons absolute alcohol in the form of wine in 1976.

The Effects of Price

The conventional wisdom regarding price and alcohol consumption is that alcohol beverages are not particularly sensitive to fluctuations in price, all other things being equal. On this point Bruun and his colleagues have this to say:

> For different countries and different periods, econometric analyses based on the classical theory of consumer demand have shown that fluctuations in the demand for alcoholic beverages can by and large be explained statistically in terms of prices and incomes, that is, in terms of the same variables as are involved in the fluctuations of demand for other commodities. Alcoholic drinks appear therefore to behave on the market like other commodities, and changes in alcohol prices and income appear to be closely related to observable changes in alcohol consumption.[54]

The relationship between price, disposable income, and the consumption of alcohol is so direct, at least in the opinion of the chief statistician for the State Alcohol Monopoly in Finland, that he is quoted as saying, "The connection between liquor consumption and economic conditions is so plain that the volume of alcohol sales has even been used in scientific economic research to register economic fluctuations."[55]

The myth that alcohol is insensitive to fluctuations in price is probably traced to notions about taxation policy and the selection of alcohol as a favorite target of taxation because it yields such important sources of revenue. Yet I was told by officials of the Swedish Alcohol Monopoly that taxation for alcohol in that country may soon reach the level at which increased taxes will clearly result in declining revenues to the state because new taxes will bring an overall decline in consumption.

Popham, Schmidt, and deLint have reviewed the literature on this topic, paying particular attention to the issue of whether the demand for alcohol is more sensitive to changes in income levels than to price.[56] H-H. Lau has also examined this issue.[57] The consensus among the researchers seems to be that some measure that combines price and income and that does not obscure the contribution of each would be the most accurate.

The most important source of criticism of the econometric studies comes from those who wonder who precisely among the drinking population is drinking less as a result of increased prices. Are the heavy consumers indifferent to the tax, with only the moderate drinkers adjusting their consumption to fluctuations in price? (There is also the question of equity: are the poor bearing an unreasonable burden of these policies?) Studies comparing the changes in the relative price of alcohol (the price of alcohol adjusted for changes in income) with changes in cirrhosis rates suggest that the impact of price changes is felt both by heavy consumers and by those who drink far less (though it would be very difficult to determine the precise differences or "elasticities" for the two groups). These studies have examined these relationships over time as well as cross-sectionally.[58]

In an important contribution to this literature, Philip Cook undertook to examine "quasi-experimentally" the impact of tax increases on distilled liquor consumption over a fifteen-year period in the United States, between 1960 and 1975, a period of rising alcohol consumption generally. For purposes of comparison, Cook limited his study only to license states and eliminated price changes of less than $.25 a gallon. (He also excluded Alaska, Hawaii, and the District of Columbia.) His procedure was to establish a twelve-month before-and-after baseline rate of consumption increase for the state in which the change occurs, and then to compare the rate of change with the median proportional change in consumption among all other license states during this same period. Of the thirty-nine price changes and subsequent changes in consumption during this period, Cook found that thirty resulted in lower rates of increase in consumption, when compared to other states and to the baseline trends for the state in which the change took place.[59]

This is very strong evidence of the impact of price on consumption. Cook went further and examined whether there was a relationship between increases in price, cirrhosis mortality, and fatal automobile crashes. Again, he found that there was a significant relationship. As he points out, these data suggest that whether the distribution of consumption thesis is correct or not, price seems on balance an effective instrument in moderating rates of cirrhosis or automobile crashes.[60]

Despite the importance of these findings, all experts caution that these relationships do not constitute the royal road to alcohol policy: the fact remains that changes in price cannot bring about dramatic reductions in total consumption for the simple reason that achieving substantial tax increases is tremendously difficult in the face of opposition from the alcohol industry and consumers generally. The rise in real income, as well as the mechanism of inflation, also constantly tends to undermine the tax policies of various governments. One suggestion might be to "index" the prices of these beverages, tying them to the inflation rate.

Popham, Schmidt, and deLint, for example, recommend the following as principles to be followed in taxation policy for alcohol:

> 1. A price structure such that the cost of a given quantity of absolute alcohol was the same for the cheapest source of alcohol in each class of beverage: beer, wine, and spirits. . . .
> 2. Adjustment of prices as often as required to maintain a constant relationship between the cost of beverage alcohol so

established and the disposable income level of the population; and

3. The ultimate establishment of a relative price level that would maximize the preventive value of this control measure.[61]

Other Restrictions

Studies of other measures to restrict the availability of alcohol have been numerous.[62] These have included such factors as whether the jurisdiction in question permits the licensed retailing of alcoholic beverages or whether some form of state monopoly is used, changes for hours of sale, restrictions on the numbers of outlets, "liquor by the drink," and so on. With perhaps the single exception of the reduction in age limitations, the findings of these studies have all been much less clear than in the case of price control.

The reasons for this are fairly complicated, but the most important is likely that—except for cases like Finland—changes in availability are seldom dramatic and sudden. Further comparisons between two areas that have differing systems for controlling the sale of alcoholic beverages (such as the difference between the monopoly states and the license or franchise states in the United States) do in fact show that the monopoly states tend to have slightly lower rates of cirrhosis and sales of alcohol.[63] This finding, however, was not statistically significant and complicated by the fact that the monopoly states tend to be states with less urbanism and where temperance sentiment remains high and where the prevailing cultural attitudes remain strongly anti-alcohol among large segments of the public.

Popham, Schmidt, and deLint suggest that there is not much evidence that control over the number of retail outlets has a marked effect on consumption.[64] One wonders, however, whether this is true, or even necessary to point out. The fact remains that in most jurisdictions alcohol is minimally available: it is difficult to develop an adequate index of availability (leaving the question of price aside) that takes into account taverns, retail stores, state stores, geographical distance. It is an extremely complicated methodological problem and not at all as easy to research as is price.

On this point, Kathy Magruder examined the various counties of North Carolina in 1972 and developed an index of availability that ranged from (1) dry (no alcohol is permitted), to (2) wine and beer, (3) state stores, and (4) wine, beer, and state stores. After controlling for income and urban-rural differences, she still found that cirrhosis rates were lowest in those counties that were dry and progressed evenly up to highest for those counties where alcohol was maximally available.[65]

The Implications for Policy

This summary of the work of researchers connecting aggregate alcohol consumption to alcohol problems has only scratched the surface. The reports coming from numerous researchers in Canada, the United States, the Nordic countries, France, and elsewhere all add up to a very strong, indeed compelling, case that the general level of consumption of alcohol beverages is of central public health significance.

The data are controversial, and it is likely that the controversy will continue. A good deal of this controversy resembles the one over smoking and health data. Opponents argue that it is purely associational or correlational, and retrospective. This is a serious criticism. But epidemiologists have long adopted decision rules to minimize the distortions that can occur when using aggregate data and where research controls are not easily found. Thus, as Popham, Schmidt, and deLint argue:

> If the associations are consistently encountered in both regional and temporal series for different populations, if the range of variation in the indices is substantial, if trends through time have been in both directions, and if the character of the relationship is in accord with expectation based on scientific knowledge, then the onus of proof shifts to those who contend that cause-and-effect is not involved. In our view this applies reasonably well to the present status of the evidence bearing on the role of economic accessibility as a determinant of rates of alcohol consumption and alcoholism.[66]

There is no doubt that the continued debate surrounding these proposals has had a salutary effect. In the first place the challenges have brought these ideas to the attention of a much wider audience within the alcoholism community than might have occurred otherwise. Also, they seem to have resulted in more modest and more reasonable statements of the central ideas involved.

This much we can say: The issue has been squarely joined. The connection between alcohol policy, total consumption levels, and at least heavy consumption and cirrhosis seems well established, although clearly subject to further refinement and clarification. Evidence seems less strong that other alcohol-related problems such as arrests for public drunkenness, or alcohol-related highway crashes would be held in check if total consumption were controlled. Certainly many more variables are at play here, and the need is to avoid overstating the case for the distribution of consumption thesis, pushing its limits too far and thereby discrediting its well-established claims.

Finally, it must always be remembered that what has been developed is a theory of aggregate consumption levels, including heavy or hazardous consumption. This approach differs sharply from the alcoholism mode of thinking in that it is a policy-oriented approach focusing on aggregate relationships that develop over time rather than seeking to explain "alcoholism" once and for all.

The irony is that if, rather than inquiring into what causes people to drink excessively (the search for a general theory of alcoholism), we ask what causes the number of those who drink heavily to rise and fall, we begin to make progress. The central questions of policy and philosophy still remain, however. It is one thing to demonstrate a relationship between alcohol policy, total consumption, and heavy consumption; it is quite another thing to consider the political and ethical questions that arise when the actual implementation of these policies is considered. This among other issues of alcohol policy will occupy us in the concluding chapter. Before this, we shall look more closely at the fascinating alcohol policy debate occurring in Finland, a debate that may be helpful in framing the debate over alcohol policy in the United States.

VI. Alcohol Policy in an International Perspective

The Case of Finland

The case of alcohol policy in the Nordic countries, particularly the legislation in Finland, Sweden, and Norway during the 1960s that was intended to liberalize the alcohol control system, is already an important and well-researched episode within alcohol policy literature. This is especially true for Finland. Data are readily available on the relationship between altering the regulation of alcohol availability and changes in total consumption, drinking for purposes of intoxication, heavy consumption, and the like. An examination of the Nordic experience is appropriate here because of the ways in which it can help frame our "ways of thinking" about alcohol policy and how alcohol policy is affected by larger forces for social and cultural change in advanced industrialized societies.

Specific data on changes in Finland may seem, at first glance, to be of minor interest to American policymakers. Many may believe that conditions in Finland or Sweden differ greatly from those in the United States. Indeed, there are important structural differences between Nordic and American politics: in the former one finds parliamentary forms, elite autonomy, multi-party traditions, a long history of dominance by the Social Democrats in most countries, and a unique form of government by consensus and consultation.[1]

It is arguable that the small size of the Nordic countries, especially Finland, makes them poor candidates for comparative research. It is true Finland is very small compared to the United States—roughly 4.5 million inhabitants, as opposed to over 200 million. On the other hand, Sweden, Norway, and Finland bear important similarities to the United States: all have had a strong Temperance tradition, Finland and Norway experienced Prohibition, and their state monopoly systems of alcohol control are similar to many state systems in the United States.

While there are always dangers in making generalizations drawn from comparative research, the case of Finnish alcohol policy remains important for the United States in two ways. The changes have been studied closely by internationally respected researchers. Their findings, summarized in this chapter, constitute an important body of alcohol policy knowledge, especially regarding alcohol availability and its control by governmental measures. This research contributes to our knowledge of the effectiveness of a small number of conventional policy instruments commonly found in the mature industrialized countries, such as tax policy, availability, and age restrictions, to name a few. The Finnish literature regarding the 1969 Alcohol Act, which liberalized alcohol restrictions, is an important part of this research.

The experience of Finland is especially interesting because of the major economic and cultural changes that occurred in that country over the past several decades. These changes brought the forces for cultural modernization and those for cultural traditionalism into conflict once more;[2] this conflict has characterized the various movements that arose in the United States and other nations as they moved toward post-industrial society, with its increasingly important services sector, high levels of affluence and consumption, and rapid urbanization and mobility.

The process of maturity is apparently occurring throughout the Western world, irrespective of political systems and cultures. If this is true, then the changes in alcohol policy occurring in Finland provide important insights for them all, not just for the impact of specific policy instruments such as taxation or availability. These changes are also important for comprehending the environment of alcohol policy—an environment that contains traditional views toward alcohol policy, as well as modern views. It may also be the case that a post-modern view of alcohol policy is developing in Finland that could help us anticipate, at least in part, trends in the United States.

The Finnish Alcohol Policy Debate

Noway, Finland, and Sweden have all had relatively restrictive systems for the control of sale of alcoholic beverages during this century. Both Finland and Norway experienced Prohibition, which lasted in Finland from 1920 to 1931. Sweden only narrowly missed Prohibition as a result of a nation-wide referendum.

The three nations also have similar systems of controlling alcohol. In each country there is a State Monopoly for the manufacture and sale of most alcoholic beverages, except for beer with a very limited alcohol content (in Finland, beer with less than 2.25 percent alcohol by weight). Generally speaking, until the liberalization legislation each country permitted only a very light form of beer to be distributed in shops and restaurants. Wine is sold through the State Monopolies.

The arrangements for the State Monopolies vary only in detail from country to country. In Finland, it is generally agreed that the Monopoly (ALKO) is more autonomous and independent from the Ministry of Social Affairs and Health. In both Finland and Sweden, the Monopoly has in recent years been headed by rather prominent figures politically (the director of ALKO is Dr. Pekka Kuusi, who served as a minister of Social Affairs and Health in the early seventies). The director of Vinmonopolet in Norway, by contrast, has been more a manager and a nonpolitical figure.

ALKO casts a formidable shadow across the Finnish economy. The revenues derived from ALKO constitute almost 8 percent of all state revenues. The comparable figure for the United States is 2.2 percent of federal, and roughly 1 percent of state and local, revenues.[3] Furthermore, ALKO also has substantial restaurant and hotel holdings: as much as 10 percent of all hotel rooms in Finland are allegedly owned by the Monopoly. ALKO is not just a retailing organization like American state monopoly systems; it is also a substantial manufacturer of alcohol beverages. The fact of ALKO's size and prominence in Finnish life leads many to speculate that there are real contradictions existing among the three purposes of ALKO: to manufacture and sell alcoholic beverages, to raise revenues, and to hold down consumption.[4]

In fact, ALKO's discretion in matters of control bears on the alcohol policy debates that began about 1948, when an Alcohol Legislation Committee was formed. ALKO anticipated the debate, and established the Finnish Foundation for Alcohol Studies (1950) as part of its response. The Committee's report came out in 1951, and prompted a wide public discussion of the usefulness of alcohol control. Soon after, ALKO supported Kuusi's study of rural prohibition, and independently liberalized wine consumption by no longer requiring identity cards for purchasing lighter wines.[5] These maneuvers signalled from the beginning ALKO's leadership role in the movement away from restrictive systems that was to follow.

The change the Alcohol Legislation Committee recommended—the end of rural Prohibition and the liberalization of beer—was to overturn a very old tradition. While Prohibition ended after an advisory referendum in 1931, rural Prohibition was instituted before national Prohibition and continued after its repeal. State Monopoly stores were permitted only in urban areas or market towns. As Kuusi points out, no sale of alcohol had taken place in rural areas in Finland since 1902.[6] When we recall the very late date for the great rural migration to the cities in Finland, rural Prohibition was very important indeed. Thus when the Committee recommended in 1951 that beer (with no more than 3.5 percent alcohol as to weight) be sold in retail shops and licensed restaurants, this was a recommendation for a change to the fifty-year-old policy. (This change did not actually occur until eighteen years later—the Alcohol Act was passed in 1968 and went into effect on January 1, 1969.)

The Finnish Drinking Style

The way in which Finns define their alcohol problems—or the Finnish drinking style—is intimately connected to the policy debate regarding making the lighter beverages more available. An excerpt from a 1958 study by Erik Allardt might help clarify the Finnish view of their alcohol problems:

> The consumption of alcohol in Finland is smaller than in most European countries. . . . More than half the adult population uses alcoholic beverages less often than once a month and the most common pattern is to use alcohol a few times in a year.

In spite of this low rate of consumption drunkenness is a comparatively common phenomenon. In 1950 the rate of arrest for drunkenness was about ten times higher in Finland than in Sweden and three times higher than in Norway. There is evidence showing that Finnish immigrants in the United States in the early nineteen-twenties had rates of arrest for drunkenness higher than any other immigrant group. . . . Studies of Finnish drinking habits reveal that the Finns drink at irregular intervals, mainly on Saturdays and Sundays, and they are apt to drink great quantities at a time. The consumption of distilled spirits is heaviest, while the consumption of wines and brewed beverages is much smaller. The drinking of alcohol is to a great extent regarded as a means of getting drunk.[7]

The Finnish alcohol problem is seen as the inclination to indulge in short, intense bouts of drinking, for the explicit purpose of intoxication, followed by rather long periods of relatively little or no use of alcohol. Survey researchers are particularly interested in the question of how much one drinks on a particular occasion—with relatively little interest in constructing a typology of drinkers. (However, and in recent years, there is some interest in what they term "big consumers.") Consequently, there has been little attempt to estimate the number of "alcoholics" in Finland. In fact, this is rather an interesting aspect of the comparative study of the definitions of problems: there seems to have been little interest in the numbers or rates of heavy drinkers in Finland until recently.

In the United States, by contrast, the magnitude of alcohol problems has long been statistically documented, and the focus has been on the long-term and chronic ingestion of alcohol, particularly manifesting itself in middle-aged males. Intoxication, even public drunkenness, is considered an alcohol problem, but there is less interest in the amount consumed on a particular occasion than on accounting for the amount. Thus, here alcoholism is judged as "loss of control" and the problem of a select, rather small minority of individuals—although that minority may be numerically quite large—and so forth.

Until the late 1960s, Finnish aggregate consumption was among the lowest totals in the world. It still remains in the middle range, despite the increases during the 1960s and the 1970s. In spite of this low overall consumption, researchers in Finland have commented on the relatively high per capita arrests for drunkenness. Finns have seen as telling the fact that many Southern European countries drink much more per capita than Finland, yet have much lower arrests for drunkenness.[8] Thus, a point of view emerged that an actual increase in consumption, specifically of wine and beer, might lead to more moderate drinking, the decline of drinking for purposes of intoxication, and a decline in drunkenness arrests.

The Proving Ground of the Debate

These two issues—the long-standing debate over the usefulness of the existing alcohol control system and the Finnish drinking style—provide the introduction to the first attempt to test the effectiveness of liberalizing alcohol measures—the rural prohibition experiment of the early 1950s.[9]

Kuusi's introduction to this early piece of field experimental research addresses the question of alcohol policy in the post-war period, taking the perspective of those individuals and groups who sought to modernize and develop Finnish society. Kuusi argues that the increase of state power to pursue collective security in many areas is a desirable and necessary attribute of modern social democracies. But Kuusi warns of the need to remove excessive restrictions in the social sphere. The need is to re-evaluate the necessity for burdensome traditional and moralistic restraints that may in fact be counter-productive. Kuusi argued that while the trend of modern social policy has been to stress social organization and collective approaches, it is often the case that the boundary line between the demonstrated needs of individuals for safety and welfare and for freedom must be carefully assessed. He went on to suggest in rather veiled terms that sometimes this line can be drawn too heavily on the side of safety and indeed may be done so to safeguard the interests of "certain groups."[10] Kuusi is clearly taking the "cultural modernist" view, referring to these restraints as categorical restrictions.

Regarding the controversy over making alcohol available in rural areas and making certain forms of beer more available in retail shops, Kuusi lists six different hypotheses about the results of change:

1. The number of temperate persons will decline.
2. The frequency of drinking will increase.
3. A shift in the consumption pattern will occur to the advantage of the light beverages.
4. The use of illicit liquors will decline.
5. The quantities consumed at one sitting will decline.
6. Drunkenness and breach of public peace will become more common. [11]

Kuusi notes that Temperance opinion tends to stress the first and second hypotheses—temperance will decline and drinking frequency will increase. The State Alcohol Monopoly tends to favor hypotheses 3 and 4, predicting a shift to light beverages and a decline in the use of illicit beverages. Kuusi also points out that the division of opinion on the decline in temperate persons and the increase in frequency of drinking was not so large as it might seem, since both sides agree that this might happen, with those favoring change arguing that more drinking and more frequent drinking are actually occurring than Temperance groups seem to believe. The sharpest point of disagreement centers around option 3, the shift in consumption to light beverages.

The actual design and implementation of the experiment is interesting but can only be discussed briefly. The experiment was to take place in four dry market towns located in rural areas (there were two control towns). Beer and wine were to be made available in state stores. A survey of the experimental and control towns was made in 1951, before the opening of the stores, and followed up with the measurements taken from 1952 to 1953, in order to determine the effects of the change. [12]

In general, Kuusi found that those who used alcohol infrequently were little affected by the opening of the experimental stores. He found that the use of beer increased sharply in some areas (particularly among those communities where drinking frequency was already higher), and that the use of illicit liquor declined. [13] There was no appreciable increase in public drunkenness, and, indeed, Kuusi questioned the relation of the control system to the frequency of excessive drinking. [14] In addition, only slight indications of an increase in the amount of alcohol consumed at a given occasion arose.[15]

Interpreting the results of the experiment was somewhat frustrated by the changes in alcohol policy ALKO put into effect at the beginning of the experimental period. However, the results were interpreted by Kuusi as generally supportive of the liberalization position (although Kuusi states his case very carefully and tentatively).

The 1969 Alcohol Act: A Sequel

It is not possible to reconstruct the complex forces that led to the changes in policy in 1968 and the Act in 1969, but, for our purposes, the broad outlines are of interest. The central point is that there were substantial forces for liberalization within Finnish society and some of those who were in a position to influence policy were in favor of these changes. It is clear that the sentiment favoring a less restrictive policy for alcohol grew stronger among the leaders of ALKO, among the experts at the Finnish Foundation for Alcohol Studies, and among the general public during the period of the sixties. It is the opinion of many experts that the rather remarkable social and demographic changes occurring in post-war Finland, accelerating during the early 1960s and culminating in the election of 1966, were major factors in the changing social climate. The left generally did well in the 1966 general election, the new government being made up of a coalition of the Center Party, the Social Democrats, and the party of the Finnish Communists.

This election was seen as a critical one among young people in Finland because it represented a break with the past, a strong commitment to growth, and a promise to liberalize Finnish society. A very popular book of this period, Kuusi's A Social Policy for the Sixties, called for a comprehensive plan for social provision for the non-producing sector (the aged, the poor, and the handicapped) in order to further expand economic growth.[16] Prevailing ideas of development and the deliberate stimulation of growth, coupled with a growing climate of permissiveness and a population that was much younger, seemed to make the existing state alcohol policy seem out of date and restrictive.

The groups opposed to change were the Temperance organizations, which have a rather long history. While their numbers have declined in the post-World War II period and their membership is older and often inactive, this decline has been somewhat offset by the tendency of Temperance members to be active politically. Also, the Temperance organizations have, in a sense, become part of the bureaucracy being subsidized by the State Ministry for Social Affairs and Health both directly and through the operation of local Temperance boards. (These boards serve mainly as local alcohol education agencies at the communal level.)

The liberalizing forces carried the day, and the changes brought by the 1969 Alcohol Act were these: The restrictions on the number of rural areas where no alcohol was permitted were abolished (in 1968 nearly 50 percent of Finns lived in areas where no state store was permitted). The state alcohol monopoly's policy toward the licensing of restaurants was changed so as to permit alcohol (beer especially) to be sold in more restaurants. And the legal drinking age was reduced from 21 to 20 for distilled beverages, and to 18 for light beer.

The Aftermath of Lifting Restrictions

What were the results of this long-anticipated and much-debated change? As a Parliamentary Commission was later to report, the results took everyone by surprise. First of all, and perhaps most spectacularly, total consumption of alcoholic beverages increased by 48 percent during the first year. Most of this initial increase was accounted for by the increase in consumption in beer. But the consumption of spirits also rose, at first moderately, and then rapidly (see Table 8).

Total consumption continued to rise over the next several years, from 2.88 liters of absolute alcohol in 1968, to 4.21 in 1969, and finally to 6.19 in 1975. In recent years alcohol consumption has apparently stabilized. As one can see, an increase in the consumption of beer from 0.94 liters of absolute alcohol in 1968 to 2.11 liters in 1969 was a rather dramatic increase. It is significant in terms of the Finnish alcohol policy debate that in that first interval the increase in strong alcoholic beverages was quite modest, but grew rather

Table 8

*Per Capita Consumption of Alcoholic Beverages in Finland,
1951–1975, in Liters of Absolute Alcohol, by Category of
Beverage, and by Mode of Distribution*

YEAR	DISTILLED SPIRITS	WINES	BEER	ALCOHOLIC BEVERAGES, TOTAL	RETAIL	CATERING
1951	1.36	0.10	0.32	1.79	1.33	0.46
1957	1.15	0.24	0.33	1.72	1.29	0.43
1962	1.42	0.26	0.43	2.11	1.63	0.48
1968	1.43	0.51	0.94	2.88	2.19	0.69
1969	1.58	0.52	2.11	4.21	3.09	1.12
1972	2.19	0.63	2.28	5.10	3.69	1.41
1975	2.81	0.97	2.41	6.19	4.73	1.46

Source: Salme Ahlström-Laakso and Esa Österberg, "Alcohol Policy and the Consumption of Alcohol Beverages in Finland in 1951–1975," *Bank of Finland Monthly Bulletin* no. 7 (Helsinki: Bank of Finland, 1976), p. 9.

strongly in the intervening years (from 1969 to 1975). As we shall see, this point is given an interesting interpretation by the Finnish researchers.

The changes in the availability structure for the distribution of medium beer were radical and sudden with the new law. The number of applicants for licenses to retail medium beer was considerable, and the policy of ALKO was to grant licenses to almost every applicant. The total number of such outlets increased from zero in 1968 to 17,431 in 1969, with about 10,000 of these located in rural municipalities.[17] The total number of outlets fell to 12,000 by 1975, for reasons unrelated to ALKO's policy. Also, the number of Monopoly stores and medium beer shops and full-licensed restaurants also increased sharply during the first three years of the change in the system. These changes are summarized in Table 9.

According to a count by Klaus Mäkelä, the number of drinking occasions during which the estimated blood alcohol level of drinkers reached at least 0.1 percent increased by about 25 percent. Another Finnish student of this period estimates the increase in heavy consumers of alcohol from 61,000 in 1961 to 91,000 in 1969, whereas the increase would likely have stopped at 71,000 had the law remained unchanged.[18]

Table 9

Finnish Distribution Network for Medium Beer, 1969–1976

YEAR	RETAIL OUTLETS	RURAL RETAIL OUTLETS	SERVICE OUTLETS	RURAL SERVICE OUTLETS
1969	17,431	9,878	2,716	1,195
1971	15,560	9,034	3,406	1,647
1973	13,550	7,374	3,319	1,524
1975	11,965	6,965	3,086	1,393

Source: Salme Ahlström-Laakso and Esa Österberg, "Alcohol Policy and the Consumption of Alcohol Beverages in Finland in 1951–1975," *Bank of Finland Monthly Bulletin* no. 7 (Helsinki: Bank of Finland, 1976), p. 9.

This sharp increase in consumption during this period in Finland has been put into historical perspective by Salme Ahlström-Laakso:

> In Finland and also obviously in other countries the concern over the increased consumption among young people is connected with the general growth of alcohol consumption. After abolishing the Prohibition Act in 1933, less than a litre of pure alcohol was consumed a year in Finland. The two-litre limit was broken after three decades in the first half of the 1960s. From the year 1968 to the year 1973, the consumption of alcohol again doubled. This took five years; in other words, one-sixth the time that it took for the previous consumption to double. Finns consumed 5.6 litres of pure alcohol per capita in 1973.[19]

This dramatic rise in consumption during the 1960s and early 1970s was not restricted to Finland; the increase occurred in most Western countries, especially those with a relatively low aggregate consumption and that had experienced Prohibition.[20]

More Recent Surveys

Jussi Simpura, another researcher with the Social Research Institute of Alcohol Studies replicated Mäkelä's 1968 and 1969 surveys in 1976 to see what further changes in drinking had occurred. In

Table 10

Data on the Previous Week's Use of Alcohol by 15- to 69-Year-Old Finns in 1968, 1969, and 1976

USE	WOMEN	MEN
Alcohol consumers (% of total)		
1968	57.00	87.00
1969	65.00	91.00
1976	80.00	91.00
*Weekly drinking instances per alcohol consumer**		
1968	0.50	0.90
1969	0.80	1.50
1976	0.70	1.40
*Average consumption of alcohol in a single instance of drinking (cl of 100% alcohol)**		
1968	3.00	7.30
1969	3.20	6.20
1976	4.40	8.40
*Average weekly consumption of alcohol (cl of 100% alcohol, all respondents)**		
1968	0.88	5.96
1969	1.66	8.37
1976	2.52	10.32

*The results are based on drinking instances within the week preceding the interview and represent a typical autumn week of the year.
Source: Jussi Simpura, "The Rise in Aggregate Alcohol Consumption and Changes in Drinking Habits: The Finnish Case in 1969 and 1976" (draft mimeo., Finnish Foundation of Alcohol Studies, Helsinki, 1978).

general, Simpura found that, during the period from 1968 to 1976, the numbers of women abstaining declined in a very dramatic fashion (see Table 10). While there was some slight decline for men in the first year of the new legislation, the number of abstainers remained constant thereafter. The mean or average number of drinking instances per alcohol consumer also tended to change, but in a rather surprising way. Not unexpectedly, the average number of drinking instances increased in the first year rather sharply. However, this number declined over the next six years.[21]

It must be recalled that, to ALKO and the experts at the Finnish Foundation, an increase in drinking frequency was regarded as a sign that drinking was becoming more moderate and that lighter drinks (such as beer) were being consumed. Thus a decline in drinking instances was not necessarily seen as a positive development.

What Simpura speculates has occurred is that there actually was an increase in drinking instances from 1969 to 1976. This was not revealed in the survey results, however, because medium beer had in the intervening period become defined as a "non-alcoholic" drink (much like the light beer that was available in Finland in retail shops prior to the change). Thus, respondents were less likely to report the drinking of medium beer in their responses.[22]

Also, regarding the average weekly consumption of alcohol, as Table 10 indicates, there has been a strong and sustained increase in alcohol consumption on average during a weekly period, increasing from 5.96 centiliters of alcohol per week to 10.32 centiliters, for men. For women the increase was, not unexpectedly, greater, from 0.88 to 2.52 centiliters. Simpura argues that "the growth in average consumption in a single instance is the overriding factor increasing consumption among men, and it is also of greater importance for women than the other chief factor, the increased number of alcohol consumers."[23]

Esa Österberg has attempted to obtain a precise understanding of the impact of these legislative changes on such problems or alcohol-related damages as public drunkenness and alcohol-related crimes, highway crashes, and the like. Here we will consider only the question of drunkenness, which is seen as a key indicator of the Finnish drinking style, because it was of special significance in the alcohol policy debate. Per capita arrests for drunkenness fell at a fairly constant rate from 1950 to 1958. There was a slight increase between 1958 and 1967, but 1967's rate still remained smaller than 1950's. For the next two-year period (1968–1969), the arrests for public drunkenness fell by 10 percent. This shift was due largely to a change in the law that removed criminal sanctions against drunkenness, and a period generally of rather lax enforcement in Helsinki and elsewhere. From 1969 to 1975 arrests for drunkenness (per capita) doubled again.[24]

Österberg is careful to point out that there are many perils in using arrest statistics. He notes, however, that arrest rates declined as a function of the per capita consumption of alcohol from 1950 to 1975, with the arrest rate for 1975 being approximately half that of

140 Beyond Alcoholism

Table 11

Per Capita Alcohol Consumption, Finland and Sweden, 1951–1973

YEAR	FINLAND		SWEDEN	
	Liters	%	Liters	%
Total				
1951	2.58		3.49	
1962	3.01		4.03	
1973	7.41		6.73	
Increase				
1951–1962	0.43	16.7	0.54	15.5
1962–1973	4.40	146.2	2.70	67.0

Source: Based on Klaus Mäkelä and Esa Österberg, "Alcohol Consumption and Policy in Finland and Sweden, 1951–1973," *Drinking and Drug Practices Surveyor* no. 12 (December 1976), p. 6.

1950. Looked at this way, the liberalization period interrupted a decline from the high point of 1950, with the period of 1969 to 1975 remaining fairly constant.

Despite the sharp increase in consumption and drinking for purposes of intoxication, the question to what extent these increases were due to the changes in law and not to a general trend in Finnish society needs addressing. Klaus Mäkelä and Esa Österberg have compared Sweden and Finland during the period 1951–1973 in terms of growth in per capita consumption, population trends, economic increases, and alcohol control policies. Their research reveals that Finland's growth in per capita alcohol consumption paralleled Sweden's until the Finnish liberalization in 1969. After this change the Finnish level rose to a point higher than Sweden's during the early seventies (see Table 11).

In comparing Finland's and Sweden's experiences with liberalizing their alcohol policies, Mäkelä and Österberg note the sharp rise in consumer expenditure in Finland in the late sixties and the timing of this increase with the Alcohol Act of 1969.[25] They also remark the sharp rise in ALKO outlets, a process that began in the 1960s outside of rural areas before the 1969 Act. (Furthermore, with the Alcohol Act in 1969, there was a tremendous expansion of Finland's restaurant network, where alcohol is available.) In 1951 there were

51,000 inhabitants per state store for the 80 stores in all of Finland. In 1973, there were 184 stores, or one store for 26,000 population. In Sweden the change has come much more gradually, with 241 stores, or one store for each 20,000 inhabitants, in 1951, and 309 stores, or one for every 26,000 inhabitants, in 1973.

Mäkelä and Österberg argue that the creation of a dense distribution network in Finland within a short period surely had a singularly negative impact on the greater increase in per capita consumption. Large areas of rural Sweden never experienced the kind of Prohibition that existed in Finland until the late 1960s. Also, the expansion of restaurants and ALKO shops everywhere—a process that began before the 1969 Act—along with the strong increase in consumer expenditures per capita, surely helped to accentuate the changes in Finland.[26]

Evaluating the Impact of the 1969 Alcohol Act

The Finnish researchers appear unanimous on three central points concerning the impact of the 1969 Act. The changes following the Act were adverse, more dramatic and much more negative than predicted. Second, there is consensus that the worsened situation of alcohol problems in the mid-1970s cannot be fairly attributed to the Act alone. There is unanimity on this point at the Finnish Foundation for Alcohol Studies. The Foundation found that while the 1969 Act clearly had significant impact on the worsening of alcohol problems, the 1970s would probably have experienced a worsening of many problems anyway. Finally, although the Temperance movement disputes it, most Finnish research concludes that the 1969 Act was more or less an inevitable product of forces for cultural change in Finnish society that were well-nigh irresistible.[27]

One force was demographic. The evidence regarding the shift toward urban preponderance is striking:

> In 1951 about 67 percent of Finns lived in the countryside, while the corresponding share in 1960 was about 60 percent and in 1973 about 43 percent. Migration has been very heavy. Moreover, there has been a rapid movement in the countryside from remote villages to population centers, and in the

cities from the center to the suburbs. Migration has been connected with changes in the vocational structure of population.[28]

The comparison between Finland, Sweden, Great Britain, and Hungary for the period 1950–1970 for the changing mix of the agricultural, industrial, and service sectors (which includes white collar) is even more revealing. These data show that the shift from primary to secondary *and* tertiary employment occurred in Finland *at much the same time*, as opposed to other Western countries (see Table 12). This period was also marked by a dramatic increase in real incomes. Ahlström-Laakso and Esa Österberg report that private consumption expenditure per capita increased by about 44 percent in real terms from 1951 to 1962, and by about 52 percent from 1962 to 1973. Disposable income also increased rapidly during the 1960s and early 1970s, the five-day work week was introduced during this period, and social legislation substantially improved the social security of the average Finnish citizen.[29]

The Rise of the "Wet Generation"

In addition to such demographic shifts in the social and economic arenas, there were some important changes in drinking styles and behavior. Data on this, particularly abstinence, has recently been analyzed by Sulkunen, using the four basic Finnish national drinking surveys: Kuusi (1946), Mäkelä (1968, 1969), and Simpura (1976). Sulkunen focuses primarily on abstinence rates and the ages at which the first drink is taken, as indices of major cultural change.[30] What emerges is a revealing picture of a society rapidly undergoing a major cultural and social transformation, and the impact of this change on drinking styles.

Sulkunen's conclusions are complex and interesting. He argues that the fact of strong economic growth during the sixties may have given impetus to the increase in consumption during that period, but that the more important changes were generational and cultural in nature. Both in terms of abstinence rates and age at which adolescents took their first drink, the post-war generation differs from its predecessors:

Table 12

Distribution of the Labor Force for Several European Countries in 1950, 1960, and 1970

COUNTRY	AGRICULTURE			MANUFACTURING			SERVICES		
	1950	1960	1970	1950	1960	1970	1950	1960	1970
Finland	46	35	20	27	31	34	27	34	46
Sweden	21	14	8	41	46	40	38	40	52
Great Britain	5	4	3	48	49	46	47	47	51
Hungary	54	38	25	22	34	45	24	28	30

Source: These data were furnished by the Research Group of Comparative Sociology of the University of Helsinki.

Drinking by adolescents seems . . . to be a phenomenon that began to emerge among those who were born in 1916–1925, and who reached their adolescence after the Prohibition and during and immediately after the war (approximately 1930–1946). Kuusi (1948, 111) estimates that probably more than 25 percent of the males in this age group had their first drink in the army or in the war.

Commenting on these data, Kuusi wondered in worry: "Is it too early now to assess whether this practice of boozing at a premature age will be found as a transitional aftermath of the war, or will it develop into a permanent custom? In any case, this is a phenomenon that deserves continuous attention."

After thirty years, the answer is somewhat distressing. Boozing at a premature age did not only develop into a permanent custom. It developed into a practice of boozing in childhood. In fact, in 1976 drinking at the age of 15–19 was no less common than at the age of 20–29, if measured by the proportion of those who had ever taken a drink.[31]

Sulkunen does not so much argue that this "wet generation" drank more on average than did the earlier generation, but rather that it tended to be more likely to drink and to begin drinking at an early age. Abstinence began to decline sharply during the period, especially during the 1960s among white-collar groups and among women. Differences between rural and urban groups began to disappear, and young persons began to take up drinking earlier.

Sulkunen's conclusions also pertain to the third major shift, after demographics and drinking habits, that Finnish researchers emphasize: He argues that declining abstinence rates and a sharp increase in the numbers who use alcohol at an early age point to a post--World War II "sea change" in the general cultural and political attitude toward alcohol, and that any evaluation of the 1969 Alcohol Act must take into account the changes already occurring in Finnish society. As Sulkunen and other Finnish researchers see it, the 1969 Alcohol Act is the result of a post-war generation enacting its values.[32] Sulkunen does not deny that the 1969 Act had an independent impact on the trend toward earlier drinking and lower rates of abstinence.

Summary and Conclusions

The most striking fact that greets an outsider speaking with various participants in the current Finnish alcohol policy debate is the consensus they share about the debate's central issues. Officials of ALKO, researchers at the Finnish Foundation, officials of the Department of Social Affairs and Health, and leaders of the Temperance organizations appear in agreement on the key issues.

First, there is widespread consensus that the impact of the 1969 Act was, on balance, not favorable, and that while many factors beyond the Act must be taken into account in explaining the rise in consumption in Finland after 1969, the Act itself was directly responsible for a significant fraction of the increase in problems.

Paradoxically, there is at least tacit acceptance by almost everyone that while the legislative changes were probably introduced too abruptly and with too much optimism, there was little likelihood that any government could have avoided these changes during this period. There is no denying that there was a remarkable change toward liberalization during the post–World War II period, with a decline in rates of abstinence, especially during the 1960s. There were similar changes in the other Nordic countries, and the move toward liberalization and the left in Finland was very popular with a young and vocal generation whose values were taken up by the major parties in Finland. Reforms of the existing alcohol system were one of those changes that enjoyed wide popularity among the general public.

It is important also to note that there is something of a consensus on just what has been learned as a result of these events. A process of "social learning" seems to have genuinely occurred among those responsible for, or attentive to, alcohol policy.[33]

Perhaps the most widely shared area of interpretation of the liberalization legislation's impact is the "addition hypothesis." Nearly everyone on the Finnish alcohol policy scene now agrees that it is not so easy simply to replace existing drinking patterns or structures with new ones, particularly by the process of enlarging the availability of lighter beverages. Thus the earlier optimism of the Finnish Committee on Alcohol Legislation, which in 1951 recommended making lighter beverages more available to stimulate the substitution of beer and wine for spirits, seems to have been the chief casualty of the aftermath of the 1969 Act. Furthermore, there is endorsement by all of the principals that per capita consumption must itself be a central feature of Finnish alcohol policy. The Parliamentary Committee formed to analyze the impact of the liberalization episode took as its central goal not only controlling consumption but also lowering it.[34] The main instruments for this control were pricing policy and restrictions on availability (mainly Saturday closings for ALKO and stricter licensing of beer establishments).

In a large sense, the Finnish case represents but another episode in the conflict between what Joseph Gusfield calls "cultural modernism" and "cultural fundamentalism," and—though this is speculation—perhaps the emergence of a new perspective in this long-standing conflict.

The post-war period in Finland found spokesmen for both viewpoints. The research community and the Finnish Foundation and the policymakers at ALKO generally endorsed a cultural modernist viewpoint, in that they not only argued for a liberalization of alcohol policy measures but voiced this support in terms of the changing cultural values and climate of the times.[35] The cultural traditionalist resisted these moves.

In a very real sense the disputants have moved somewhat closer to one another in this debate. It is misleading to depict this episode as typical of contending interest groups of roughly equal size, especially today. By and large, the groups who are concerned with alcohol policy are quite small in Finland, and alcohol policy issues—while enjoying wide coverage in the press—have become defined as a secondary problem in Finnish society. It is the terms of the debate that have narrowed considerably, the issues becoming much more a matter of specifics and detail than of broad policy.

What seems to have occurred is that all sides recognize (with different degrees of regret) that the times have changed in Finland. Most parties seem to sense the permanence of the post-industrial society and its values—even the rejection of Temperance and abstinence. At the same time, all sides now realize that modernity is not a process of replacing old values and structures with new ones. Rather, modern values and traditional values regarding alcohol tend to co-exist with one another; traditional patterns of drinking are not only not replaced; they endure and, as we have seen, are even magnified. One is reminded of a quotation from Joseph Schumpeter regarding the process of economic modernization:

> Social structures, types and attitudes are coins that do not readily melt. Once they are formed they persist, possibly for centuries, and since different structures and types display different degrees of ability to survive, we almost always find that actual group and national behavior more or less departs from what we should expect it to be if we tried to infer it from the dominant forms of the productive process.[36]

The dominant form to which Schumpeter refers for our case is the shift from traditional values where there is a predominance of rural and industrial occupational structures undergirded and overlaid by the values of localism, religious fundamentalism, and an ethic of work, productivity, thrift, and abstemiousness. This shift, which has been occurring for a very long number of decades in many Western societies (and for a very much shorter period in Finland) brought a marked decline in both the agricultural sector and the industrial sector (happening almost simultaneously in Finland in the space of two decades).

The current period in Finland represents something of a retreat from the heady optimism of the 1960s, and not just for alcohol policy. In fact the rate of growth has slowed considerably, and the general debate concerning the wisdom of rapid, continuous growth espoused by nearly all parties during the 1960s is heard in Finland, as elsewhere. Furthermore, these changes have brought something of a cultural and social reassessment and retrenchment. But it would be a serious mistake to see the shift in Finland regarding alcohol policy as a return to earlier and traditional positions. In Finland, the principle of the freedom of the individual from onerous and too restrictive alcohol policy measures that are justified ultimately in terms of cultural norms rather than public health or safety seems to have been firmly established. It seems clear those who supported the liberalization measures have on balance prevailed.

What seems to have occurred is that the old traditional-modern split is being replaced by another one, one that represents different issues in the post-industrial culture. Now that personal lifestyle choices remain solidly established and the goal of closely determining appropriate or normative styles for drinking has been firmly rejected, the central issues for alcohol policy turn away from the specific models of drinking that are seen as harmful and instead rely on macro policy and regulatory mechanisms to prevent those harmful aspects of the model from worsening.

One of the surprising, if implicit, areas of agreement that can be discerned is the gradual recognition of the benefits of the Finnish style of drinking. One of the virtues of episodic drinking is that it minimizes the adverse impact on productivity and also the effects of chronic ingestion on the liver and other physical structures. I found this view expressed by both the Temperance movement spokesmen and alcohol policy researchers.

This is an interesting if paradoxical development. It represents an increased acceptance of the goal of substantial freedom for the citizen in matters of alcohol use and the abandonment of attempts to shape directly the modal pattern of drinking. The traditional, predominantly rural values that stress abstemious, if not abstinent, conduct have begun to disappear. (The Parliamentary Committee did, however, suggest that, as an educational goal, the government should attempt to reduce "admiration for alcohol, and especially drunkenness.") At the same time, there is far less belief that liberalization will result in an improved situation for alcohol problems. Hence the paradox: the commitment to liberating individuals from excessively restrictive policy for alcohol (e.g., rural prohibition as a national policy) as a matter of basic principle combined with the re-

appearance of the necessity of broad and aggregate control mechanisms. There is, at the same time, a growing emphasis on such
issues as health and safety, which are apparently enlarging the previous preoccupation with the Finnish drinking style. The attempt
to find a better marriage between alcohol policy and larger economic policy, especially incomes policy, is also a new central part of
the alcohol policy debate.

The issue of medium beer represents something of a problem for
alcohol policymakers, with the Temperance groups anxious to find
some way to retreat from the current situation of widespread availability. But here, one senses that medium beer has become a symbolic issue, and that, other than a general tightening up of the
availability structure through stricter controls over licensing, the removal of medium beer from the retail shops is not likely to occur.
This debate in the Parliament continues at this writing, with the
trend seeming to be more control over the policymaking apparatus
of ALKO, primarily by strengthening the administrative controls of
the Ministry. The challenge for alcohol policy for Finland seems to
be to strike the proper balance between an enduring interest in
Finnish society to hold alcohol problems as low as possible while
respecting the new boundaries for personal autonomy and freedom
from too restrictive alcohol measures.

Implications for the United States

While the federal government's power over alcohol policy in the United States is a great deal more limited than is the case
in Finland, and the debate here is conducted in somewhat different
terms, the evidence that the Finnish liberalization episode did have
a significant impact on alcohol problems is important for the growing discussion of alcohol policy in the United States. But it may
not—in and of itself—be the most important lesson of the episode.
The principal value of the Finnish experience, beyond the light it
sheds on the general issues regarding alcohol availability and other
control measures, may well lie in providing an illuminating context
for those who might wish to consider alcoholism policy in the
United States.

In the debate in the United States, policy measures to restrict the availability of alcohol or to attempt to influence per capita consumption will likely be seen by some as a retreat from the values of cultural modernism and a return to rural, traditional viewpoints. The entry of several new factors into the debate on alcohol problems in post-industrial society, however, may well force a reconsideration of the post-repeal model for alcohol policy (the alcoholism model). What has arisen in post-industrial society is a fundamental concern with the quality of the environment, with the social costs of unrestricted growth, inflation, and unchecked consumption. A broad and diverse body of support has grown up around the ecology movement, and there seems to be little diminution of support for this issue, even as its economic impact becomes more manifest. Likewise, the impact of inflation and expensive and depleting energy sources has called to account the central assumptions for the modal personality of post-industrialism—consumption as a central and relatively unrestricted right. In the area of health policy, specifically, there is increased awareness of the limits to medicine and health care, and attention to lifestyle and environmental hazards as a threat to health. Alcohol policy is as likely as other issues to be reexamined in this new light.

In post-industrial culture, the extreme privacy and anonymity of the individual has already undergone some pressures for alteration. It is true that this debate still contains many of the lines of the old traditional-modernist conflict. The lifestyle debate in health policy, for example, is often challenged by some as one more example of the attempts by public health reformers to conduct campaigns of moral reform against the infidels—a jihad.[37]

The dominant view appears to be that there is an appropriate place for reasonable limits over threats to health in the lifestyle area. These limits will likely be established along the lines of the struggle for consumer or environmental protection: strong advocacy against certain practices of industrial concerns, especially in pollution, the manufacturing of hazardous products, and advertising practices.

What is crucial about this emerging concern with the quality of life is the struggle to find a new language for appropriate limits to consumption while at the same time preserving the gains of the post-industrial society in abandoning counter-productive moralistic restraints. In fact, it might be said that the most suggestive way in which to view the emerging conflict between those who might advocate a re-examination of alcohol policy and those opposed is the attempt of the first group to persuade the second that their desires are not part of a general programmatic return to traditional systems of control and restraints but rather part of the general trend toward heightened concern for environmental protection, safety in transportation, and consumer protection.

The shifts in alcohol policy in Finland can be seen as preliminary skirmishes in the larger cultural struggle to define post-industrial values, in our case particularly for alcohol. In the early period in Finland, the struggle between traditional and modern values predominated. In the most recent period, this tension has begun to fade (but not disappear). There seems to be greater readiness for at least a discussion of limits to alcohol consumption, but in ways that reject traditional approaches. For Finnish policy this means reliance on tax measures and broad regulatory policy (licensing, limiting ALKO's marketing pressures, education, etc.) but rejection of measures like personal identity cards and the return to a system of sharply restricted availability. Ironically, there is a heightened appreciation for the health benefits of the current Finnish style of drinking and even a deepened respect for the inability of available and acceptable social policy measures to influence these radically in a favorable direction.

The Finnish case suggests that there is significant value in retaining the present structure of alcohol consumption in the United States. Ours is an enormously pluralistic structure that shows important variation from region to region and ethnic group to ethnic group. Nevertheless, a fundamental attribute of that structure is a modal drinker who either drinks not at all or very little indeed.

This modal pattern cannot be treated as a norm in the strict sense, representing an attempt to closely shape and limit lifestyles for drinkers. That approach, which is the approach of cultural fundamentalism, must be rejected and the modernist emphasis on freedom from close restraint and individual choice must be firmly upheld. Nevertheless, government policymakers should seek to protect and strengthen this structure of alcohol consumption against further erosion.

The policy implication of this for the United States is that a cornerstone of that policy might well take the form not just of attempting to minimize adverse consequences from alcohol consumption but also of attempting to discourage—mainly through media campaigns and the like—drinking models that attempt to undermine the dominant or modal pattern of limited drinking. This should always be undertaken as an explicit attempt to work out in a new way an appropriate model for alcohol use that is congruent with shifting values and dominant images of post-industrial culture. It is to this task that we turn in the concluding chapter.

VII. Beyond Alcoholism:
Alcohol Policy for the 1980s

In September 1979, in his first appearance before the Senate Subcommittee on Alcoholism and Drug Abuse after being named director of the NIAAA, John DeLuca endorsed the fixing of warning labels on alcoholic beverages. The label, to be placed on all alcoholic beverages containing at least 24 percent alcohol, would read: "Caution: Consumption of alcoholic beverages may be hazardous to your health."[1] Given the long history of the alcoholism movement's basic hostility toward alcohol policy, this was a rather astonishing development. Sitting in the audience were not only the representatives of the alcoholic beverage industry but also Dr. Morris Chafetz, the first director of the NIAAA, and other leaders within the alcoholism movement, who later strongly opposed the official HEW position. Despite this opposition, the overwhelming majority of sentiment expressed regarding this legislation (passed by the Senate in May 1979) was favorable.[2]

What is more, since 1977 the directors of the National Institute on Alcohol Abuse and Alcoholism have advocated stabilizing per capita consumption, have urged use of warning labels to advise pregnant mothers of the risks of fetal alcohol syndrome, and have increasingly criticized the advertising practices of segments of the alcohol industry.[3] It has also become common practice for the leadership of the NIAAA to preface many of their statements regarding policy, especially for prevention, with announcements that the framework within which the NIAAA operates is the public health perspective. While there has been increasing opposition to some of these changes within the NIAAA, what is remarkable is the widespread support that has been manifested for the "public health approach." If there is to be a new paradigm for alcohol problems and for alcoholism policy, perhaps public health is the leading candidate.

These forces for change cannot be explained simply as the result of a rethinking of the alcoholism paradigm. These imperatives arise from the search for support by federal health agencies.[4] There is much to suggest that the NIAAA is forced by dint of its position within HEW to move away from a strict disease and treatment orientation to embrace a philosophy that explicitly emphasizes prevention, advocacy, and increasing conflict with the alcohol industry. That position is founded on a number of forces: the need to state maximally the magnitude of the agency's fundamental problems, the need to compete with other federal agencies for jurisdiction of the agency's own problem areas, and the imperative to see the agency's role as, in part, an adversary role in relation to the alcohol industry, which is, after all, an important force in society.[5] These policy imperatives create strong incentives for an agency like the NIAAA to embrace a philosophy that is consistent with the currents of change. It will be argued here that the most likely candidate is a public health perspective.

The New Public Health

The high priority given prevention and public health by the NIAAA seems influenced by a number of other factors in the agency's environment, in addition to the glaring anomalies of the alcoholism paradigm.

First, there is renewed interest in prevention everywhere, as the costs of treatment continue to soar. Although this interest sometimes sees prevention as a panacea and replacement for treatment, it is nonetheless clearly evident and can be found across the board in social policy.

Second, there is a growing sophistication about the limits to treatment programs per se, quite aside from their costs.[6] This attention to the "limits to medicine" is paralleled by the questions regarding the effectiveness of therapy for the mentally ill and rehabilitation for the criminal, to mention only two key areas.

Third, as we noted in Chapters 5 and 6, there has been a resurgence of interest internationally in public health measures to limit per capita consumption as a strategy to control certain alcohol problems such as cirrhosis. The proposal has certainly not been received without controversy among leaders in the alcoholism field in the United States and elsewhere, and the indications are that interest and debate about this proposal will likely increase. This factor alone may account for a renewed interest in public health in the alcoholism field.

The purpose of this concluding chapter, then, is to explore in some detail the implications of a public health model for alcohol problems. No attempt will be made to demonstrate conclusively that this version will in fact be the next basic paradigm for alcoholism policy. If this shift is to occur, it will only be, on the one hand, because the new public health paradigm provides an adequate structure, or framework, to account for the basic anomalies that have developed for the alcoholism model and, on the other, because this new model better explains and justifies the NIAAA's objectives and interests and can assist in mobilizing a widening base of public support.

What Is Public Health?

What is meant by a *public health perspective* or philosophy? The principles of public health cannot be simply inferred from the practice of those institutions in the public sector that can be distinguished from "private" medicine. We usually do refer to these organizations as "public health," and, at the federal level, the organization that has played an important role in the development of federal health policy and of assisting these state and local public institutions is termed the Public Health Service.[7] While it is true that these public organizations and programs differ sharply from private and clinical medicine (for example, the emphasis on prevention, education, and community health), however, one is sometimes hard pressed to find a coherent and consistent set of principles behind their development and policies. Whatever influence the philosophy of public health has had on the establishment of these services, that influence has often been lost in the details of political or administrative history.

It may be more helpful to define public health in terms of the contrast of its approach to that of clinical medicine. Clinical medicine is concerned with individuals and the treatment of patients who present conditions directly to the physician or other health care providers. Public health, on the other hand, is concerned with the occurrence of disease and early death as it arises in populations. The goal of public health is to apply strategies and programs that reduce the rates of disease and early death among total groups and aggregates of individuals.

During the last century, public health was identified with the sanitary movement and then later with the struggle against communicable infectious disease. In fact, many distinguished public health figures such as Herman Biggs are noted for their political activism in the fight against tuberculosis.[8] In sharp contrast with the campaign against alcoholism, the campaign against tuberculosis was seen as requiring "social technology" of a preventative nature, and early public health activists explicitly espoused a major governmental role in combatting the disease.[9]

Edward McGavran has argued that the distinctive feature of public health is its focus on communities, not individuals, and that communities are more than populations or aggregates of individuals.[10] He sees the health sciences as evolving through four distinct phases: the first was an empirical era, existing until approximately 1850, that was essentially devoted to the amelioration of symptoms. Next was the rise of the basic sciences in the last half of the nineteenth century, which Milton Terris has called the "first epidemiological revolution."[11] During this period of great triumph of public health, the focus shifted from symptoms to specific diseases and bacterial agents.

The period from 1900 to 1950 witnessed the ascendancy of medicine and the preoccupation with the total patient. This period saw the greatest advances in drugs, diagnostic techniques, and therapies. While McGavran ends this period at mid-century, some might argue that it extends to the present period, with its advances in surgery, in the development of tranquilizers, and in diagnostic technology (the CAT scanning device). Yet McGavran may have the last word, since the past decade has witnessed a growing body of literature that is critical of the impact of this technology for the health of the public. Indeed, some have seen modern medicine as a "nemesis."[12]

McGavran sees the present period as the true beginning of public health. For McGavran, the distinctive attribute of public health is its focus on the health of "the total community, the body politic."[13] I would suggest that McGavran's formulation could be modified slightly to take into account the conflict between a traditional culture and cultural modernism.

In fact, one can see a traditional form of public health, with primary location at the state and local government level and a minimal federal role, lasting until the conclusion of World War II. Typical of this traditional form is Haven Emerson's codification of "public health" implementation during the period. He suggests that public health consisted of six key elements: vital statistics, public health laboratories, health education, services for mothers and children, sanitation, and communicable disease control.[14]

The expansion of the federal involvement in health in the postwar period, particularly with the Great Society programs of the sixties, had its origins in the New Deal philosophy of social welfare, which was an expression of cultural modernism. The major emphasis in public health shifted from local areas to the federal government, and the chief emphasis was on the expansion of personal health services for the underserved, the poor and minority groups, health planning, the building of hospitals, research, and expanding the supply of health manpower. Prevention as an ideal, however, was not salient during this period.

While traditional public health often waged warfare against entrenched community interests in the name of better housing, sanitation, or a safer food supply, gradually the public health organizations at the state and local level accommodated and lived in rather peaceful coexistence with the dominant interest groups, especially the medical community. The emergence of the New Deal and its push to increase health and welfare legislation saw more conflict, especially at the federal level. The crucial issue was the legitimacy of the expansion of the welfare state to include health policy, with the opposition of the medical community intense even to the present period.

A "new public health" emerged in the sixties, and in many, if not most, instances this occurred outside the traditional community of public health. This movement has been broad, loosely connected, and not always self-consciously public health-oriented. I have in mind the ecology movement, the campaigns for consumer protection and product safety, the anti-nuclear movement, the emergence of a limits-to-medicine debate, and a broad concern with the quality of life and egalitarian values. What is distinctive about these developments is the post-modern orientation of many of these movements. These groups see uncontrolled technology, intensive consumption, and the "profits before safety" viewpoint as central characteristics of modern American society and a problem for the health and welfare of the public and the protection of the environment. For the first time, a broad series of social movements began to break from the embrace of cultural modernism and its values of consumption, technology, and affluence, and instead speak of the necessity for limits and the hazards of our man-made environment. More than the earlier periods of traditionalism and modernism, the emphasis is on adversary relations with an industry or industrial sector, legal stratagems, and the expansion of the federal government's regulatory power. It is interesting that for most of these endeavors there is a sharp shift in emphasis away from remonstrating with the individual (with safety campaigns, education, or slogans) to regulating industries. William Ryan, in his *Blaming the Victim*, for example, has the following to say about this way of viewing the public health perspective:

> Adherents of this approach tended to search for defects in the community and the environment rather than in the individual; to emphasize predictability and usualness rather than random deviance; they tried to think about preventing problems rather than merely repairing or treating—to see social problems, in a word, as social.[15]

This view of public health, with its strong emphasis on the "social," was less clearly articulated in the early years of American public health, although one can certainly find strong statements or endorsements of this view among early public health leaders.[16] Also, the expansion of the welfare state during the modern period of public health can be seen as a further, if still partial, endorsement of the "social," when social means the commitment to expanding welfare services to include medical care for the elderly or the needy, at least rudimentary planning, and increased public sector involvement in research and facilities. But Ryan's emphasis was not clearly articulated until the emergence of what is labeled here as the new public health.

Public Health as Ethic

While public health has always had ethical foundations, implicitly, if not explicitly, it is only with the emergence of post-modern public health that the distinctly ethical commitments of public health have become more visible. Although public health is rooted ultimately in the tradition of social justice, it has seldom been explicitly treated in philosophical literature on social philosophy. Traditional public health measures, such as sanitation and protection of the air and water supply, have been treated as "public goods," a case in which the question of distribution does not come up, and as established fixtures of the modern state. The allocation of scarce medical care resources has, however, been seen as more problematic, and as raising the issue of social justice.[17]

The question of social justice arises in a rather unique way for post-modern public health. The question for public health here is not the distribution of specific benefits to identifiable individuals, but rather the improvements of levels or rates of health among the entire population or among specific groups. The standards for public health are based on an ideal situation in which the rates of early death or serious disability are substantially lowered, or in which the situation in American society is compared with another society with substantially better levels of health and safety.[18] Furthermore, public health stands closer to a communitarian ethic than does the stark individualistic perspective of most treatments of social justice. Social justice has traditionally allocated the benefits and burdens of society to individuals based on need and rights.[19] The community as a category was mistrusted by many social justice commentators because the task of justice was seen as liberating the individual from the bonds of the community.[20]

With the emergence of a post-modern perspective in which the values of the untrammeled self are seriously being questioned, the categories of community and social justice will likely seem more compatible with each other. In the post-modern era, the category of community may begin to lose some of its identity as an oppressor of individuals, and become accepted as an ally for securing such fundamental interests as health, safety, a protected environment, a safe marketplace. This ideal of community is not a paraphrase of the utilitarian vision, in which the emphasis is on maximizing the welfare of the majority, but is rather one aimed at minimizing the number who suffer serious disability and early death—given other basic societal commitments such as fundamental liberties, privacy, and autonomy.

In the following sections four central attributes that are likely to be encountered in post-modern public health will be discussed: hazards, prevention, shared responsibility, and the limits of public health set by other key societal values. The new public health discussed here is not yet found as an explicit philosophy; rather it is an extrapolation from the emergence of a variety of social movements arising here and in other Western industrial nations, and attempts to achieve higher levels of health and safety for the public and the environment. Nevertheless, we can best understand the application of the new public health to such topics and to alcohol control if we position the development within a larger social movement to re-evaluate our unquestioning commitment to growth, the unbounded self, and ever-increasing personal consumption.

Focus on the Hazards

A key principle of the new public health is to *identify and control the hazards and dangers* of modern post-industrial societies, instead of focusing on problems as the lot of a minority population of difficulty-prone people. Against this principle it has usually been argued that the causes of death and disability are multiple and frequently behavioral in origin.[21] Furthermore, since it is usually only a minority of the public who are casualties of most known hazards, additional controls on those hazards would not seem effective or just. Instead we should ask why some (kinds of) people expose themselves to known hazards or peril, or act in an unsafe or careless manner.

Post-modern public health would tend to reject the behavioral explanations so prominent in modernist perspectives, since such explanations blame the victim and unfairly protect powerful groups from the burdens of prevention. Whether the issue is alcohol, other drugs, large dogs, noxious chemicals, infectious diseases, exploding bombs, crashing automobiles, damaging levels of noise, avalanches, earthquakes, polluted air, radiation, contaminated water, starvation, the unjust distribution of medical care, or the "escape of tigers," the focus of any public health ethic seeking to minimize injury would never be on explaining "why" some individuals fall victim to perils.[22] Rather, its point would be to ensure that all hazards and all essential goods were controlled by fair and equitable community rules to minimize the risks of death and disability.

Prevention

Post-modern public health sees community alcohol problems as the predictable and expected consequence of the consumption ethic, which urges the maximum legal availability of alcohol as a consumer product, and of the manifold commercial pressures for the integration of alcohol into our culture and the "alcoholization of everyday life." In the context of the transition from a modernist to a postmodern perspective, the new public health traces many serious public health problems directly to the "dark side" of an unlimited commitment to the values of growth, personal consumption, technology, and affluence. The second principle of a new public health, therefore, is *prevention*.

Prevention is a central feature of all public health, and is based directly on the ethical commitment to minimize the numbers of persons who suffer disability and early death. The classic public health options for prevention are as follows: creating rules to minimize the exposure of groups of individuals to hazards and thereby to reduce the rates of hazardous exchanges; creating rules to provide safeguards against damage in the event that hazardous exchanges occur anyway, in cases in which such techniques (for example, fluoridation, seat belts, or immunization) are feasible; and organizing treatment resources in the community so as to minimize damage that does occur, since damage can rarely be prevented totally for most modern public health problems.

William Haddon, Jr., has called attention to the fact that for many kinds of public health hazards we can reduce losses even if we do not control per capita exposure to hazards; we can use techniques (sometimes called technological shortcuts)[23] that are socially and politically less disruptive. Seat belts, as a strategy against highway injuries, may be unpopular, but the planned reduction of exposure of the public to the private automobile might be significantly more unpopular. If such techniques were available for alcohol problems, we would be justified in using them, if for no other reason than that they usually disrupt other values less than do direct controls over exposure to hazards.

But in the case of drugs—and perhaps many other chemical hazards of man's environment—there seem to be few known techniques to protect individuals without controlling exposure to the substance. As Terris has pointed out, there seems to be no presently available technology for "immunizing" individuals against hazardous chemical exposures.[24] Even if such techniques were available, it is clear that there would be problems in implementing them as collective policies. For all hazardous drugs then, including alcohol, it seems that much of the focus of preventive strategy must be aimed at controlling exposure in the first place.

Collective Responsibility

The third principle of a new public health is collective responsibility. The initiative and major burden for controlling injury and death lies within the community and the society. This does not mean that legislated measures are set against private measures; both the public and private sectors are visualized as working jointly to strengthen existing mechanisms for controlling aggregate consumption and for affirming norms for minimal alcohol use.

The policy of collective responsibility is based on the belief that the control of hazards cannot be substantially achieved by voluntary mechanisms, but must be undertaken primarily by governmental or non-governmental agencies through planned, organized, and collective action that is non-voluntary. Market or voluntary action is typically inadequate for providing what are called public goods— public policies such as national defense, police and fire protection, and the reduction of rates of alcohol-related problems. These policies are often universal in their impacts and effects, distributing benefits in the form of lowered risks. A typical individual might choose to withhold his support, reasoning that the community could not deny him the benefit anyway (this is called the "free rider" problem). Also, individual holdouts might plausibly reason that their small contribution might not prevent the public good from being offered.[25]

But perhaps the most serious reason lies elsewhere. As societies become freer from risks, holdouts might plausibly reason that the odds are very good that someone else will suffer the harm—even though it is known that thousands in the society will suffer harm if the collective policy is not adopted. Thus, many public health problems can be viewed as something akin to a lottery in which the overwhelming majority win (in the short run at least), and the individual acting out of self-interest rationalizes that he does not need the benefit. The rule of self-interest often leads to a rejection of measures that would save the lives of thousands in the society because many millions will win the bet.[26]

Limits to Alcohol Policy

Legislated measures are likely to be represented, especially by the alcohol industry, as another instance of gross governmental interference with the private decisions of individual citizens. If public acceptance of these measures is to be won, this issue must be faced, and the *limits and boundaries to a fair alcohol policy* must be clearly communicated. For example, the public must be reassured that a community ethic for alcohol is strictly opposed to prohibition. Prohibition not only entails the risk of jeopardizing other basic values, such as the protection of individual autonomy and privacy; it also encourages the false supposition that the alcohol issue is our leading or only health or social problem.

While limits to consumption should indeed be the norm for policy, the pluralistic nature of American culture would prevent this norm from being advocated except to point out a direction, to indicate what lies beyond the norm. Recognition of pluralism will be a basic check against new forms of intolerance.

In broad terms the basic limits to a community policy for alcohol problems are these:[27]

1. The broad injunction against public health measures that unreasonably and coercively interfere with the fundamental rights of privacy of individual citizens.

2. The avoidance of a tendency to deny the genuine pluralism that exists in the United States, especially for drinking: no attempt to specify the norm for drinking should become another exercise in "status" or symbolic politics.

3. The injunction against the undue emphasis on alcohol problems to the exclusion of other equally serious problems, especially where the control of other problems might achieve more dramatic results in terms of minimizing disability or early death.

4. The injunction against measures that increase, over the long run, the risks of death and disability.

5. The injunction to consider the problems of "redistributive justice," or the special problems of achieving a transition from one model of justice to another (a corollary of this injunction would seem to be that where two or more policy options promise roughly equivalent results, the option should be chosen that is least disruptive of other social or economic values).

6. The final principle would be one of realism. One of the greatest dangers confronting alcohol policy is that of utopianism. Prohibition is a form of utopianism. But utopianism can also take the form of imagining a world where alcohol is made available and where—somehow—serious alcohol problems would be avoided if only individuals were more responsible (perhaps with more education or training).

The principle of realism, however, also carries a paradox within it. There are only limited and partially effective tools available to society to control or to reduce alcohol-related problems. The focus, then, should be upon those instruments that make a difference; even so, these measures will not make radical changes in the rates of problems. The lesson to be drawn from the principle of realism is to be conservative and skeptical about innovative techniques that blithely promise marked change in the rates of problems. If the most important and effective changes—changes that are typically passive and mandatory—will only realize containment or at best partial reductions in aggregate consumption and rates of problems, we should be extremely suspicious of other methods that are voluntary and promise more effective results.

Recommendations for Policy

A serious obstacle to implementing and developing any new policy for alcohol, whether it takes the form of increased alcohol taxation, controls over advertising, or other limits or restrictions on the availability of alcohol, is a lack of immediate jurisdiction for the NIAAA in these matters. In each case, the primary responsibility for implementing these policies lies with an agency outside of the NIAAA and in most cases, even outside of the jurisdiction of the Department of Health and Human Services (as HEW was renamed in 1980).

But this may not be the most serious obstacle to prevention facing the NIAAA. The NIAAA must work diligently at forming a consensus on alcohol. Although the long-term goal for the NIAAA and other federal and local agencies is the reduction of the aggregate rate of alcohol problems, this goal in itself provides little sense of direction either for agencies or for the average citizen about how these goals are to be achieved and what norms are appropriate for drinking.

Limiting Per Capita Consumption

The question of a consensus for drinking has been a major issue in the alcoholism movement for over fifteen years, as we have seen. The findings of the Cooperative Commission on Alcoholism raised just this concern, emphasizing the need to establish a new drinking consensus.[28] In fact, the entire movement to establish "responsible drinking" was an outgrowth of the integration hypothesis and the notion that normal (and normative) drinking patterns have important consequences for rates of at-risk, that is, heavy, drinking. As the Cooperative Commission's report, *Alcohol Problems*, indicated:

> One major shortcoming of current American drinking patterns is the absence of agreed-upon norms or rules about which kinds of drinking are socially acceptable. If this situation could be changed, consistent social disapproval of irresponsible drinking could be expressed and various sanctions instituted to reduce the likelihood of its occurrence.[29]

This goal has often been counter-productive, particularly since the goal of a drinking consensus usually downplays the role of alcohol per se, disapproving only of the behavioral consequences of heavy drinking.

This criticism holds if the consensus is exclusively individual, a consensus that ignores alcohol. Yet the idea of a normative consensus for alcohol—particularly if it includes a consensus on the collective dynamics of alcohol problems—is vital to the preventive role of the NIAAA, other government agencies, and private groups like the NCA.

A consensus on alcohol would help in the following ways: It would, above all, help legitimate the attempt by the government at all levels to legislate policies such as taxation, control advertising, and control availability. If the government's policy is to restrict and limit the availability of alcohol, the prevailing consensus on alcohol must permit, and also anticipate and legitimate, that change.

This point pertains to the first specific policy recommendation of the present study:

> *The federal government should take the initiative, working with other levels of government and concerned private parties, to develop a consensus on alcohol. This consensus would concern both the question of the collective dynamics of alcohol problems and the measures needed to control consumption. The primary message would be minimal or non-use of alcohol and zero growth in per capita alcohol consumption.*

This consensus necessarily would be developed collaboratively (with the NIAAA taking the lead), and would reflect the necessary pluralism and complexity of drinking in American society. But it would also have to take a stand on the substantive issue of how alcohol problems occur in society, and what models of drinking would lead to deterioration of the present situation.

The overall goal of alcohol control policy would be to encourage high rates of minimal or non-use of alcohol, so as to promote low rates of excessive use of alcohol. If at first glance this goal seems unduly stringent or utopian, we need to remember that most American drinkers do not drink very much. At any given time, roughly 70 percent of all adults either do not drink, or can be categorized as infrequent or light drinkers.[30] To repeat a point made in Chapter IV, if the drinking habits of American adults were to be represented by ten adults, assuming a mean annual consumption of 2.7 gallons of absolute alcohol per person, this twenty-seven gallons would be distributed among the ten as follows: three abstaining, three drinking one and one-half gallons between them, and the others drinking one and one-half, three, six, and fifteen gallons each.[31] Clearly the first seven people either abstain or have minimal involvement with alcohol. Of the remaining three, one is a "moderate" drinker, one a heavy drinker, and one a very heavy or alcoholic drinker.

This picture is repeated in almost every survey taken of American drinking habits. We must remember, of course, that this is a picture of the total population; there are age, sex, regional, urban-rural, and individual variations, with much instability and change over time. These differences in the United States must be taken into account: the inhabitants of San Francisco or New York City clearly drink more than the citizens of Birmingham; the Pacific and New England regions consume the greatest amount of alcohol, while the East South Central region consumes the least. But too much can be made of the differences. Figure 4, taken from the *Second Special Report to the U.S. Congress on Alcohol and Health*, illustrates the differences among the regions. There is diversity, but one is struck by the similarities, also. With the average national per capita consumption of alcohol being roughly 2.7 gallons of absolute alcohol, California stands at 3.24. This is significantly more than the average, but not so much as to invalidate the thesis that the United States is, on balance, a culture of constraint when it comes to alcohol. The overall pattern of minimal alcohol use provides a point of

Figure 4

Apparent Per Capita Consumption of Absolute Alcohol, by the Drinking-Age Population, in U.S. Gallons, by Region, United States, 1972*

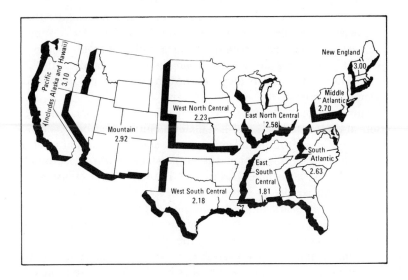

*The regions are the standard regions of the U.S. Census Bureau.
Source: HEW and NIAAA, *The Second Special Report to the U.S. Congress on Alcohol and Health* (Washington, D.C.: G.P.O., 1975), p. 3.

departure for establishing a national consensus on alcohol, one that includes not just community constraints on alcohol but also a shared understanding of the essential dynamics of our society's alcohol problems.[32]

After controlling aggregate or per capita consumption, as a corollary there must be increased recognition that the overall structure of consumption in the United States needs to be protected and strengthened, and that the control policies reviewed here greatly increase the health and safety of the public. While our political tradition and experience with Prohibition requires us to reject defining specifically approved drinking behavior, nevertheless, a national consensus for alcohol policy must recognize that, as far as personal alcohol use is concerned, less is better.

Second, a national consensus on alcohol must also recognize that, in a mature industrial society such as ours, pressures for continual increases in personal consumption of a wide range of consumer products, including alcohol, are a fundamental dynamic of the society. Therefore, a goal of all public health policy should be to moderate these pressures.

Third, while Prohibition has been rejected, a generation after Repeal the United States still remains a culture that limits alcohol use. Regulating the manufacture, sale, and consumption of alcoholic beverages falls within the well-established and legitimate powers of the government to protect the health and safety of the public and is consistent with the goal of social justice to reduce the harms of early death and serious disability to a minimum.

These broad principles clearly suggest that the goal of reducing problems can never be realized if the norm for drinking shifted to frequent drinking. While frequent, or what we sometimes call social, drinking need not be regarded as problematic in itself, the evidence in Chapters V and VI clearly suggests that as alcohol consumption increases so do the rates of heavy consumption and problems. This is a problem with any policy that would seek to expand the size of the frequent-drinker group or to establish frequent (social) drinking as a normative ideal. It is clear that the goal of the alcohol industry is to encourage the spread of frequent, "social," drinking norms and to expand substantially the small minority who at present are classified as frequent drinkers. The industry bases its campaign on the assumption that its product will be frequently but not harmfully used while not seeming to solicit at-risk users directly. The image of social drinking as the frequent but nonproblematic use of alcohol is well suited to the industry's purposes. But this ideal is the ideal of the magazine advertisement, not the experience of most American adults. In formulating its policy, the government must not be misled into defining social drinking as the ideal or principal goal of public policy. To summarize, the overall goal of alcohol policy should be to encourage high rates of minimal or non-use of alcohol, so as to promote low rates of excessive use of alcohol. Frequent but nonproblematic use of alcohol would not be defined as harmful or deviant drinking, but it would also not be encouraged as a model for individual adults.

The Question of "Safe" Drinking

Encouraging minimal alcohol use as a normative ideal and empirical achievement helps avoid the crucial confusion between a norm for what is "safe" for individuals to drink (assuming that they will never drink more than the safe limit) and a norm for what individuals ought to drink (assuming that there will be imperfect compliance). When asked to define the level of "safe" drinking on the occasion of the release of the second *Alcohol and Health* report, Morris Chafetz responded by endorsing the norm set by the nineteenth-century physician Francis Anstie, who argued that persons who drank no more than the equivalent of three ounces of whiskey a day did not seem to suffer an increase in health problems or mortality.[33] The interesting thing about this response is that fewer than 10 percent of Americans drink as much as the equivalent of three ounces of whiskey daily. In fact, the NIAAA's *Second Special Report to Congress on Alcohol and Health* classified a daily intake of three ounces of whiskey as heavy drinking.[34]

The entire notion of "safe drinking" ignores the fact that the rules governing what is safe drinking for a given individual are different from the rules governing what individuals "should" drink in order to minimize alcohol problems in the community. This is essentially the difference between prudential or "self-regarding" rules and ethical rules that are designed to achieve a much lower rate of alcohol problems in the community. Ethical norms are much more conservative, allowing for a factor of failure, and require that individuals drink at rates that are far lower than might be safe for them individually. The empirical evidence from the work of researchers suggests that cultural and social norms are rooted not in prudence but in the common good.

Alcohol Taxation

Focusing on legislated measures to achieve a stabilized or, even more optimistically, a lowered level of consumption as a principal goal of public policy, the evidence presented in Chapter V suggests that taxation is a leading tool. The use of federal, state, and local powers of taxation to check the growth of per capita consumption would surely be one cornerstone of a new policy for alcohol. This leads to my second specific policy recommendation:

> *The federal government must seek over a scheduled period a substantial increase in the current tax applied to alcohol. The goal should be to seek parity with the level obtaining prior to substantial consumption increases in 1960, and should keep pace with the continuing inflationary pressures.*

The present level of federal tax for distilled spirits of $10.50 per proof gallon was established in 1950 as an excise tax added during the Korean war. The level has not been adjusted since that time. Since the federal tax constitutes a substantial proportion of the total price of all distilled beverages, both inflation and rising disposable incomes make alcohol cheaper relative to other goods with each passing year. Thus a policy of neglect by the government is actually a policy of making alcohol cheaper. Initially, I would propose that the tax on alcohol be increased to $20 per gallon by 1985, and thereafter indexed to the inflation rate.

At present, such a policy may seem visionary, especially given the current anti-tax atmosphere in the states and in Washington, but it may also be that what Americans are seeking are more legitimate sources of taxation rather than a simple reduction of the total tax burden. Certainly, the current discussion of consumption taxes, or what is referred to as "value-added" taxes, lends credence to the view that taxes on consumption may come to be viewed more favorably by the public than income or property taxes.

The recurrent questions regarding the rising costs of health care and how alcohol and tobacco use contributes to that increased burden also create more support for targeting these substances for purposes of public health policy. One possibility might be the use of revenues from creation of special taxes on alcohol and tobacco to replace some of the present social security taxes. It is likely that any support for increased taxation will be part of a broad-based effort at overhauling the tax structure to find new revenues for established programs, such as social security. Opposition to these measures may be formidable, however, and may come from such diverse sources as tax reduction organizations, the Treasury, and the industry (certainly), to name just a few. Supporters will likely include public health groups, some consumer organizations, churches, and hopefully, the alcoholism treatment constituency. It must also be remembered that the burden of this taxation will likely be felt most by the heavy users of alcohol, a group that represents 10–15 percent of all adults. For most voters the increase in taxes will be of little or no consequence, since so many adults use alcohol either minimally or not at all. This would likely be a crucial factor in securing passage of such legislation.

Here we can visualize the connection between tax policy and a normative model for drinking that stresses minimal use. Tax policy is designed not just to prevent problems but also to affirm and encourage minimal alcohol use as a widely supported norm. The fundamental purpose of such taxes is threefold: to encourage minimal use, to reduce problems, and to tax nonessential consumption more heavily.[35] While alcohol taxes have a regressive character, the individual's per capita tax expenditure relative to average income is small, and even smaller when one allocates this per capita tax according to consumption. Thus the argument that those who use more of the substance and are more at risk for problems ought bear the greater burden seems consistent with the objectives of promoting minimal use and is roughly fair.

The argument that alcohol taxes fall most heavily on the poor is an objection to consumption or sales taxes generally. At least theoretically, the income tax will be more progressive in its incidence. It is no doubt true that these arguments have merit, but they exaggerate the magnitude of the burden on the poor as well as ignore the distribution of benefits from these policies. For example, Milton Terris reports that, in England, the highest rates of cirrhosis are found among the upper classes, while in the United States the opposite is the case. Terris argues that this difference is due in part to the high taxation imposed on alcoholic beverages in England. As he puts it, only the wealthy can afford the luxury of cirrhosis.[36] Perhaps more importantly, if we seek to improve the condition of the poor, this is best accomplished by economic policies that directly and dramatically benefit this group. Avoiding the imposition of taxation policies to improve the public's health because the economic burden might fall unequally on one group is not likely to substantially benefit the poor. As a general principle, however, public health should, in fairness, set as a primary goal strong economic measures to advance the health and welfare of the poor.

Alcohol Control Laws

The third specific policy recommendation deals with the existing systems controlling the availability and consumption of alcohol beverages, the so-called "ABC" systems. The assumption here is that the goal of the various state alcohol control laws is to hold the line against increases in consumption and to prevent problems. More specifically, these laws and systems should reflect, as a minimum, a commitment to "regulated minimum availability" as a national policy.[37] But what is needed is some process by which national guidelines are developed that specify the content of regulated minimum availability. This leads to my third policy recommendation:

> *The NIAAA should develop on a cooperative basis with the various states guidelines that specify the broad institutional implications of what is meant by "regulated minimum availability."*

The NIAAA can play an indirect but powerful role in shaping and directing the trends for these systems. The purpose of these standards is to facilitate the larger involvement of the public and public officials in monitoring, evaluating, and improving laws and the regulatory process.

The purpose of establishing guidelines for state policy regarding age limits, location, hours of sale, density, taxation, and off-premises regulation is to provide states, localities, and private groups with tools with which to evaluate the current status of their alcohol control policy and to discern trends and patterns in regulation and enforcement. While there have been attempts to assess the impact of state regulations on drinking behavior, consumption, and alcohol-related problems, the situation is still one in which substantially more research is needed to measure the effects of legal restraints on drinking.

But the process being outlined here would not depend nor wait upon conclusive scientific evidence for the effectiveness of each element of the control structure. Effectiveness is not the only criterion; there is the question of fairness to producers and retailers as well as the important question of the contribution of ABC laws to reinforcing the normative consensus on limiting consumption and signifying the public health role as primary. Prime consideration should also be given to developing simple, consistent guidelines that would assist private organizations as well as public health agencies to monitor and participate in ABC activity effectively.

What is clearly needed is some understanding of what is important and what is trivial and even counter-productive about state and federal alcohol control policies. Age restrictions seem to be very important; it is not clear whether changes that permit "liquor by the drink" will have a significant impact on consumption or alcohol-related problems. The fact is that we simply do not know very much about the specific workings of the states' alcohol control legislation and we need more research to untangle these problems. This will not be an easy task and in some cases it might be hopelessly complicated.

As Robin Room and James Mosher point out, we also need to remember that there are numerous agencies and jurisdictions that have rather impressive alcohol-related policy-making powers.[38] The authors have in mind such instances as the Defense Department's power to control the retailing and consumption of alcoholic beverages for service personnel, the Civil Aeronautics Board's power over airline policies for serving alcoholic beverages, the Park Service's regulatory powers over the use of alcoholic beverages in the nation's parks, local zoning commissions' powers to regulate the location of retail outlets for alcoholic beverages, and the regulation of advertising by the Department of the Treasury. Mosher and Room argue that these nontraditional sources of alcohol policy may, taken separately, represent only small increments of change but in total could result in important substantive progress as well as symbolize society's posture toward alcohol.[39]

Until we have more precise information about these policy relationships, however, the prudent course at all levels of government would be to resist major changes in the existing structure that promise to relax or liberalize the availability of alcohol. Since the central features of public policy would be the limits and restrictions on alcohol use, this would seem to be axiomatic.

The Control of Advertising

The fourth major policy recommendation for legislated change focuses on the control of the advertising of alcoholic beverages. A substantial amount of control over these matters already exists, either by the industry or by the government. The 1979 decision by the Congress instructing HEW and the Treasury to determine the need for health warning labels on alcoholic beverages suggests that sentiment is building to expand and strengthen this policy. If this occurs, it would place the United States in conformance with a growing number of Western democracies that are tightening up on alcohol advertising. The most stringent policies have been established in Norway, Sweden, and Finland, where for all practical purposes alcohol advertising is not permitted. This trend, of course, accompanies tightening regulations on the advertising of tobacco here and abroad, and is a major factor itself in bringing policy toward these two commodities into conformity.

The fourth policy recommendation then, is:

> *The federal government must seek to limit advertising appeals for beer and wine that are aimed at youth or heavy users. Furthermore, the NIAAA should develop a counter-advertising campaign that portrays the dominant pattern of limited or no involvement with alcohol in a positive light.*

This recommendation is based squarely on the experience with smoking, which seems to indicate that "counter-advertising" campaigns that directly oppose the claims of the industry are most effective when combined with sustained information about the public health consequences of use.[40] The purpose of the control of advertising would not be to eliminate such advertising—at least for the time being—but to seek its modification. The justification for these measures would be the provision of full information about products

found in the marketplace to the consumer, as well as information
regarding normative patterns of drinking. [41]

Education and the Alcohol Problems of Teenagers

A primary instrument to reduce alcohol problems has been education, and especially alcohol education for teenagers. A chief focus of
alcohol education has been to "innoculate" teenagers against alcohol problems in adult life. [42] This approach is consistent with our belief that character and individual behavior are fixed early in life and
that education is a primary force in establishing these characteristics. Therefore, or so the argument goes, the case for teenage alcohol education is almost self-evident. But a central perspective of
this study has been on direct effects of the surrounding environment
on the drinking behavior of individuals and the "waxing and waning" of many drinking problems. This perspective challenges the
assumption that adult behavior is mainly determined early in life
and persists no matter what environment the individual encounters.

The increased public attention to drug use among teenagers, including alcohol use and alcohol problems in recent years, has forced
a higher priority for these problems among public officials. [43] The
perspective here encourages a new approach—addressing teenage
alcohol problems and problems with other drugs as current and
pressing problems in their own right, and not merely as symptoms
of future problems later in adult life. This suggests that alcohol education is not mainly "teenage alcohol education," and that teenage
drinking and drinking problems should be considered as current
problems for this group and the institutions and settings that are of
direct concern for them. Thus, our fifth policy recommendation:

> *Policies should be devised to reduce alcohol-related problems
> for the schools, recreational activities and other focal points
> of the life of teenagers. These policies should not be solely or
> even mainly educational in nature; they should include the
> full range of policy alternatives: legal age restrictions, alcohol
> availability, advertising, and education. These policies should
> be coordinated with other policies to reduce the spectrum of*

teenage and young adult drug use—alcohol, tobacco, and marijuana.

This approach shifts attention away from educational programs to prevent alcohol problems in adult life—a goal that is hopelessly difficult to measure. The policy orientation broadens to include the most common drugs, the question of drinking by minors, alcohol and the automobile, alcohol and recreational activities, and so forth.

Making the World Safe for Drunks

The measures we have discussed so far have been focused on alcohol. There are important policy measures that are non-alcohol-specific and that promise substantial reduction in alcohol-related casualties. I have in mind interventions such as airbags for automobiles or the reduction of handgun ownership. Room, who has done most of the advanced thinking in this area, labels this approach the *disaggregation strategy.*[44] Room argues that in addition to focusing on reducing aggregate consumption, we seek to reduce specific outcomes (such as highway crashes or firearms casualties), and seek strategies that will reduce those outcomes.

A public health paradigm for alcohol problems policy should not narrowly construe its mission as limited to alcohol-specific measures and should give high priority and support to other policy options that achieve even greater results. Accordingly, and focusing on the most outstanding example in this class of policies, the sixth policy recommendation is as follows:

> *The NIAAA should lend its aggressive support for mandatory airbag laws and legislated measures for passive restraints to protect all who are on the highways, including those who are driving while drunk.*

No number of slogans or amount of piety will achieve the results of passive restraints for automobiles; when combined with mandatory seat belts, the safety of the passenger would be even more substantially increased. Indeed, with the entire energy crisis and an anticipated decline in use of the automobile, we can anticipate a decline in alcohol-connected fatalities. While these passive mechanisms are demonstrably effective, this recommendation should not be construed as lack of support for the intensified surveillance of drunk driving by law enforcement agencies.

The Participation of the Community

The measures we have outlined here are not free from major problems of jurisdiction or mission. But the path does seem clear for alcohol problems to become defined—like inflation, crime, unemployment—as an issue for which the size or rate is a matter of common discussion, and for which government at all levels recognizes its own key regulatory role.

At the same time, government does not possess the sole interest or competence in this field. Responsibility also rests with the community, that wide variety of groups that play an active role in developing, legitimating, and implementing policy for alcohol and alcohol problems. Under the alcoholism model this activity was primarily limited to the National Council on Alcoholism (in the early years) and to the lobbying of governmental grant recipients (after the establishment of the NIAAA). If we consider only briefly the community beyond government, using the churches as an example of a group that has historically played a role in alcohol policy, we can see that new assumptions may well portend a significantly increased role for many groups in the private sector.

Most of the mainstream churches have adopted something of a "hands off" stand toward alcohol policy, in part because of the unhappy experience of Prohibition and the attempt to move away from a point of view—the position of total abstinence—that clearly was not supported by their congregations. On the other hand, the position of the alcoholism movement, that the topic of alcohol was not an issue of public policy, has clearly posed something of a problem for many churches. Consequently, the position of the churches on the subject of alcohol and alcoholism policy seems to range from silence to benign neglect, but is mostly characterized by confusion and conflict. Some denominations have disestablished alcohol from their national agendas because the "alcohol issue" has so often worked to suppress interest in other issues of social justice.

The concept of limits to consumption outlined here represents a possible compromise for the churches. First, it is more consistent with their traditional emphasis on community, as opposed to prudential, ethics. Also, it is consistent with their emphasis on limits, simpler lifestyles, and resistance to the demands of a consumer society, dictated by a concern not only for one's own health but also for the well-being of the larger community. The churches would of necessity have to reject the error of defining "total abstinence" as the only "correct" moral posture toward alcohol, just as they would have to reject "social" drinking as beyond the scope of moral concerns. A social policy that stressed limits to alcohol consumption would take its reference point from the context of the community— the necessity to maintain covenant with other members of the community.

The intriguing aspect of the church's refocusing on the issue of community limits to alcohol use is that it helps create a constructive dialogue within an institution with enormous scope and influence in many sectors of American life, and one that demonstrates signs of a re-awakening. These issues were put aside after the coming of Repeal, and in many ways the churches turned to other issues with something close to relief. But the fact remains that this issue is not likely to disappear. The initiation of a new national discussion of the topic of alcohol would be helpful from the standpoint of public policy and from the standpoint of renewing and re-awakening a sense of community and one's common or shared obligations. This dialogue also would be intimately connected to such policy changes as taxation, advertising restrictions, local and state reforms, and the like, since the question of community norms for drinking cannot be treated separately from these questions.

The character of the dialogue within the churches (and many other private groups) would take it from the realm of experts and techniques, where prevention as an issue is currently lodged. Although responsible drinking has been rejected because of its vagueness, the current state of the art in prevention relies on some general psychological services that are vaguely reminiscent of responsible drinking, if not precisely that concept. These services are seen as increasing individual competence, coping skills, rational decision-making, or self-esteem, as well as imparting some basic information about alcohol. The rationale for these stratagems is that it is difficult, if not wrong, to determine what to tell people about how much they should drink; the best we can do is make them more capable as human beings, increase their sense of self-respect and their decision-making capacities. Thus strengthened, they will surely make better decisions about alcohol.

The notion that the community should say nothing about how much its members should drink is based in part on the distinctively modernist view that it should not intrude on the private lives of its members. This view tends to define all alcohol use as essentially private in nature, and thus off-limits to the larger community, except for some instances, such as drunk driving, in which this behavior constitutes a direct threat to the well-being of others. But, in truth, the community historically has had an important role in determining very broad limits regarding alcohol use for individuals. While cultural modernism has ignored the community role, the indications are for a return to a legitimate role for the society in limiting alcohol consumption. A post-modern alcohol policy that would legitimate reasonable societal limits to consumption will probably increase the role of community groups and broaden the base of attention and interest in alcohol problems. This is to be hoped for, since in the current situation, alcohol policy remains the preserve of social science researchers and other experts.

A Community Approach to Alcohol Education

Although a community alcohol policy would reject educational campaigns aiming to teach individuals "how to drink"—as if avoiding alcohol problems were a skill analogous to driving—education would play a vital role in such a policy. Education is needed for two key purposes: first, to increase the visibility of alcohol problems and, especially, the collective or structural basis of these problems; and, second, to promote public acceptance of the fairness of more effective control structures and a more equitable distribution of responsibility for prevention among all those who manufacture, import, distribute, advertise, market, or consume alcoholic beverages.

Alcohol problems will automatically be made more visible to the entire society if we focus on the control of the substance itself rather than on the failures of the minority who suffer problems. The frank focus on alcohol dictated by a public health perspective, and the stress upon the need for controlling per capita consumption would in themselves begin to communicate the collective aspects of alcohol problems.

The problem has sorely lacked visibility in the past, mainly because of the ideological biases of the "alcoholism paradigm." As this paradigm defines the situation, alcohol, drinking, the neighborhood bar, the cocktail hour, and the dry martini are all seen only as aspects of a widespread and legitimate social custom. But under the new policy outlined here, with its emphasis on controlling overall consumption, these aspects of drinking would no longer be taken as safe and innocent practices but as having reference to the strong forces found everywhere in our society that contribute to ever-increasing levels of per capita consumption.

The prevailing definition of the problem of alcoholism has the explicit ideological function of restricting public attention and concern to the problem group. This helps in part to explain why alcohol problems—our most serious drug problems—have never reached the national agenda. This is in sharp contrast to other drug problems, such as heroin and marijuana, that receive massive political attention. Redefining alcoholism in terms of the availability of alcohol and the need for all persons to bear the burden of its restriction expands the issue. Such expansion would occur through the redirection of public attention from an exclusive focus on those suffering an "illness" to the much broader and more general issue of the public health, fairness, and the question of reasonable controls. Expanding the issue of alcohol problems is a precondition for moving alcohol problems to the public agenda and is necessary for the adoption and implementation of a new alcohol policy.

Such a redefinition of alcohol problems will help achieve the second goal of education for alcohol—public acceptance of the principle of a shared responsibility for preventing alcohol problems. As long as the myth persists that alcohol problems result from the "failure" of a minority, public acceptance of the fairness of alcohol control policies that affect all drinkers and the industry will be frustrated. By placing alcohol at the center of policy, and by refusing to resort to blaming the alcoholic exclusively for society's alcohol problems, we also will help remove some of the stigma implied in the current approach, which still locates the problem within the skin of

the alcoholic. Under the current paradigm the alcoholic is still stigmatized: the disease label indicates that the alcoholic cannot successfully perform a widely legitimate social practice.

The norm of minimal alcohol use must be articulated within the
larger framework of concern for the community and in pursuit of
the goals of the public welfare and the public health. It is clear that
this norm entails some measure of self-restraint and the sharing of
burdens. It is not only the alcohol industry and the advertising media who must shoulder the burdens of moving toward a higher level
of welfare and health; it is also a burden for the individual consumer
of alcoholic beverages—a burden that is expressed and made manifest in a social norm.

Conclusion

One is struck over and over again by how much conflict
over alcohol is woven into our national history and how these con-
flicts have so often stood for more than the harm alcohol has caused
to individuals and groups. But there is one question that deserves
mention if only briefly. What are we to make after all of those persons in our midst who drink to excess—indeed, beyond all sense
and reason? Will not a renewed focus on alcohol only turn the entire issue back to a narrow "moralism"?

This is always a possibility, but I think that the signs are for a
more hopeful outcome. The basic contradictions in our thinking
about alcohol flow from viewing these problems in terms of fundamentally opposed types, with the normal drinker and the deviant
drinker inhabiting two very different worlds. With this approach we
are confronted with either believing that the alcoholic could have
acted otherwise and could have retained their membership in
the world of the normal drinkers or seeing the alcoholic as fundamentally different in that they could *not* have acted differently. The
first path leads to a heightened sense of individual responsibility,
but also to a strong condemnation and stigmatization of the alcoholic. The second view, the path of the alcoholism movement,
makes the alcoholic a sort of immanent reality in our midst who,
once lost to the "other side," can never expect to inhabit the world
of normalcy and "social drinking." One kind of stigma is replaced

with another, still leaving alcoholics condemned as fundamentally different from normal drinkers.

Our only hope is to stop seeing the alcoholic and the normal drinker as two fundamentally different types inhabiting two different worlds. Raising the issue of alcohol and its availability in society should help us to begin to reject these commonsensical but harmful definitions of the situation. The alcoholic and the social drinkers are members of the same world; there is no difference of kind. It is neither conceivable nor plausible to imagine a world in which alcohol is made commercially available—even minimally available—but one does not encounter people with alcohol problems. As pessimistic as this judgment might seem, realism leads to hope and compassion. To say that alcoholics could have acted otherwise—where this means a world without alcoholics—is to speak contrary to what we know empirically. Yet, at the individual level, we must always hold out hope and courage, remembering that, while alcohol problems are often enduring and intractable, they are just as often transitory and changing. Our task as a society is to recognize our common obligations to reduce early death and serious disability as much as possible, while retaining the basic minimums of a free society in which an individual enjoys personal autonomy and privacy. In this sense, the problem of alcoholism in society is always a moral question. The worst thing we can do is to continue to insist on the freedom to enjoy the use of alcohol or other drugs with only minimal constraint from the community, and then in a self-serving manner stigmatize the alcoholic by labeling him as morally inferior or permanently diminished in his capacities. The dark side of the benefits of alcohol cannot be wished away; if we are to have alcohol in our society (and I support this choice), then we should in courage and in humility agree to pay the price in terms of reasonable restrictions over its availability and consumption, as well as provide treatment for the casualties that we know will occur.

Notes

Chapter I

1. See Dan Beauchamp, "Precarious Politics: Alcoholism and Public Policy" (Ph.D. diss., The Johns Hopkins University, 1973), pp. 337–373. See also Eric Redman, *The Dance of Legislation* (New York: Simon and Schuster, 1973), pp. 284–285.
2. The 1980 budget estimates for the National Institute on Alcohol Abuse and Alcoholism (NIAAA) are obtained from the January 11, 1980, issue of *The Alcoholism Report*, vol. 8, no. 6. *The Alcoholism Report* is the newsletter of record for the alcoholism constituency and is published in Washington, D.C. Legislation renewing the authority for the NIAAA and establishing the authorized ceilings of $198 million for the 1980 fiscal year and $217 million for the 1981 fiscal year was signed on January 2, 1980. However, the NIAAA is operating in FY 1980 under a continuing resolution that sets an actual ceiling of $175 million in appropriations. The January 28, 1980, issue of *Alcoholism Report* reports that President Carter's budget cuts to fight inflation propose $175 million for the 1980 fiscal year, with a further reduction to approximately $150 million for the 1981 fiscal year.
3. For a breakdown of the various programs and funding levels see the January 28, 1980, issue of *The Alcoholism Report*.
4. See Beauchamp, "Precarious Politics," pp. 337–373.
5. See HEW and NIAAA, *The Second Special Report to the U.S. Congress on Alcohol and Health* (Washington, D.C.: G.P.O., 1976); HEW and NIAAA, *The Third Special Report to the U.S. Congress on Alcohol and Health* (Washington, D.C.: G.P.O., 1978).
6. Ibid., especially the *Third Special Report*.
7. Kettil Bruun et al., *Alcohol Control Policies in Public Health Perspective* (Helsinki, Finland: Finnish Foundation for Alcohol Studies, 1975).
8. While this concept has been repeatedly criticized in the professional

literature, among the wider public the major debate has centered on the definition of alcoholism as a disease or illness, and the constant repetition of that theme to everyone who will hear it.

9. John P. Hewitt and Peter M. Hall, "Social Problems, Problematic Situations, and Quasi-Theories," *American Sociological Review* 38 (June 1973), pp. 367–374.

10. Ibid., pp. 370–371.

11. James D. Thompson and William J. McEwen, "Organizational Goals and Environment: Goal Setting as an Interaction Process," *American Sociological Review* 23 (February 1958), pp. 23–31.

12. This "official history" of the disease theory is based mainly on Juan Marconi, "The Concept of Alcoholism," *Quarterly Journal of Studies on Alcohol* 20 (1959), pp. 216–235; A. E. Wilkerson, Jr., "A History of the Concept of Alcoholism as a Disease" (Ph.D. diss., University of Pennsylvania, 1966); and E. M. Jellinek, *The Disease Concept of Alcoholism* (New Haven: College and University Press, 1960). I have also relied on Craig MacAndrew, "On the Notion That Certain Persons Who Are Given to Frequent Drunkenness Suffer from a Disease Called Alcoholism," in *Changing Perspectives in Mental Illness*, ed. Stanley C. Plog and Robert B. Edgerton (New York: Holt, Rinehart, and Winston, 1969); Joseph Schneider, "Deviant Drinking as Disease: Alcoholism as a Social Accomplishment," *Social Problems* 15 (1976), pp. 326–392; Robert Straus, "Problem Drinking in the Perspective of Social Change: 1940– 1973," in *Alcohol and Alcohol Problems*, ed. William J. Filstead, Jean J. Rossi, and Mark Keller (Cambridge: Ballinger, 1976), pp. 29–56; and Harry Gene Levine, "The Discovery of Addiction," *Journal of Studies on Alcohol* 39 (1978), pp. 143–174.

13. Marconi, "Concept of Alcoholism."

14. Quoted in ibid., p. 223.

15. Quoted in ibid., p. 228.

16. Ibid. See also Jellinek, *Disease Concept of Alcoholism*, pp. 1–12, for another history of the disease concept.

17. See Jellinek, *Disease Concept of Alcoholism*, p. 1.

18. Wilkerson, "History of the Concept of Alcoholism."

19. See Chapter III for a discussion of the Washingtonians.

20. Jellinek, *Disease Concept of Alcoholism*, p. 1.

21. Levine, "Discovery of Addiction."

22. Jellinek suggested this in *Disease Concept of Alcoholism*, p. 1. See also Levine, "Discovery of Addiction," and Mark E. Lender, "Jellinek's Typology of Alcoholism," *Journal of Studies on Alcohol* 40 (1979), pp. 361–375.

23. Mark Keller, "Alcoholism: Nature and Extent of the Problem," *Annals of the American Academy of Political and Social Sciences* 315 (1958), p. 2, n. 6.

24. Norman H. Clark, *Deliver Us from Evil* (New York: Norton, 1976), especially chs. 8–10.

25. Andrew Sinclair, *Prohibition: The Era of Excess* (Boston: Little, Brown, 1962).

26. Frederick Lewis Allen, *The Big Change* (New York: Harper, 1952); Daniel Bell, *The Cultural Contradictions of Capitalism* (New York: Basic Books, 1976), esp. pp. 54–76.

27. See Joseph Gusfield, *Symbolic Crusade: Status Politics and the American Temperance Movement* (Urbana, Ill.: University of Illinois Press, 1963).

28. The early history of this group has been recounted in Mark Keller, *Manual of the Classified Abstract Archive of the Alcohol Literature* (New Haven: Quarterly Journal of Studies on Alcohol, 1962).

29. The "Current Notes" section of the early years of the *Quarterly Journal of Studies on Alcohol*, vols. 1–10 (1940–1949), is the source of data on the early activities of the Council.

30. See Ernest B. Gordon, *Alcohol Reaction at Yale* (Francestown, N.H.: Alcohol Information Press, 1946), for a Temperance view of the alcohol section at Yale. But see Jay L. Rubin, "Shifting Perspectives on the Alcoholism Treatment Movement, 1940–1955," *Journal of Studies on Alcohol* 40 (1979), pp. 376–386, for evidence that some Temperance groups welcomed the Yale group.

31. This change was made in 1975.

32. The information for this section on the developments at Yale was taken from the "Current Notes" section of the *Quarterly Journal of Studies on Alcohol*, vols. 1–10. The information on the Yale Plan clinics is from "Current Notes," *Quarterly Journal of Studies on Alcohol* 4 (1943–1944), pp. 496–508.

33. See "Current Notes," *Quarterly Journal of Studies on Alcohol* 5 (1944–1945), pp. 354–358.

34. Ibid., p. 356.

35. See Sidney Cahn, *The Treatment of Alcoholics* (New York: Oxford University Press, 1970), p. 96.

36. Samples of Seeley's and Lemert's writings on alcoholism may be found in David J. Pittman and Charles R. Snyder, eds., *Society, Culture, and Drinking Patterns* (New York: J. Wiley, 1962), pp. 330–344, 553–571.

37. See Robert Straus, "Problem Drinking in the Perspective of Social Change: 1940–1973," for a discussion of this move.

38. Joint Commission on Mental Illness and Health, *Action for Mental Health: Final Report of the Joint Commission on Mental Illness and Health* (New York: Basic Books, 1961).

39. Thomas F. A. Plaut, *Alcohol Problems—A Report to the Nation* (Report of the Cooperative Commission on the Study of Alcoholism; New York: Oxford University Press, 1967.) This history of the commission is based on an interview with Plaut, currently with the National Institute of Mental Health. See also Bruce Johnson, "The Alcoholism Movement in America: A Study in Cultural Innovation" (Ph.D. diss., University of Illinois at Urbana-Champaign, 1973).

40. See the 1962 and 1973 *Annual Reports* of the National Council on Alcoholism. The Smithers Foundation, established by a wealthy recovered alcoholic, is the sole national foundation that focuses exclusively on alcohol problems.
41. Selden Bacon, "The Mobilization of Community Resources for the Attack on Alcoholism," *Quarterly Journal of Studies on Alcohol* 8 (1947–1948), pp. 473–497.
42. Ibid., p. 474.
43. Ibid., p. 477.
44. Marty Mann, "The Citizen's Part in the Problem of Alcoholism," *Quarterly Journal of Studies on Alcohol* 6 (1945–1946), pp. 249–255.
45. Selden Bacon, "Alcoholism," in *Man Alone: Alienation in Modern Society*, ed. Eric Josephson and Mary Josephson (New York: Dell, 1962), pp. 393–410.
46. Keller, "Alcoholism," p. 3.
47. Robert F. Bales, "Cultural Differences in Rates of Alcoholism," *Quarterly Journal of Studies on Alcohol* 6 (1945–1946), pp. 480–499.
48. Nils Christie and Kettil Bruun, "Alcohol Problems: The Conceptual Framework," *Proceedings of the 28th International Congress on Alcohol and Alcoholism*, Washington, D.C., Sept. 15–20, 1968, ed. Mark Keller and Timothy Coffey (Highland Park, N.J.: Hillhouse Press, 1969), pp. 65–73.
49. Alcoholics Anonymous, *Alcoholics Anonymous* (New York: Alcoholics Anonymous World Services, 1955), p. 59.
50. Marty Mann, *Primer on Alcoholism* (New York: Rinehart, 1950), p. 9.
51. Mark Keller, "Definition of Alcoholism," *Quarterly Journal of Studies on Alcohol* 21 (1960), p. 127.
52. Plaut, *Alcohol Problems*, p. 39. Plaut goes on to say that "since the vast majority of alcohol users do not become problem drinkers, other factors—biological, psychological, and sociological—must be involved in the development of the disorder" (p. 49). Again the implication is that most drinkers exhibit personal control over their drinking.
53. Marconi, "Concept of Alcoholism."
54. Mark Keller, "On the Loss-of-Control Phenomenon in Alcoholism," *British Journal of Addiction* 67 (1972), p. 154.
55. World Health Organization, Expert Committee on Mental Health, Alcoholism Subcommittee, *Second Report* (World Health Organization Technical Rep. Ser., no. 48; August 1952).
56. Keller, "Alcoholism."
57. John Seeley, "The WHO Definition of Alcoholism," *Quarterly Journal of Studies on Alcohol* 20 (1959), pp. 352–356.
58. Gusfield, *Symbolic Crusade*; Daniel Bell, *Cultural Contradictions of Capitalism*; Daniel Bell, "Interpretations of American Politics," and "The Dispossessed," in *The Radical Right*, ed. Daniel Bell (Garden City, N.Y.: Anchor, 1964), pp. 1–73; and Richard Hofstadter, "The Pseudo-Conservative Revolt" and "Pseudo-Conservatism Revisited," in *The Radical Right*, ed. Daniel Bell, pp. 75–103.

Chapter II

1. Rupert Wilkinson's *The Prevention of Drinking Problems* (New York: Oxford, 1970), an outgrowth of the Cooperative Commission, is the exception. The Yale group did not ignore matters of alcohol policy and law. The *Quarterly Journal of Studies on Alcohol* has presented many articles on this topic over the years. The public health consequences of these laws, however, were seldom of significant interest. There were scattered efforts to investigate the impact of state alcohol control policies, such as the Moreland Commission in New York State, in the early 1960s. See L. E. Walsh, Chairman, *Report and Recommendations* (New York: New York State Moreland Commission on the Alcoholic Beverage Control Law, January 1964).

   The first major article on the per capita consumption thesis in this country was by Jan deLint and Wolfgang Schmidt, "The Distribution of Alcohol Consumption in Ontario," *Quarterly Journal of Studies on Alcohol* 29 (1968), pp. 968–973. At about the same time, Max Hayman challenged this silence over social drinking with "The Myth of Social Drinking," *American Journal of Psychiatry* 124 (November 1967), pp. 585–594.

2. Norman Clark, *Deliver Us from Evil* (New York: Norton, 1976), pp. 178, 209.

3. John Kaplan, *Marijuana—The New Prohibition* (New York: World Publishing, 1970).

4. National Commission on Marihuana and Drug Abuse, *Drug Use in America: Problem in Perspective* (Second Report of the National Commission, March 1973; Washington, D.C.: G.P.O., 1973), pp. 382–383.

5. See Dan Beauchamp, "Precarious Politics: Alcoholism and Public Policy" (Ph.D. diss., The Johns Hopkins University, 1973), pp. 252–336, regarding the issue of public drunkenness in Washington, D.C.

6. Ibid.

7. Joseph Timberlake, *Prohibition and the Progressive Movement: 1910–1920* (Cambridge: Harvard University Press, 1963); Norman Clark, *Deliver Us from Evil*; John C. Burnham, "New Perspectives on the Prohibition 'Experiment' of the 1920s," *Journal of Social History* 2 (1968–1969), pp. 51–68; Richard Hofstadter, *The Paranoid Style in American Politics* (New York: Knopf, 1965) and Daniel Bell, ed., *The Radical Right* (New York: Anchor, 1964). *The Radical Right* is a good source for essays by Bell, Hofstadter, David Reisman, Nathan Glazer, and others on "status politics" and the struggle between modernity and traditionalism in American politics. See also Bell's *The Cultural Contradictions of Capitalism* (New York: Basic Books, 1976), especially pp. 33–84.

8. Clark, *Deliver Us from Evil*, pp. 18–22.

9. Ibid., pp. 17–18.

10. Ibid., pp. 19–21. See W. J. Rorabaugh, "Estimated U.S. Alcoholic Beverage Consumption, 1790–1860," *Journal of Studies on Alcohol* 37 (1976), p. 361, for a somewhat more conservative estimate of six gallons,

absolute alcohol. Rorabaugh points out that even his estimate may be high because children may have consumed more during this earlier period in the United States.

11. Clark, *Deliver Us from Evil*, p. 29.
12. Bell, *Cultural Contradictions of Capitalism*, p. 64.
13. Gusfield, *Symbolic Crusade*, p. 140.
14. Daniel Bell, "The Dispossessed," in *The Radical Right*, ed. Daniel Bell (New York: Anchor, 1964), p. 25. Bell defines as rural places with fewer than 2,500 persons.
15. H. G. Levine, "The Discovery of Addiction," *Journal of Studies on Alcohol* 39 (1978), pp. 143–174.
16. W. J. Rorabaugh, *The Alcoholic Republic* (New York: Oxford University Press, 1979), pp. 25–92.
17. Quoted in Levine, "Discovery of Addiction," p. 149.
18. Quoted in ibid., pp. 149–150.
19. Levine, of course, does not ignore this emphasis on saloons and the industry in Temperance thought.
20. Quoted in ibid., p. 152.
21. Quoted in ibid., p. 168.
22. Ibid., pp. 164–165. See Mark E. Lender, "Jellinek's Typology of Alcoholism," *Journal of Studies on Alcohol* 40 (1979), pp. 361–375, for nineteenth-century precursors of the disease concept.
23. Levine does indeed remark on the shift to "person-specific" explanations for alcoholism, and notes that this is an important shift from the perspectives on addiction developed by the Temperance movement. As he says, "for the first time, the source of addiction lay in the individual body, and not in the drug per se" (p. 162). I see this shift, however, as a great deal more important than Levine apparently does, because it amounts to the "discovery of alcoholism" or the idea that alcoholism strikes only the few. Again, the discovery of alcoholism is more than the "discovery of addiction." Addiction is a behavioral loss of control. Alcoholism is a theory about the vulnerability to, or risk for, this loss of control.
24. Ibid., p. 165.
25. Albert Cohen, *Deviance and Control* (Englewood Cliffs, N.J.: Prentice-Hall, 1966), pp. 42–44.
26. The classic statement remains that of Talcott Parsons, *The Social System* (Chicago: Free Press, 1951).
27. Vilhem Aubert and Sheldon Messinger, "The Criminal and the Sick," *Inquiry* (Oslo) 1 (1958), pp. 137–160.
28. Aubert and Messinger, "The Criminal and the Sick," pp. 142–143.
29. Ibid.
30. Geoffrey Vickers, "What Sets the Goals of Public Health?" *The New England Journal of Medicine* 258 (March 1958), pp. 589–596.
31. Ibid.
32. Lewis Thomas, *The Lives of a Cell* (New York: Bantam, 1974), especially pp. 88–101.

33. Ibid., p. 89.
34. Ibid., p. 90. My italics.
35. René Dubos, *Man Adapting* (New Haven: Yale University Press, 1965), pp. 163–164.
36. John E. Gordon, "The Epidemiology of Alcoholism," *New York State Journal of Medicine* 58 (1958), pp. 1911–1918. See also Jack Mendelson and Stefan Stein, "The Definition of Alcoholism," *International Psychiatry Clinics* 3, no. 2 (Summer 1966), pp. 8–10; and Alan F. Williams, "Epidemiology and Ecology of Alcoholism," *International Psychiatry Clinics* 3, no. 2 (Summer 1966), p. 19. Williams relies on John Gordon's essay, "The Epidemiology of Alcoholism," to make his point.
37. National Center for Prevention and Control of Alcoholism, National Institute of Mental Health, *Alcohol and Alcoholism* (Washington, D.C.: G.P.O., 1969), p. 24.
38. Morris Chafetz, *Why Drinking Can Be Good for You* (New York: Stein and Day, 1976), pp. 109–110.
39. National Center for Prevention and Control of Alcoholism, *Alcohol and Alcoholism*, p. 5.
40. Thomas F. A. Plaut, *Alcohol Problems—A Report to the Nation* (New York: Oxford University Press, 1967), p. 49.
41. Selden Bacon, "The Process of Addiction to Alcohol," *Quarterly Journal of Studies on Alcohol* 34 (March 1973), p. 2.
42. Ibid., p. 3.
43. Bacon, "Alcoholics Do Not Drink," *Annals of the American Academy of Political and Social Science* 315 (January 1958), p. 63.
44. Ibid., pp. 58–59.
45. Ibid.
46. Ibid., p. 56.
47. Bruce H. Johnson, "The Alcoholism Movement in America: A Study in Cultural Innovation" (Ph.D. diss., University of Illinois at Urbana-Champaign, 1973).
48. See Morris Chafetz, "The Prevention of Alcoholism," *International Journal of Psychiatry* 9 (1970–1971), pp. 329–348.
49. Abraham Myerson, "Alcohol: A Study of Social Ambivalence," *Quarterly Journal of Studies on Alcohol* 1 (1940–1941), pp. 13–20.
50. Robert F. Bales, "Cultural Differences in Rates of Alcoholism," *Quarterly Journal of Studies on Alcohol* 6 (1945–1946), pp. 480–499.
51. The following are some of the key references in the integration literature: Albert D. Ullman, "Sociocultural Backgrounds Conducive to Alcoholism," *Annals of the American Academy of Political and Social Science* 315 (1958), pp. 48–54; Selden Bacon, "Social Settings Conducive to Alcoholism: A Sociological Approach to a Medical Problem," *Journal of the American Medical Association* 164 (1957), pp. 177–181; Robert F. Bales, "Attitudes toward Drinking in the Irish Culture," in *Society, Culture, and Drinking Patterns*, ed. David J. Pittman and Charles R. Snyder (New York: J. Wiley, 1962); Edward Blacker, "Sociocultural Factors in Alcoholism," *International Psychiatry Clinics* 3 (1966),

pp. 51–80; Giorgi Lolli, Edmidio Serianni, Grace M. Golder, and P. Luzzatto-Fegiz, *Alcohol in Italian Culture* (Yale Center of Alcohol Studies Monograph no. 3; Glencoe, Ill.: Free Press, 1958); Roland Sadoun, Giorgi Lolli, and Milton Silverman, *Drinking in French Culture* (New Brunswick, N.J.: Rutgers Center of Alcohol Studies, 1965); Jerome H. Skolnick, "Religious Affiliation and Drinking Behavior," *Quarterly Journal of Studies on Alcohol* 19 (1958), pp. 452–470; and Charles R. Snyder, *Alcohol and the Jews* (Glencoe, Ill.: Free Press, 1958).

52. Ullman, "Sociocultural Backgrounds Conducive to Alcoholism," pp. 48–54.

53. Plaut, *Alcohol Problems*, pp. 125–159.

54. Skolnick, "Religious Affiliation and Drinking Behavior."

55. See note 51 for the major studies conducted at Yale.

56. As quoted from Selden Bacon in National Center for Prevention and Control of Alcoholism, *Alcohol and Alcoholism*, pp. 26–27.

57. Morris Chafetz, *Liquor: The Servant of Man* (Boston: Little, Brown 1965).

58. Morris Chafetz, "Alcoholism Prevention and Reality," *Quarterly Journal of Studies on Alcohol* 28 (1967), pp. 345–348. Also, Chafetz, "The Prevention of Alcoholism," pp. 329–348.

59. Morris Chafetz, "Alcoholism Prevention and Reality," p. 349. Cited in Robin Room, "Evaluating the Effect of Drinking Laws on Drinking," in *Drinking*, ed. John Ewing and Beatrice Rouse (Chicago: Nelson-Hall, 1978), p. 281.

60. I am using the term "alibi" simply to point to the ideological functions of the concept of alcoholism, putting alcohol somewhere else than with alcohol problems. See Roland Barthes, *Mythologies* (New York: Hill and Wang, 1972), for a similar use of alibi.

Chapter III

1. The principal sources for this account of A.A. are the official history, Alcoholics Anonymous, *Alcoholics Anonymous Comes of Age* (New York: Alcoholics Anonymous World Services, 1957); Irving Peter Gellman, *The Sober Alcoholic* (New Haven: College and University Press, 1964); Robert Thomsen's biography of Bill Wilson, *Bill W.* (New York: Harper and Row, 1975); Ernest Kurtz, *Not-God* (Center City, Minn.: Hazeldon, 1979); and Barry Leach and John Norris, "Factors in the Development of Alcoholics Anonymous (A.A.)," in *Treatment and Rehabilitation of the Chronic Alcoholic*, ed. Benjamin Kissin and Henri Begleiter (New York: Plenum, 1977), pp. 441–543. See also John Lofland, *Deviance and Identity* (Englewood Cliffs, N.J.: Prentice-Hall, 1969), and Paul Roman, "Delabeling, Relabeling, and Alcoholics Anonymous," *Social Problems* 17 (1970), pp. 538–546.

2. Organizational anonymity refers to the withdrawal of A.A. both from

the public view and from the controversy over alcohol problems, a policy that serves the ideological function of supporting the new status quo for alcohol since Prohibition.

3. Marty Mann, *Primer on Alcoholism* (New York: Rinehart, 1950), pp. 109–117. See U.S., Congress, Senate, Special Subcommittee on Alcoholism and Narcotics, *Examination of the Impact of Alcoholism*, Hearings before the Special Subcommittee on Alcoholism and Narcotics, 91st Cong., 1st Sess. (Washington, D.C.: G.P.O., 1969); July 23–25, 1969, pp. 107–129.
4. Alcoholics Anonymous, *Alcoholics Anonymous* (New York: Alcoholics Anonymous World Services, 1939), p. 30.
5. The book by Lewis Yablonsky, *The Tunnel Back: Synanon* (Baltimore: Penguin Books, 1967), is a case in point. See also Joseph Kessel, *The Road Back* (New York: Knopf, 1962), a book about Alcoholics Anonymous. The "bible" of A.A.—*Alcoholics Anonymous*—was originally to be called "The Way Out."
6. This was a common expression in A.A. groups in the Washington, D.C., area, at any rate. Information on Alcoholics Anonymous that appears in this section was gathered by attending over 300 open and closed meetings of A.A. over a three-year period in the Washington, D.C., area.
7. See Lofland, *Deviance and Identity*, pp. 66–117.
8. Nicholas Kittrie, *The Right to Be Different* (Baltimore: The Johns Hopkins University Press, 1971).
9. The only option for the alcoholic to challenge his or her fundamental difference would be by opposing the existing order for alcohol, which defines alcohol problems purely in personal terms.
10. Selden Bacon, "New Legislation for the Control of Alcoholism: The Connecticut Law of 1945," *Quarterly Journal of Studies on Alcohol* 6 (1945–1946), p. 191.
11. Hannah Arendt, *The Human Condition* (Chicago: University of Chicago Press, 1958), p. 113.
12. Rarely, however, do these persons mention their connection to A.A.
13. See the page one obituary on Wilson in the *New York Times*, January 27, 1971.
14. Vilhelm Aubert, *The Hidden Society* (Totowa, N.J.: Bedminster Press, 1965). See ch. 10, "Secrecy: The Underground as a Social System," pp. 288–310.
15. Georg Simmel, *The Sociology of Georg Simmel*, trans. and ed. Kurt Wolff (New York: Free Press, 1950), pp. 330–375.
16. See Harry Gene Levine, "The Discovery of Addiction," *Journal of Studies on Alcohol* 39 (1978), p. 160. But A.A. and Temperance orders differ sharply on the issue of alcohol in society.
17. Kurtz, *Not-God*, pp. 199–230.
18. The history in this section is taken from the sources indicated in note 1.
19. See A.A., *Alcoholics Anonymous Comes of Age*, p. 290.
20. See Tom Driberg, *The Mystery of Moral Re-armament* (New York:

Knopf, 1965), for a discussion of this group. See also Kurtz, *Not-God*, pp. 9–36.

21. Thomsen, *Bill W.*, pp. 290–312.
22. Ibid., p. 295.
23. Jack Alexander, "Alcoholics Anonymous," *Saturday Evening Post* 213 (March 1, 1941), pp. 9–11, 89–92.
24. Thomsen, *Bill W.*, p. 315.
25. Kurtz, *Not-God*, p. 119.
26. Alcoholics Anonymous, *Twelve Steps and Twelve Traditions* (New York: Alcoholics Anonymous Publishing, 1952), pp. 9–13.
27. A.A., *Alcoholics Anonymous Comes of Age*, pp. 286–294.
28. Ibid., p. 288. Actually, these traditions were formulated and published in 1946, but not officially adopted until 1950. See ibid., p. viii.
29. Ibid.
30. Kurtz, *Not-God*, p. 197. Chapter 2 of A.A., *Alcoholics Anonymous Comes of Age*, pp. 49–221, discusses the evolution of the tradition of anonymity. See also the pamphlet by Bill Wilson, *A.A. Tradition: How It Developed* (New York: Alcoholics Anonymous World Series, 1955), for a good discussion of the gradual evolution of the doctrine of anonymity and the need to protect individual identities.
31. See Talcott Parsons, "Definitions of Health and Illness in the Light of American Values and Social Structure," in *Patients, Physicians and Illness*, ed. E. Gartley Jaco (Glencoe, Ill.: Free Press, 1958), pp. 165–187, for a discussion of "collectivities," as non-organized groupings.
32. The Twelve Steps are the foundation of the A.A. Program of Recovery. They are: "(1) We admitted we were powerless over alcohol—that our lives had become unmanageable. (2) Came to believe that a Power greater than ourselves could restore us to sanity. (3) Made a decision to turn our will and our lives over to the care of God *as we understood Him*. (4) Made a searching and fearless moral inventory of ourselves. (5) Admitted to God, to ourselves, and to another human being, the exact nature of our wrongs. (6) Were entirely ready to have God remove all these defects of character. (7) Humbly asked Him to remove our shortcomings. (8) Made a list of all persons we had harmed, and became willing to make amends to them all. (9) Made direct amends to such people whenever possible, except when to do so would injure them or others. (10) Continued to take personal inventory and when we were wrong promptly admitted it. (11) Sought through prayer and meditation to improve our conscious contact with God *as we understood Him*, praying only for knowledge of His will for us and the power to carry that out. (12) Having had a spiritual awakening as the result of these steps, we tried to carry this message to alcoholics, and to practice these principles in all our affairs" (from A.A., *Alcoholics Anonymous*), pp. 59–60.
33. See Harvey G. Cox, *The Secular City* (New York: Macmillan, 1966), pp. 46–51, for discussion of anonymity as a central feature of modern existence.
34. Matt. 6:1 (Auth. King James Version).

35. This account of the Washingtonian Movement leans heavily on Milton
    A. Maxwell's "The Washingtonian Movement," *Quarterly Journal of
    Studies on Alcohol* 11 (September 1950), pp. 410–451, and my own doc-
    toral dissertation, "Precarious Politics: Alcoholism and Public Policy"
    (The Johns Hopkins University, 1973).
36. Alexis DeTocqueville, in his *Democracy In America*, makes this point
    repeatedly. See the edition edited by J. P. Mayer and Max Lerner,
    translated by George Lawrence (New York: Harper and Row, 1966).
37. See A.A., *Alcoholics Anonymous Comes of Age*, p. 125.
38. See Simmel's essays on secrecy and the secret society in Simmel, *So-
    ciology of Georg Simmel*, pp. 330–376.
39. Jesse Pitts, "Social Control," *International Encyclopedia of the Social
    Sciences*, vol. 14, ed. David L. Sills (New York: Macmillan, 1968), pp.
    381–396.

Chapter IV

1. Harry Gene Levine, in his "The Discovery of Addiction," *Journal of
   Studies on Alcohol* 39 (1978), pp. 143–174, anticipates a new model for
   alcoholism, one that is more loosely and flexibly constructed than the
   present one. See my "Post Alcoholism Models of Prevention" (paper
   presented to the Society for General Systems Research and the American Association for the Advancement of Science, February 13–16, 1978;
   Washington, D.C.), for an earlier attempt to understand the changes
   overtaking our ideas about alcoholism.
2. Craig McAndrew, "On the Notion that Certain Persons Who Are Given
   to Frequent Drunkenness Suffer from a Disease Called Alcoholism,"
   in *Changing Perspectives in Mental Illness*, ed. Stanley C. Plog and
   Robert B. Edgerton (New York: Holt, Rinehart, and Winston, 1969),
   pp. 487–488.
3. The best short discussion of typifications is found in Peter L. Berger
   and Thomas Luckmann, *The Social Construction of Reality* (Garden
   City, N.Y.: Anchor, 1967), pp. 3–34 and passim.
4. David Robinson, "The Alcoholigist's Addiction," *Quarterly Journal of
   Studies on Alcohol* 33 (1972), p. 1041.
5. See Howard Becker, "Labelling Theory Reconsidered," in *Deviance
   and Social Control*, ed. Paul Rock and Mary McIntosh (London:
   Tavistock, 1974), pp. 41–66.
6. Quoted in Edwin M. Schur, *Labeling Deviant Behavior* (New York:
   Harper and Row, 1971), p. 12. Italics in original.
7. For the best analysis of dispositional explanations and their status in social science, see Robert Brown, *Explanation in Social Science* (Chicago:
   Aldine, 1963), pp. 75–88.
8. This literature is too extensive to treat here. The best starting place for
   the social scientist is Gilbert Ryle's *The Concept of Mind* (New York:
   Barnes and Noble, 1949). See also Irving Thalberg, *Enigmas of Agency*

(New York: Humanities Press, 1972); John L. Austin, *Philosophical Papers*, ed. J. O. Urmson and G. J. Warnock (Oxford, England: Clarendon Press, 1961), especially pp. 153–180. Geoffrey Mortimore, ed., *Weakness of Will* (London, England: Macmillan, 1971), is a good collection of papers on the ideas of will and willpower. The recent and extensive influence of Wittgenstein among social scientists does not overturn the point that, by and large, there has been little interest in the literature in testing the limits of the dispositional and ability explanations that are in such widespread use.

9. See the various essays in Mortimore, *Weakness of Will*, esp. the essay by Gwynneth Matthews, "Weakness of Will," pp. 160–174.
10. Jellinek is quoted in Robinson, "The Alcoholigist's Addiction," pp. 1029–1030.
11. Arnold Kaufman, "Ability," *Journal of Philosophy* 60 (1963), pp. 537–551; and J. L. Austin, "Ifs and Cans," in his *Philosophical Papers*, pp. 153–180.
12. Vilhelm Aubert and Sheldon Messinger, "The Criminal and the Sick," *Inquiry* (Oslo) 1 (1958), pp. 142–143.
13. Thomas Szasz, *The Myth of Mental Illness* (New York: Dell, 1961). See also Szasz, *Ceremonial Chemistry: The Ritual Persecution of Drugs, Addicts, and Pushers* (New York: Doubleday, 1975).
14. Claude Steiner, *Games Alcoholics Play* (New York: Grove, 1971), p. xvi.
15. Ibid.
16. William Rohan, "Drinking Behavior and 'Alcoholism,'" *Journal of Studies on Alcohol* 36 (1975), p. 908.
17. Ibid., p. 909.
18. Robinson, "Alcoholigist's Addiction."
19. Ibid., p. 1037.
20. Claude Steiner, "The Alcoholic Game," *Quarterly Journal of Studies on Alcohol* 30 (1969), p. 921.
21. Robin Room, "Comment on 'The Alcoholigist's Addiction,'" *Quarterly Journal of Studies on Alcohol* 33 (1972), pp. 1049–1059.
22. Nancy Mello, "Behavioral Studies of Alcoholism," in *The Biology of Alcoholism*, vol. 2, ed. Benjamin Kissin and Henri Begleiter (New York: Plenum, 1972), pp. 219–291.
23. Mark Keller, in *Emerging Concepts in Alcohol Dependence*, ed. E. Mansell Pattison, Mark Sobell, and Linda Sobell (New York: Springer, 1977), pp. 63–64. It is striking, however, that Keller fails to realize that the concept of alcoholism that he helped develop and defend rests on the idea that alcoholics are similar beyond the fact that they are dependent on alcohol. For Keller, alcoholics may be different but they are first of all similar in their incapacities—incapacities that explain their difference from nonproblem drinkers.
24. Pattison et al., *Emerging Concepts*, pp. 61–63, cites the literature. Blaine asserts that while a variety of personality factors "are not centrally present in all alcoholics, [they] are common enough to merit attention" (Pattison et al., *Emerging Concepts*, p. 63). Williams is unwill-

ing to dismiss the possibility that there might be basic personality differences between alcoholics and the rest of the drinking population. He notes that even if differences are found, the comparison of the alcoholic and all other drinkers still encounters the objection that any differences noted might be due to years of heavy drinking. To meet this objection, Williams argues that we need better longitudinal studies of young persons before they become alcoholic to see if there are some predisposing factors in alcoholism. See his "Personality Factors in Alcoholism," in *Social Aspects of Alcoholism*, ed. Benjamin Kissin and Henri Begleiter (New York: Plenum, 1976), pp. 243–274.

25. Mello, "Behavioral Studies of Alcoholism," pp. 219–291.
26. Ibid., p. 259.
27. Pattison et al., *Emerging Concepts*, p. 99.
28. Ibid., p. 100.
29. Ibid.
30. Ibid., pp. 102–103.
31. Ibid., p. 63.
32. A. H. Cain, *The Cured Alcoholic* (New York: John Day, 1964).
33. Reports of "spontaneous remission" have been around for some time. One of the earliest was D. L. Davies, "Normal Drinking in Recovered Alcohol Addicts," *Quarterly Journal of Studies on Alcohol* 23 (1962), pp. 94–104. See also L. R. H. Drew, "Alcoholism as a Self-Limiting Disease," *Quarterly Journal of Studies on Alcohol* 29 (1968), pp. 956–967.
34. This research is reported in David J. Armor, J. Michael Polich, and Harriet B. Stambull's *Alcoholism and Treatment* (New York: John Wiley, 1978).
35. Ibid., pp. 294–295.
36. See ibid., app. B, "Reaction to the Rand Report on 'Alcoholism and Treatment,'" pp. 212–292.
37. J. Michael Polich, David Armor, and Harriet Braiker, "Patterns of Alcoholism over Four Years," *Journal of Studies on Alcohol* 31 (1980), pp. 397–416.
38. Don Cahalan, *Problem Drinkers* (San Francisco: Jossey-Bass, 1970), pp. 35–62.
39. Ibid., pp. 36–38.
40. Ibid.
41. Ibid., p. 142.
42. Walter B. Clark and Don Cahalan, "Changes in Problem Drinking over a Four-Year Span," *Addictive Behaviors* 1 (1976), p. 258. See also Josephine Williams, "Waxing and Waning Drinkers," paper presented at the Annual Meeting for the Study of Social Problems, August 27, 1967.
43. Personal communication, September 1979.
44. MacAndrew, "On the Notion That Certain Persons," p. 496; Joseph Schneider, "Deviant Drinking as Disease: Alcoholism as a Social Accomplishment," *Social Problems* 15 (1976), pp. 361–372.
45. MacAndrew, "On the Notion That Certain Persons," p. 487.

46. Morris Janowitz, *The Last Half-Century* (Chicago: University of Chicago Press, 1978), p. 29.
47. For a brief discussion of "Anstie's limit" see Howard W. Haggard and E. M. Jellinek, *Alcohol Explored* (Garden City, N.Y: Doubleday, 1942), pp. 9–10.
48. Don Cahalan, Ira H. Cisin, and Helen M. Crossley, *American Drinking Practices* (New Brunswick, N.J.: Rutgers Center of Alcohol Studies, 1969), p. 19. The categories have the following meanings: *abstainers* either do not drink or do not drink as much as once a year; *infrequent drinkers* drink at least once a year but not as much as once a month; *light drinkers* drink at least once a month but typically no more than one or two drinks at a single occasion; *moderate drinkers* drink at least once a month, but typically no more than three or four drinks on a single occasion; and *heavy drinkers* drink every day with at least five or more drinks at least once in a while or about once weekly with about five or more drinks per occasion.
49. See Armor et al., *Alcoholism and Treatment*, pp. 173–211, for a discussion of this issue.
50. Dean Gerstein, "Alcohol Use and Consequences" (paper prepared for the Panel on Alternative Policies Affecting the Prevention of Alcohol Abuse and Alcoholism, the National Academy of Sciences; Washington, D.C., September 1979), p. 14.
51. Eliot Freidson, *Professional Dominance* (Chicago: Aldine, 1970), p. 63.
52. Ibid., pp. 64–65.
53. Ibid., p. 64.
54. Ryle, *Concept of Mind*, pp. 17–18.
55. William Ryan, *Blaming the Victim* (New York: Vintage, 1971), discusses this form of reductionism, pp. 3–29 and passim.
56. Ibid., pp. 61–85.
57. Ibid., p. 8.
58. Ibid., p. 9.

Chapter V

1. Robert Popham, Wolfgang Schmidt, and Jan deLint, "The Effects of Legal Restraint on Drinking," in *Social Aspects of Alcoholism*, ed. Benjamin Kissin and Henri Begleiter (New York: Plenum, 1976), p. 581.
2. Robin Room, "Social Science and Alcohol Policy Making" (paper delivered at the Conference on the Utilization of Social Research in Drug Policy Making, Center for Socio-Cultural Research on Drug Use, Columbia University; Washington, D.C., May 3–5, 1978).
3. Milton Terris, "Epidemiology of Cirrhosis of the Liver: National Mortality Data," *American Journal of Public Health* 57 (1967), pp. 2076–2088.
4. Ibid., p. 2077.
5. Ibid., pp. 2082–2083.

6. Ibid., pp. 2087–2088.
7. Jack Elinson, "Epidemiologic Studies and Control Programs in Alcoholism: Discussion," *American Journal of Public Health* 57 (1967), pp. 991–996.
8. Ibid., p. 992. Interestingly, Terris' article was not printed with the other papers by the *American Journal of Public Health*, appearing several months later in the December issue.
9. John Kaplan, *Marijuana—The New Prohibition* (New York: World, 1970).
10. John C. Burnham, "New Perspectives on the Prohibition 'Experiment' of the 1920s," *Journal of Social History* 2 (1968–1969), pp. 51–68; Norman Clark, *Deliver Us from Evil* (New York: Norton, 1976); Joseph Gusfield, *Symbolic Crusade: Status Politics and the American Temperance Movement* (Urbana, Ill.: University of Illinois Press, 1963); Gusfield in *Change and Continuity in Twentieth-Century America: The 1920s*, ed. John Braeman et al. (Columbus: Ohio State, 1968), pp. 257–308; Clark Warburton, *The Economic Results of Prohibition* (Columbia University Studies in History, Economics and Public Law, no. 379; New York: Columbia University Press, 1932); Norman Joliffe and E. M. Jellinek, "Vitamin Deficiencies in Alcoholism," *Quarterly Journal of Studies on Alcohol* 2 (1941), pp. 544–583; and E. M. Jellinek, "Recent Trends in Alcoholism and Alcohol Consumption," *Quarterly Journal of Studies on Alcohol* 8 (1947–1948), pp. 1–42.
11. Morris Chafetz, *Liquor: Servant of Man* (Boston: Little, Brown, 1965), pp. 173–174.
12. See references at note 10.
13. Terris, "Epidemiology of Cirrhosis of the Liver," pp. 2077–2078.
14. Clark, *Deliver Us from Evil*, pp. 140–180.
15. Ibid., pp. 181–208.
16. Burnham, "New Perspectives on the Prohibition 'Experiment.'"
17. Jan deLint and Wolfgang Schmidt, "The Distribution of Alcohol Consumption in Ontario," *Quarterly Journal of Studies on Alcohol* 29 (1968), p. 968.
18. Ibid., pp. 968–973.
19. Ibid., p. 971.
20. Ibid. The citation for Ledermann is Sully Ledermann, *Alcool, Alcoolisme, Alcoolisation* (Données scientifiques de caractère physiologique, économique et social, Institut National d'Etudes Démographiques, Travaux et Documents, Cahier no. 29; Paris: Presses Universitaires de France, 1956). See also Sully Ledermann, "Can One Reduce Alcoholism without Changing Total Alcohol Consumption in a Population?" (paper presented at the 27th International Congress on Alcohol and Alcoholism, Frankfurt-am-Main, 1964).
21. Quoted in Gary H. Miller and Neil Agnew, "The Ledermann Model of Alcohol Consumption," *Quarterly Journal of Alcohol Studies* 35 (1974), pp. 886–887.
22. The principal documents discussing this line of research are: deLint

and Schmidt, "Distribution of Alcohol Consumption in Ontario"; Wolfgang Schmidt and Jan deLint, "Estimating the Prevalence of Alcoholism from Alcohol Consumption and Mortality Data," *Quarterly Journal of Studies on Alcohol* 31 (1970), pp. 957–964; Jan de Lint and Wolfgang Schmidt, "Consumption Averages and Alcoholism Prevalence: A Brief Review of Epidemiological Investigations," *British Journal of Addiction* 66 (1971), pp. 97–107; Kettil Bruun et al., *Alcohol Control Policies in Public Health Perspective* (Helsinki, Finland: Finnish Foundation for Alcohol Studies, 1975); A. K. J. Cartwright, S. J. Shaw, and T. A. Spratley, "The Validity of Per Capita Alcohol Consumption as an Indicator of the Prevalence of Alcohol Related Problems: An Evaluation Based on National Statistics and Survey Data," in *Alcoholism and Drug Dependence: A Multidisciplinary Approach*, ed. J. S. Madden, Robin Walker, and W. H. Kenyon (New York: Plenum, 1977), pp. 71–84; O-J. Skog, "On the Distribution of Alcohol Consumption" (paper delivered at the symposium, "The Epidemiological Approach to the Prevention of Alcoholism"; London, England, 1977); and O-J. Skog, "Less Alcohol— Fewer Alcoholics?" *The Drinking and Drug Practices Surveyor* 7 (1973), pp. 7–14.

23. See Miller and Agnew, "Ledermann Model of Alcohol Consumption," p. 887, for a critique of this feature of Ledermann's model.

24. Wolfgang Schmidt and Robert Popham, "The Single Distribution Model of Alcohol Consumption: A Rejoinder to the Critique of Parker and Harman" (paper delivered at the Conference on Normative Approaches to Alcoholism and Alcohol Problems; Coronado, Calif., April 26–28, 1977).

25. See Douglas Parker and Marsha Harman, "The Distribution of Consumption Model of Prevention: A Critical Assessment" (paper delivered at the Conference on Normative Approaches to Alcoholism and Alcohol Problems; Coronado, Calif., April 26–28, 1977). See also Miller and Agnew, "Ledermann Model of Alcohol Consumption," pp. 877–898, for another critical view of the "distribution of consumption thesis." Also, see Michael Lauderdale, "An Analysis of the Control Theory of Alcoholism" (report of a study sponsored by the Education Commission of the States and the Distilled Spirits Council of the U.S., June 13, 1977).

26. Miller and Agnew, "Ledermann Model of Alcohol Consumption," pp. 893–895.

27. Parker and Harman, "Distribution of Consumption Model of Prevention," pp. 1–16; and N. M. H. Smith, "Research Note on the Ledermann Formula and Its Recent Applications," *The Drinking and Drug Practices Surveyor* 12 (1976), pp. 15–22.

28. Parker and Harman, "Distribution of Consumption Model of Prevention," pp. 9–10, 17.

29. Schmidt and Popham, "Single Distribution Model."

30. O-J. Skog, "On the Distribution of Alcohol Consumption," quoted in

Schmidt and Popham, "Single Distribution Model," p. 23.
31. Bruun et al., *Alcohol Control Policies*, p. 31.
32. Ibid., p. 34.
33. Ibid., p. 34.
34. Schmidt and Popham, "Single Distribution Model," pp. 3–4.
35. Room, "Social Science," pp. 16–17.
36. Floyd H. Allport, "The J–Curve Hypothesis of Conforming Behavior," *Journal of Social Psychology* 5 (May 1934), pp. 141–183.
37. Cartwright, Shaw, and Spratley, "Validity of Per Capita," pp. 71–72.
38. But O-J. Skog in "Liver Cirrhosis Mortality as an Indicator of Prevalence of Heavy Alcohol Use," *British Journal of Addiction* (forthcoming, 1980), argues that the British case is due to a "lagged" effect.
39. See n. 3. See L. Massé, J. M. Jullian, and A. Chisloup, "Trends in Mortality from Cirrhosis of the Liver, 1950–1971," *World Health Statistics Report* 29 (1976), pp. 40–67.
40. Klaus Mäkelä, "Types of Alcohol Restrictions, Types of Drinkers and Types of Alcohol Damages: The Case of the Personnel Strike in the Stores of the Finnish Alcohol Monopoly" (paper presented at the Twentieth International Institute on the Prevention and Treatment of Alcoholism, Manchester, England, June 23–28, 1974).
41. Ibid., p. 13.
42. Ibid., p. 16.
43. Ibid., p. 6. The wife of a Finnish acquaintance of mine was working in one of these polyclinics during the strike. She reported that the older personnel there said that the quiet during the period of the strike was much like that at the end of the war in Finland several decades before.
44. C. W. Bryant, "Effects of Sale of Liquor by the Drink in the State of Washington," *Quarterly Journal of Studies on Alcohol* 15 (1954), pp. 320–324.
45. This section draws heavily on Richard Douglass' article, "The Legal Drinking Age and Traffic Casualties," *Alcohol Health and Research World* 4 (Winter 1979–1980), pp. 18–25.
46. Paul Whitehead and Roberta Ferrence, "Women and Children Last: Implications of Trends in Consumption for Women and Young People," in *Alcoholism Problems in Women and Children*, ed. Milton Greenblatt and Mark Schukett (New York: Grune and Stratton, 1976), pp. 163–192.
47. Richard Douglass and Jay A. Freedman, *Alcohol-Related Casualties and Alcohol Beverage Market Response to Beverage Alcohol Availability Policies in Michigan*, vol. 1 (UM-HRS1-77-37; Ann Arbor: The University of Michigan Press, 1977).
48. Richard Zylman, "Fatal Crashes among Michigan Youth Following Reduction of Legal Drinking Age," *Quarterly Journal of Studies on Alcohol* 35 (1974), pp. 283–286.
49. Whitehead and Ferrence, "Fatal Crashes among Michigan Youth," pp. 171–173.
50. Pekka Sulkunen, "Drinking Patterns and the Level of Alcohol Con-

200   Beyond Alcoholism

sumption: An International Overview," in *Research Advances in Alcohol and Drug Problems*, vol. 3, ed. R. J. Gibbins et al. (New York: John Wiley, 1976), pp. 223–281.

51. Ibid., p. 233.
52. Ibid., pp. 250–251.
53. Ibid., p. 265.
54. See Bruun et al., *Alcohol Control Policies*, p. 74.
55. Popham, Schmidt, and deLint, "Effects of Legal Restraints on Drinking," p. 595.
56. Ibid., pp. 597–598.
57. H-H. Lau, "Cost of Alcoholic Beverages as a Determinant of Alcohol Consumption," in *Research Advances in Alcohol and Drug Problems*, vol. 2, ed. R. J. Gibbins et al. (New York: John Wiley, 1975), pp. 211–245.
58. See Bruun et al., *Alcohol Control Policies*, pp. 74–180. See also Popham, Schmidt, and deLint, "Effects of Legal Restraints on Drinking," pp. 595–601.
59. Philip Cook, "The Effect of Liquor Taxes on Drinking, Cirrhosis, and Auto Accidents" (paper prepared for the Panel on Alternative Policies for the Prevention of Alcohol Abuse and Alcoholism, the National Academy of Sciences; Washington, D.C., February 1980), pp. 15–18.
60. Ibid., pp. 29–31.
61. Popham, Schmidt, and deLint, "Effects of Legal Restraint on Drinking," p. 600.
62. See ibid., pp. 579–584.
63. Ibid., pp. 608–609.
64. Ibid., pp. 581–586.
65. Kathy Magruder, "The Association of Alcoholism Mortality with Legal Availability of Alcoholic Beverages," *Journal of Alcohol and Drug Education* 21 (Spring 1976), pp. 27–37.
66. Popham, Schmidt, and deLint, "Effects of Legal Restraints on Drinking," pp. 559–560.

Chapter VI

1. Francis G. Castles, *The Social Democratic Image of Society* (London: Routledge, Kegan Paul, 1978); M. Donald Hancock, *Sweden: The Politics of Postindustrial Change* (Hinsdale, Ill.: Druden Press, 1972); Harry Eckstein, *Division and Cohesion in Democracy* (Princeton, N.J.: Princeton University Press, 1966); Pertti Pesonen, "Finland: Party Support in a Fragmented System," in *Electoral Behavior: A Comparative Handbook*, ed. Richard Rose (New York: Free Press, 1974), pp. 271–314. The dominance of the Social Democrats is less true for Finland than for Sweden and Norway. Social Democrats in all these countries suffered setbacks in the mid-1970s.
2. Joseph Gusfield, *Symbolic Crusade: Status Politics and the American*

Temperance Movement (Urbana, Ill.: University of Illinois Press, 1963).
3. U.S. Bureau of the Census, *Statistical Abstract of the United States* (Washington, D.C.: G.P.O., 1978), p. 290.
4. This is perhaps the most commonly voiced concern about the role of ALKO in Finnish alcohol policy.
5. Pekka Kuusi, *Alcohol Sales Experiment in Rural Finland* (Finnish Foundation of Alcohol Studies Publication no. 3; Helsinki, Finland: Finnish Foundation of Alcohol Studies, 1957).
6. Ibid.
7. Erik Allardt, "Drinking Norms and Drinking Habits," in *Drinking and Drinkers: Three Papers in Behavioral Sciences*, ed. Erik Allardt, Touko Markkanen, and Marti Takala (Stockholm, Sweden: Almquist and Wiksell, 1958), pp. 7–109.
8. Salme Ahlström-Laakso and Esa Österberg, "Alcohol Policy and the Consumption of Alcohol Beverages in Finland in 1951–1975," *Bank of Finland Monthly Bulletin* no. 7 (Helsinki, Finland: Bank of Finland, 1976), pp. 3–11.
9. Kuusi, *Alcohol Sales Experiment*.
10. Ibid., p. 3.
11. Ibid., pp. 22–23. A seventh hypothesis, that time and money will be saved if the ALKO stores are more widely distributed, is not relevant to our discussion.
12. Ibid., p. 12.
13. Ibid., p. 189.
14. Ibid., p. 217.
15. Ibid., p. 200.
16. Pekka Kuusi, *Social Policy for the Sixties: A Plan for Finland* (Helsinki, Finland: Finnish Social Policy Association, 1964).
17. Ahlström-Laakso and Österberg, "Alcohol Policy," p. 6.
18. Jorma Purontaus, "Cost-Benefit Analysis and the Finnish Alcohol Policy" (M.A. thesis, University of Helsinki, 1970), cited in Kettil Bruun et al., *Alcohol Control Policies in Public Health Perspective* (Helsinki, Finland: Finnish Foundation for Alcohol Studies, 1975), p. 81.
19. Ahlström-Laakso, "Changing Drinking Habits among Finnish Youth" (paper presented at the 31st International Congress on Alcoholism and Drug Dependence, Bangkok, Thailand, February 23–28, 1975), p. 1.
20. Pekka Sulkunen, "Drinking Patterns and the Level of Alcohol Consumption: An International Overview," in *Research Advances in Alcohol and Drug Problems*, vol. 3, ed. R. J. Gibbins et al. (New York: John Wiley, 1976), pp. 223–281.
21. Jussi Simpura, "The Rise in Aggregate Alcohol Consumption and Changes in Drinking Habits: The Finnish Case in 1969 and 1976" (mimeo, Social Research Institute of Alcohol Studies, Helsinki, Finland, 1978); Jussi Simpura, "Who Are the Heavy Consumers of Alcohol?" (mimeo, International Study of Alcohol Control Experiences, Finnish Foundation for Alcohol Studies; Helsinki, Finland, March

1979); Jussi Simpura, "Study of Finnish Drinking Habits in 1976: Summaries of Main Reports" (mimeo, Social Research Institute of Alcohol Studies; Helsinki, Finland, 1979).

22. Simpura, "The Rise in Aggregate Alcohol Consumption," p. 3.

23. Ibid., p. 11.

24. Esa Österberg, "Indicators of Damage and the Development of Alcohol Conditions . . . , 1950–1975" (mimeo, International Study of Alcohol Control Experiences, Finnish Foundation for Alcohol Studies; Helsinki, Finland, January 1979), p. 32.

25. Klaus Mäkelä and Esa Österberg, "Alcohol Consumption and Policy in Finland and Sweden, 1951–1973," Drinking and Drug Practices Surveyor, no. 12 (December 1976), pp. 4–7, 37–45.

26. Ibid., p. 37.

27. These conclusions were sampled in two visits by the author to Finland, Norway, and Sweden in 1976, and to Finland in 1979.

28. Ahlström-Laakso and Österberg, "Alcohol Policy," p. 9.

29. Ibid., p. 10.

30. Pekka Sulkunen, "Abstainers in Finland, 1946–1976: A Study in Social and Cultural Transition" (Social Research Institute of Alcohol Studies Report no. 126; Helsinki, Finland: The Finnish Foundation for Alcohol Studies, August 1979); Pekka Sulkunen, "Drinking Populations, Institutions, and Patterns, Part 2: Individual Drinking Patterns" (draft mimeo, Social Research Institute of Alcohol Studies; Helsinki, Finland: Finnish Foundation for Alcohol Studies, July 31, 1979).

31. Sulkunen, "Abstainers in Finland," pp. 36–37.

32. Ibid., p. 72.

33. Hugh Heclo, Modern Social Politics in Britain and Sweden (New Haven: Yale University Press, 1974).

34. Gov't of Finland, Council of State, The Report of the Alcohol Committee, 1978 (English version prepared by Oy Alko Ab Information Service; Helsinki, Finland, 1978).

35. Kuusi, Alcohol Sales Experiment, pp. 1–3.

36. Reinhard Bendix, Nation-Building and Citizenship (New York: Anchor, 1964), p. 10.

37. Leon Kass, "Regarding the End of Medicine and the Pursuit of Health," Public Interest 40 (1975), pp. 11–42; John Knowles, "Individual Responsibility," in Doing Better and Feeling Worse, ed. John Knowles (New York: Norton, 1977), pp. 57–80.

Chapter VII

1. For a discussion of the labeling controversy and a compilation of the sentiments pro and con regarding the Senate passage of this measure in May of 1979, see U.S., Senate, Committee on Labor and Human Resources, Subcommittee on Alcoholism and Drug Abuse, Report on Consumer Health Warnings for Alcoholic Beverages and Related Is-

sues, 96th Cong., 1st Sess. (Washington, D.C.: G.P.O., 1979). The outcome of this issue is still in doubt. The Congress authorized HEW and the Department of the Treasury to conduct a joint study on the necessity for health warnings on alcoholic beverages.

2. Ibid.
3. What is more, Congress and the Senate Subcommittee on Alcoholism and Drug Abuse have taken an increasingly harder line toward the industry. See ibid. for a discussion of the industry's recent involvement with the alcoholism constituency.
4. See Francis E. Rourke, *Bureaucracy, Politics, and Public Policy* (Boston: Little, Brown, 1969), pp. 11–37, for the best analysis of the search for public support by public agencies.
5. Ibid.
6. The leading references in the policy debate for the "limits to medicine" have been: Ivan Illich, *Medical Nemesis: The Expropriation of Health* (New York: Pantheon, 1976); Victor Fuchs, *Who Shall Live?* (New York: Basic Books, 1974); A. L. Cochrane, *Effectiveness and Efficiency* (Abingdon, Berkshire, U.K.: Burgess and Sons, 1972); and Marc Lalonde, *A New Perspective on the Health of Canadians* (Ottawa, Canada: Government of Canada, 1974).
7. See George D. Greenberg, "Reorganization Reconsidered," *Public Policy* 23 (1975), pp. 483–522. See also Sidney S. Lee and Curtis P. McLaughlin, "Changing Views of Public Health Services as a System," in *Systems and Medical Care*, ed. Alan Sheldon, Frank Baker, and Curtis P. McLaughlin (Cambridge, Mass.: M.I.T. Press, 1970), pp. 126–142.
8. One of the most interesting studies of early public health campaigns is contained in C.-E. A. Winslow, *The Life of Herman Biggs, Physician and Statesman of the Public Health* (Philadelphia: Lea and Febiger, 1929). See also Stephen Smith's *The City That Was* (Metuchen, N.J.: Scarecrow, 1973). The classic history is C.-E. A. Winslow's *The Conquest of Epidemic Disease* (New York: Hafner, 1967).
9. See René Dubos and Jean Dubos, *The White Plague* (Boston: Little, Brown, 1952), pp. 208–210.
10. Edward McGavran, "What Is Public Health?" *Canadian Journal of Public Health* 44 (1953), pp. 441–451.
11. Milton Terris, "The Epidemiological Revolution, National Health Insurance, and the Role of the Health Departments," *American Journal of Public Health* 66 (1976), pp. 1155–1164.
12. Illich, *Medical Nemesis*.
13. McGavran, "What Is Public Health?" p. 445.
14. Haven Emerson, *Local Health Units for the Nation* (New York: Commonwealth Fund, 1945).
15. William Ryan, *Blaming the Victim* (New York: Vintage, 1971), pp. 15–16.
16. Milton Terris, a former president of the American Public Health Association, points to the truly radical and advanced thinking that was developed by some of the pioneers of American public health (C.-E. A. Winslow, Josephine Baker, Herman Biggs, Charles Chapin, and Ste-

phen Smith). The following quotation is from Dr. Hermann Biggs, and is drawn from an October 1911 issue of the New York City Health Department *Bulletin* (cited in Winslow, *Life of Hermann Biggs*, p. 230): "Disease is largely a removable evil. It continues to afflict humanity, not only because of incomplete knowledge of its causes and lack of adequate individual and public hygiene, but also because it is extensively fostered by harsh economic and industrial conditions and by wretched housing in congested communities. These conditions and consequently the diseases which spring from them can be removed by better social organization. No duty of society, acting through its governmental agencies, is paramount to this obligation to attack the removable causes of disease. The duty of leading this attack and bringing home to public opinion the fact that the community can buy its own health protection is laid upon all in public health movements. For the protection of the public health must come in the last analysis through the education of public opinion so that the community shall vividly realize both its needs and powers."

17. I have addressed some of these issues in earlier articles, including "Exploring New Ethics for Public Health: Developing a Fair Alcohol Policy," *The Journal of Health Politics, Policy and Law* 1 (Fall 1976), pp. 338–354; "Blood Sports," *The Christian Century* 94 (1977), pp. 237–238; and "Fallen Idol," *Inquiry* 15 (1977), pp. 103–105.

18. See my "Public Health and Individual Liberty," *Annual Review of Public Health* 1 (1980), pp. 121–136.

19. See David Miller, *Social Justice* (Oxford, England: Clarendon Press, 1976). For other treatments of social justice see Joel Feinberg, *Social Philosophy* (Englewood Cliffs, N.J.: Prentice-Hall, 1973), and John Rawls, *A Theory of Justice* (Cambridge, Mass.: Harvard University Press, 1971).

20. See the essay by Michael Tietleman in *Reading Rawls*, ed. Norman Daniels (New York: Basic Books, 1975). The merging of the ideal of social justice and community has often been more explicit in the Judeo-Christian ethical tradition, where the ideal of community is that of meeting the needs of others and justice is the project of building a safer future for humankind.

21. Richard Brotman and Frances Suffet, "The Concept of Prevention and Its Limitations," *Annals* 417 (1975), pp. 53–65.

22. The "escape of tigers" is from the articles of William Haddon, Jr. For his excellent discussions of the strategies of public health, see William Haddon, Jr., "Energy Damage and the Ten Countermeasure Strategies," *Journal of Trauma* 13 (1973), pp. 321–331; and his "The Changing Approach to the Epidemiology, Prevention, and Amelioration of Trauma," *American Journal of Public Health* 58 (1968), pp. 1431–1438.

23. See Amitai Etzioni and Richard Remp, "Technological 'Shortcuts' to Social Change," *Science* 175 (1972), pp. 31–38.

24. Terris, "Epidemiological Revolution," p. 1156.
25. Mancur Olson, *The Logic of Collective Action* (Cambridge, Mass.: Harvard University Press, 1965), pp. 5–52.
26. See my "Blood Sports," pp. 237–238, for a discussion of the lottery and the ethics of collective action.
27. These limits to alcohol policy are taken in part from my "Exploring New Ethics for Public Health," pp. 345–346.
28. Thomas F. A. Plaut, *Alcohol Problems—A Report to the Nation* (New York: Oxford University Press, 1967), p. 144.
29. Ibid., p. 142.
30. Don Cahalan, Ira H. Cisin, and Helen M. Crossley, *American Drinking Practices* (New Brunswick, N.J.: Rutgers Center for Alcohol Studies, 1969), p. 19.
31. This example is taken from Dean Gerstein, "Alcohol Use and Consequences," (paper prepared for the Panel on Alternative Policies Affecting the Prevention of Alcohol Abuse and Alcoholism, the National Academy of Sciences; Washington, D.C., September 1979), p. 14.
32. This is the issue of paternalism. I am aware that this does not constitute a systematic philosophical defense justifying limits to consumption. For a preliminary attempt to review some of these issues see my "Public Health and Individual Liberty," and "Exploring New Ethics for Public Health."
33. Anstie's Limit is "not more than 1½ ounces of absolute alcohol (approximately 3 oz. of whiskey, ½ bottle of wine, or 4 glasses of beer) taken only with meals or food, and with all hard liquor in well diluted form. This is the amount calculated by Francis Anstie (1862) that an adult man could drink daily without being adversely affected in general health" (statement made by Morris Chafetz, M.D., at the Seminar for Health Writers, The White House, Washington, D.C., July 10, 1974, as cited in Eleanor Edelstein, "Dr. Anstie's Magic Formula," *Addictions* 3 [September 1974], p. 10).
34. HEW and NIAAA, *The Second Special Report to the U.S. Congress on Alcohol and Health* (Washington, D.C.: G.P.O., 1978), p. 7.
35. One of the few published studies of the various justifications for taxes placed on alcoholic beverages is the report of the (Canadian) Alcohol Beverage Study Committee, "Beer, Wine and Spirits: Beverage Differences and Public Policy in Canada," 1972, pp. 128–152. This report was funded by the Brewers Association of Canada.
36. Milton Terris, "Epidemiology of Cirrhosis of the Liver: National Mortality Data," *American Journal of Public Health* 57 (1967), p. 2086.
37. Medicine in the Public Interest, *The Effects of Alcoholic-Beverage Control Laws* (Washington, D.C.: Medicine in the Public Interest, 1979). The "MIPI" study argues that "regulated minimal availability" is not widely endorsed as a goal in the U.S. I would suggest that our dominant drinking norms imply "regulated minimal availability" as a sup-

porting set of enforcement mechanisms and sanctions, but that these sanctions have been allowed to deteriorate over the years due to official inattention and neglect.

38. Robin Room and James Mosher, "Out of the Shadow of Treatment: A Role for Regulatory Agencies in the Treatment of Alcohol Problems," *Alcohol and Health World* 4 (Winter 1979–1980), pp. 11–17.

39. Ibid.

40. See K. E. Warner, "The Effects of the Anti-Smoking Campaign on Cigarette Consumption," *American Journal of Public Health* 67 (1977), pp. 645–650.

41. In U.S., Congress, Senate, *Report on Consumer Health Warnings*, many of the justifications of labeling are founded on the consumer's right to full and accurate information.

42. See Morris Chafetz, "Alcoholism Prevention and Reality," *Quarterly Journal of Studies on Alcohol* 28 (1967), pp. 345–350.

43. See Howard T. Blane and Morris Chafetz, *Youth, Alcohol, and Social Policy* (New York: Plenum, 1979).

44. In a personal communication, Room attributed the slogan, "making the world safe for drunks," to Joseph Gusfield.

Bibliography

Ahlström-Laakso, Salme, and Österberg, Esa. "Alcohol Policy and the Consumption of Alcohol Beverages in Finland in 1951–1975." *Bank of Finland Monthly Bulletin*, no. 7, pp. 3–11. Helsinki: Bank of Finland, 1976.

Alcoholics Anonymous. *Alcoholics Anonymous*. New York: Alcoholics Anonymous World Services, 1939.

―――. *Alcoholics Anonymous Comes of Age*. New York: Alcoholics Anonymous World Services, 1957.

―――. *Twelve Steps and Twelve Traditions*. New York: Alcoholics Anonymous Publishing, 1952.

Allardt, Erik. "Drinking Norms and Drinking Habits." In *Drinking and Drinkers: Three Papers in Behavioral Sciences*, ed. Erik Allardt, Touko Markkanen, and Marti Takala, pp. 7–109. Stockholm: Almquist and Wiksell, 1958.

Allen, Frederick Lewis. *The Big Change*. New York: Harper, 1952.

Arendt, Hannah. *The Human Condition*. Chicago: University of Chicago Press, 1958.

Armor, David; Polich, J. Michael; and Stambull, Harriet B. *Alcoholism and Treatment*. New York: John Wiley, 1978.

Aubert, Vilhelm. *The Hidden Society*. Totowa, N.J.: Bedminster Press, 1965.

Aubert, Vilhelm, and Messinger, Sheldon. "The Criminal and the Sick." *Inquiry* (Oslo) 1 (1958): 137–160.

Austin, John L. *Philosophical Papers*. Ed. J. O. Urmson and G. J. Warnock. Oxford, England: Clarendon Press, 1961.

Bacon, Selden. "Alcoholics Do Not Drink." *Annals of the American Academy of Political and Social Science* 315 (January 1958): 55–64.

―――. "Social Settings Conducive to Alcoholism: A Sociological Approach to a Medical Problem." *Journal of the American Medical Association* 164 (1957): 177–181.

―――. "The Mobilization of Community Resources for the Attack on Alcoholism." *Quarterly Journal of Studies on Alcohol* 8 (1947–1948): 473–497.

Bales, Robert F. "Cultural Differences in Rates of Alcoholism." *Quarterly Journal of Studies on Alcohol* 6 (1945–1946): 480–499.

Barthes, Roland. *Mythologies.* New York: Hill and Wang, 1972.

Beauchamp, Dan. "Public Health and Individual Liberty." *Annual Review of Public Health* 1 (1980): 121–136.

———. "Blood Sports." *The Christian Century* 94 (1977): 237–238.

———. "Fallen Idol." *Inquiry* 15 (1977): 103–105.

———. "Exploring New Ethics for Public Health: Developing a Fair Alcohol Policy." *The Journal of Health Politics, Policy and Law* 1 (Fall 1976): 338–354.

———. "Precarious Politics: Alcoholism and Public Policy." Ph.D. diss., The Johns Hopkins University, 1973.

Becker, Howard, "Labelling Theory Reconsidered." In *Deviance and Social Control,* ed. Paul Rock and Mary McIntosh, pp. 41–66. London: Tavistock, 1974.

Bell, Daniel. *The Cultural Contradictions of Capitalism.* New York: Basic Books, 1976.

———. "Interpretations of American Politics" and "The Dispossessed." In *The Radical Right,* ed. Daniel Bell, pp. 1–73. Garden City, N.Y.: Anchor, 1964.

Bendix, Reinhard. *Nation-Building and Citizenship.* Garden City, N.Y.: Anchor, 1964.

Berger, Peter L., and Luckmann, Thomas. *The Social Construction of Reality.* Garden City, N.Y.: Anchor, 1967.

Brotman, Richard, and Suffet, Frances. "The Concept of Prevention and Its Limitations." *Annals* 417 (1975): 53–65.

Brown, Robert. *Explanation in Social Science.* Chicago: Aldine, 1963.

Bruun, Kettil, et al. *Alcohol Control Policies in Public Health Perspective.* Helsinki: Finnish Foundation for Alcohol Studies, 1975.

Bryant, C. W. "Effects of Sale of Liquor by the Drink in the State of Washington." *Quarterly Journal of Studies on Alcohol* 15 (1954): 320–324.

Burnham, John C. "New Perspectives on the Prohibition 'Experiment' of the 1920s." *Journal of Social History* 2 (1968–1969): pp. 51–68.

Cahalan, Don. *Problem Drinkers.* San Francisco: Jossey-Bass, 1970.

Cahalan, Don; Cisin, Ira H.; and Crossley, Helen M. *American Drinking Practices.* New Brunswick, N.J.: Rutgers Center of Alcohol Studies, 1969.

Cahalan, Don, and Roizen, Ron. "Changes in Drinking Problems in a National Sample of Men." Paper delivered at Conference on Social Research in Alcohol and Drug Use, San Francisco, December 16, 1974.

Cain, A. H. *The Cured Alcoholic.* New York: John Day, 1964.

Cartwright, A. K. J.; Shaw, S. J.; and Spratley, T. A. "The Validity of Per Capita Alcohol Consumption as an Indicator of the Prevalence of Alcohol Related Problems: An Evaluation Based on National Statistics and Survey Data." In *Alcoholism and Drug Dependence: A Multidisciplin-*

ary Approach, ed. J. S. Madden, Robin Walker, and W. H. Kenyon, pp. 71–84. New York: Plenum, 1977.

Castles, Francis G. *The Social Democratic Image of Society*. London: Routledge, Kegan Paul, 1978.

Chafetz, Morris. *Why Drinking Can Be Good for You*. New York: Stein and Day, 1976.

———. "The Prevention of Alcoholism." *International Journal of Psychiatry* 9 (1970–1971): 329–348.

———. "Alcoholism Prevention and Reality." *Quarterly Journal of Studies on Alcohol* 28 (1967): 345–348.

———. *Liquor: The Servant of Man*. Boston: Little, Brown, 1965.

Christie, Nils, and Bruun, Kettil. "Alcohol Problems: The Conceptual Framework." In *Proceedings of the 28th International Congress on Alcohol and Alcoholism*, ed. Mark Keller and Timothy Coffey, pp. 65–73. Highland Park, N.J.: Hillhouse Press, 1969.

Clark, Norman H. *Deliver Us from Evil*. New York: Norton, 1976.

Clark, Walter B., and Cahalan, Don. "Changes In Problem Drinking Over a Four-Year Span." *Addictive Behaviors* 1 (1976): 251–259.

Cochrane, A. L. *Effectiveness and Efficiency*. Abingdon, Berkshire, U.K.: Burgess and Sons, 1972.

Cohen, Albert. *Deviance and Control*. Englewood Cliffs, N.J.: Prentice-Hall, 1966.

Cook, Philip. "The Effect of Liquor Taxes on Drinking, Cirrhosis, and Auto Accidents." Paper prepared for the Panel on Alternative Policies for the Prevention of Alcohol Abuse and Alcoholism, the National Academy of Sciences, Washington, D.C., February 1980.

Davies, E. L. "Normal Drinking in Recovered Alcohol Addicts." *Quarterly Journal of Studies on Alcohol* 23 (1962): 94–104.

deLint, Jan, and Schmidt, Wolfgang. "Consumption Averages and Alcoholism Prevalence: A Brief Review of Epidemiological Investigations." *British Journal of Addiction* 66 (1971): 97–107.

———. "The Distribution of Alcohol Consumption in Ontario." *Quarterly Journal of Studies on Alcohol* 29 (1968): 968–973.

DHEW, NIAAA. *The Third Special Report to the U.S. Congress on Alcohol and Health*. Washington, D.C.: G.P.O., 1978.

———. *The Second Special Report to the U.S. Congress on Alcohol and Health*. Washington, D.C.: G.P.O., 1976.

Douglass, Richard. "The Legal Drinking Age and Traffic Casualties." *Alcohol Health and Research World* 4 (Winter 1979–1980): 18–25.

Douglass, Richard, and Freedman, Jay A. *Alcohol-Related Casualties and Alcohol Beverage Market Response to Beverage Alcohol Availability Policies in Michigan*. Vol. 1. UM-HRS1-77-37. Ann Arbor: The University of Michigan, 1977.

Drew, L. R. H. "Alcoholism as a Self-Limiting Disease." *Quarterly Journal of Studies on Alcohol* 29 (1968): 956–967.

Dubos, René. *Man Adapting*. New Haven: Yale University Press, 1965.

Dubos, René and Jean. *The White Plague*. Boston: Little, Brown, 1952.

Elinson, Jack. "Epidemiologic Studies and Control Programs in Alcoholism: Discussion." *American Journal of Public Health* 57 (1967): 991–996.

Emerson, Haven. *Local Health Units for the Nation.* New York: Commonwealth Fund, 1945.

Etzioni, Amitai, and Remp, Richard. "Technological 'Shortcuts' to Social Change." *Science* 175 (1972): 31–38.

Feinberg, Joel. *Social Philosophy.* Englewood Cliffs, N.J.: Prentice-Hall, 1973.

Freidson, Eliot. *Professional Dominance.* Chicago: Aldine, 1970.

Fuchs, Victor. *Who Shall Live?* New York: Basic Books, 1974.

Gellman, Irving Peter. *The Sober Alcoholic.* New Haven: College and University Press, 1964.

Gerstein, Dean. "Alcohol Use and Consequences." Paper prepared for the Panel on Alternative Policies Affecting the Prevention of Alcohol Abuse and Alcoholism, The National Academy of Sciences, Washington, D.C., September 1979.

Gordon, John E. "The Epidemiology of Alcoholism." *New York State Journal of Medicine* 58 (1958): 1911–1918.

Greenberg, George D. "Reorganization Reconsidered." *Public Policy* 23 (1975): 483–522.

Gusfield, Joseph. "Prohibition: The Impact of Political Utopianism." In *Change and Continuity in Twentieth-Century America: The 1920s,* ed. John Braeman, Robert H. Bremner, and David Brody, pp. 257–308. Columbus, Ohio: Ohio State University Press, 1968.

———. *Symbolic Crusade: Status Politics and the American Temperance Movement.* Urbana, Ill.: University of Illinois Press, 1963.

Haddon, William, Jr. "Energy Damage and the Ten Countermeasure Strategies." *Journal of Trauma* 13 (1973): 321–331.

———. "The Changing Approach to the Epidemiology, Prevention, and Amelioration of Trauma." *American Journal of Public Health* 58 (1968): 1431–1438.

Haggard, Howard W., and Jellinek, E. M. *Alcohol Explored.* Garden City, N.Y.: Doubleday, Doran, 1942.

Hancock, M. Donald. *Sweden: The Politics of Postindustrial Change.* Hinsdale, Ill.: Druden Press, 1972.

Hayman, Max. "The Myth of Social Drinking." *American Journal of Psychiatry* 124 (November 1967): 585–594.

Heclo, Hugh. *Modern Social Politics in Britain and Sweden.* New Haven, Conn.: Yale University Press, 1974.

Hewitt, John, and Hall, Peter. "Social Problems, Problematic Situations, and Quasi-Theories." *American Sociological Review* 38 (June 1973): 367–374.

Hofstadter, Richard. *The Paranoid Style in American Politics.* New York: Knopf, 1965.

Illich, Ivan. *Medical Nemesis: The Expropriation of Health.* New York: Pantheon, 1976.

Janowitz, Morris. *The Last Half-Century*. Chicago: University of Chicago Press, 1978.

Jellinek, E. M. *The Disease Concept of Alcoholism*. New Haven: College and University Press, 1960.

———. "Recent Trends in Alcoholism and Alcohol Consumption." *Quarterly Journal of Studies on Alcohol* 8 (1947–1948): 1–42.

Johnson, Bruce. "The Alcoholism Movement in America: A Study in Cultural Innovation." Ph.D. diss., University of Illinois at Urbana-Champaign, 1973.

Kaplan, John. *Marijuana—The New Prohibition*. New York: World, 1970.

Kaufman, Arnold. "Ability." *Journal of Philosophy* 60 (1963): 537–551.

Keller, Mark. "On the Loss-of-Control Phenomenon in Alcoholism." *British Journal of Addiction* 67 (1972): 153–66.

———. "The Definition of Alcoholism." *Quarterly Journal of Studies on Alcohol* 21 (1960): 125–134.

———. "Alcoholism: Extent and Nature of the Problem." *Annals of the American Academy of Political and Social Sciences* 315 (1958): 1–11.

Kittrie, Nicholas. *The Right to Be Different*. Baltimore: The Johns Hopkins University Press, 1971.

Kurtz, Ernest. *Not-God*. Center City, Minn.: Hazeldon, 1979.

Kuusi, Pekka. *Social Policy for the Sixties: A Plan for Finland*. Helsinki: Finnish Social Policy Association, 1964.

———. *Alcohol Sales Experiment in Rural Finland*. Publication no. 3, the Finnish Foundation of Alcohol Studies. Helsinki: Finnish Foundation of Alcohol Studies, 1957.

Lalonde, Marc. *A New Perspective on the Health of Canadians*. Ottawa: Government of Canada, 1974.

Lau, H-H. "Cost of Alcoholic Beverages as a Determinant of Alcohol Consumption." In *Research Advances in Alcohol and Drug Problems*, vol. 2, ed. R. J. Gibbins et al., pp. 211–245. New York: John Wiley, 1975.

Leach, Barry, and Norris, John. "Factors in the Development of Alcoholics Anonymous (A.A.)." In *Treatment and Rehabilitation of the Chronic Alcoholic*, ed. Benjamin Kissin and Henri Begleiter, pp. 441–543. New York: Plenum, 1977.

Ledermann, Sully. "Can One Reduce Alcoholism without Changing Total Alcohol Consumption in a Population?" Paper presented at the 27th International Congress on Alcohol and Alcoholism, Frankfurt-am-Main, 1964.

———. *Alcool, Alcoolisme, Alcoolisation*. Institut National d'Etudes Démographiques, Travaux et Documents. Données scientifiques de caractère physiologique, économique et social, Cahier no. 29. Paris: Presses Universitaires de France, 1956.

Lee, Sidney S., and McLaughlin, Curtis P. "Changing Views of Public Health Services as a System." In *Systems and Medical Care*, ed. Alan Sheldon, Frank Baker, and Curtis P. McLaughlin, pp. 126–142. Cambridge, Mass.: M.I.T. Press, 1970.

Lender, Mark E. "Jellinek's Typology of Alcoholism." *Journal of Studies on Alcohol* 40 (1979): 361–375.

Levine, Harry Gene. "The Discovery of Addiction." *Journal of Studies on Alcohol* 39 (1978): 143–174.

Lofland, John. *Deviance and Identity.* Englewood Cliffs, N.J.: Prentice-Hall, 1969.

Lolli, Giorgi; Serianni, Edmidio; Golder, Grace M.; and Luzzatto-Fegiz, P. *Alcohol in Italian Culture.* Yale Center of Alcohol Studies, monograph no. 3. Chicago: Free Press, 1958.

MacAndrew, Craig. "On the Notion that Certain Persons Who Are Given to Frequent Drunkenness Suffer from a Disease Called Alcoholism." In *Changing Perspectives in Mental Illness,* ed. Stanley C. Plog and Robert B. Edgerton, pp. 483–501. New York: Holt, Rinehart and Winston, 1969.

McGavran, Edward. "What Is Public Health?" *Canadian Journal of Public Health* 44 (1953): 441–451.

Magruder, Kathy. "The Association of Alcoholism Mortality with Legal Availability of Alcoholic Beverages." *Journal of Alcohol and Drug Education* 21 (Spring 1976): 27–37.

Mäkelä, Klaus. "Types of Alcohol Restrictions, Types of Drinkers, and Types of Alcohol Damages: The Case of the Personnel Strike in the Stores of the Finnish Alcohol Monopoly." Paper presented at the 20th International Institute on the Prevention and Treatment of Alcoholism, Manchester, England, June 23–28, 1974.

Mäkelä, Klaus, and Österberg, Esa. "Alcohol Consumption and Policy in Finland and Sweden, 1951–1973." *Drinking and Drug Practices Surveyor,* no. 12 (December, 1976): 4–7, 37–45.

Mann, Marty. "The Citizen's Part in the Problem of Alcoholism." *Quarterly Journal of Studies on Alcohol* 6 (1945–1946): 249–255.

———. *Primer on Alcoholism.* New York: Holt, Rinehart, 1950.

Marconi, Juan. "The Concept of Alcoholism." *Quarterly Journal of Studies on Alcohol* 20 (1959): 216–235.

Medicine in the Public Interest. *The Effects of Alcoholic-Beverage Control Laws.* Washington, D.C.: Medicine in the Public Interest, 1979.

Mello, Nancy. "Behavioral Studies of Alcoholism." In *The Biology of Alcoholism,* vol. 2, ed. Benjamin Kissin and Henri Begleiter, pp. 219–291. New York: Plenum, 1972.

Mendelson, Jack, and Stein, Stefan. "The Definition of Alcoholism." *International Psychiatry Clinics* 3, no. 2 (Summer 1966): 3–16.

Miller, David. *Social Justice.* Oxford, England: Clarendon, 1976.

Miller, Gary H., and Agnew, Neil. "The Ledermann Model of Alcohol Consumption." *Quarterly Journal of Alcohol Studies* 35 (1974): 886–887.

Mortimore, Geoffrey, ed. *Weakness of Will.* London: Macmillan, 1971.

Myerson, Abraham. "Alcoholism: A Study of Social Ambivalence." *Quarterly Journal of Studies on Alcohol* 1 (1940–1941): 13–20.

National Center for Prevention and Control of Alcoholism. *Alcohol and Alcoholism.* Washington, D.C.: G.P.O., 1970.

National Commission on Marihuana and Drug Abuse. *Drug Use in America: Problem in Perspective.* Second Report of the Commission. Washington, D.C.: G.P.O., 1973.

Olson, Mancur. *The Logic of Collective Action.* Cambridge, Mass.: Harvard University Press, 1965.

Österberg, Esa. "Indicators of Damage and the Development of Alcohol Conditions . . . , 1950–1975." Mimeographed. Helsinki: International Study of Alcohol Control Experiences, Finnish Foundation for Alcohol Studies, January 1979.

Parker, Douglas, and Harman, Marsha. "The Distribution of Consumption Model of Prevention: A Critical Assessment." Paper delivered at the Conference on Normative Approaches to Alcoholism and Alcohol Problems, Coronado, Calif., April 26–28, 1977.

Parsons, Talcott. *The Social System.* Chicago: Free Press, 1951.

Pattison, E. Mansell; Sobell, Mark; and Sobell, Linda. *Emerging Concepts in Alcohol Dependence.* New York: Springer, 1977.

Pittman, David J., and Snyder, Charles R., eds. *Society, Culture, and Drinking Patterns.* New York: J. Wiley, 1962.

Pitts, Jesse. "Social Control." In *International Encyclopedia of the Social Sciences,* vol. 14, ed. David Sills. New York: Macmillan, 1968.

Plaut, Thomas F. A., ed. *Alcohol Problems—A Report to the Nation.* Report of the Cooperative Commission on the Study of Alcoholism. New York: Oxford University Press, 1967.

Popham, Robert; Schmidt, Wolfgang; and deLint, Jan. "The Effects of Legal Restraint on Drinking." In *Social Aspects of Alcoholism,* ed. Benjamin Kissin and Henri Begleiter, pp. 579–625. New York: Plenum, 1976.

Rawls, John. *A Theory of Justice.* Cambridge: Harvard University Press, 1971.

Redman, Eric. *The Dance of Legislation.* New York: Simon and Schuster, 1973.

Robinson, David. "The Alcoholgist's Addiction." *Quarterly Journal of Studies on Alcohol* 33 (1972): 1028–1042.

Rohan, William. "Drinking Behavior and 'Alcoholism.'" *Journal of Studies on Alcohol* 36 (1975): 908–916.

Roman, Paul. "Delabeling, Relabeling, and Alcoholics Anonymous." *Social Problems* 17 (1970): 538–546.

Room, Robin. "Social Science and Alcohol Policy Making." Paper prepared for a Conference on the Utilization of Social Research in Drug Policy Making, Center for Socio-Cultural Research on Drug Use, Columbia University, Washington, D.C., May 3–5, 1978.

————. "Evaluating the Effect of Drinking Laws on Drinking." In *Drinking,* ed. John Ewing and Beatrice Rouse, pp. 267–289. Chicago: Nelson-Hall, 1978.

————. "Ambivalence as a Sociological Explanation: The Case of Cultural

Explanation of Alcohol Problems." *American Sociological Review* 41 (1976): 1047–1065.

———. "Comment on 'The Alcoholologist's Addiction.'" *Quarterly Journal of Studies on Alcohol* 33 (1972): 1049–1059.

Rorabaugh, W. J. *The Alcoholic Republic*. New York: Oxford University Press, 1978.

———. "Estimated U.S. Alcoholic Beverage Consumption, 1790–1860." *Journal of Studies on Alcohol* 37 (1976): 357–364.

Rourke, Francis E. *Bureaucracy, Politics, and Public Policy*. Boston: Little, Brown, 1969.

Rubin, Jay L. "Shifting Perspectives on the Alcoholism Treatment Movement, 1940–1955." *Journal of Studies on Alcohol* 40 (1979): 376–386.

Ryan, William. *Blaming the Victim*. New York: Vintage, 1971.

Ryle, Gilbert. *The Concept of Mind*. New York: Barnes and Noble, 1949.

Sadoun, Roland; Lolli, Giorgi; and Silverman, Milton. *Drinking in French Culture*. New Brunswick, N.J.: Rutgers Center of Alcohol Studies, 1965.

Schmidt, Wolfgang, and Popham, Robert. "The Single Distribution Model of Alcohol Consumption: A Rejoinder to the Critique of Parker and Harman." Paper delivered at the conference on Normative Approaches to Alcoholism and Alcohol Problems, Coronado, Calif., April 26–28, 1977.

Schneider, Joseph. "Deviant Drinking as Disease: Alcoholism as a Social Accomplishment." *Social Problems* 15 (1976): 326–392.

Schur, Edwin. *Labeling Deviant Behavior*. New York: Harper and Row, 1971.

Seeley, John. "The W.H.O. Definition of Alcoholism." *Quarterly Journal of Studies on Alcohol* 20 (1959): 352–356.

Simmel, Georg. *The Sociology of Georg Simmel*. Translated and edited by Kurt Wolff. New York: The Free Press, 1950.

Simpura, Juusi. "Study of Finnish Drinking Habits in 1976: Summaries of Main Reports." Mimeographed. Helsinki: Social Research Institute of Alcohol Studies, 1979.

———. "Who Are the Heavy Consumers of Alcohol?" Mimeographed. International Study of Alcohol Control Experiences. Helsinki: The Finnish Foundation for Alcohol Studies, March 1979.

———. "The Rise in Aggregate Alcohol Consumption and Changes in Drinking Habits: The Finnish Case in 1969 and 1976." Mimeographed. Helsinki: Social Research Institute of Alcohol Studies, 1978.

Sinclair, Andrew. *Prohibition: The Era of Excess*. Boston: Little, Brown, 1962.

Skog, O-J. "Liver Cirrhosis Mortality as an Indicator of Prevalence of Heavy Alcohol Use: Some Methodological Problems." *British Journal of Addiction* (forthcoming).

———. "On the Distribution of Alcohol Consumption." Paper delivered at the symposium "The Epidemiological Approach to the Prevention of Alcoholism," London, England 1977.

————. "Less Alcohol—Fewer Alcoholics?" *The Drinking and Drug Practices Surveyor* (1973), pp. 7–14.

Skolnick, Jerome H. "Religious Affiliation and Drinking Behavior." *Quarterly Journal of Studies on Alcohol* 19 (1958): 452–470.

Smith, N. M. H. "Research Note on the Ledermann Formula and Its Recent Applications." *The Drinking and Drug Practices Surveyor* 12 (1976): 15–22.

Smith, Stephen. *The City That Was.* Metuchen, N.J.: Scarecrow, 1973.

Snyder, Charles R. *Alcohol and the Jews.* Glencoe, Ill.: Free Press, 1958.

Steiner, Claude. *Games Alcoholics Play.* New York: Grove, 1971.

Straus, Robert. "Problem Drinking in the Perspective of Social Change: 1940–1973." In *Alcohol and Alcohol Problems,* ed. William J. Filstead, Jean J. Rossi, and Mark Keller. Cambridge: Ballinger, 1976.

Sulkunen, Pekka. "Abstainers in Finland, 1946–1976: A Study in Social and Cultural Transition." Report no. 126 from the Social Research Institute of Alcohol Studies. Helsinki: The State Alcohol Monopoly, August 1979.

————. "Drinking Patterns and the Level of Alcohol Consumption: An International Overview." In *Research Advances in Alcohol and Drug Problems,* vol. 3, ed. R. J. Gibbins et al., pp. 223–281. New York: John Wiley, 1976.

Szasz, Thomas. *Ceremonial Chemistry: The Ritual Persecution of Drugs, Addicts, and Pushers.* New York: Doubleday, 1975.

————. *The Myth of Mental Illness.* New York: Dell, 1961.

Terris, Milton. "The Epidemiological Revolution, National Health Insurance, and the Role of the Health Department." *American Journal of Public Health* 66 (1976): 1155–1164.

————. "Epidemiology of Cirrhosis of the Liver: National Mortality Data." *American Journal of Public Health* 57 (1967): 2076–2088.

Thalberg, Irving. *Enigmas of Agency.* New York: Humanities Press, 1972.

Thomas, Lewis. *The Lives of a Cell.* New York: Bantam, 1974.

Thompson, James D., and McEwen, William J. "Organizational Goals and Environment: Goalsetting as an Interaction Process." *American Sociological Review* 23 (February 1958): 23–31.

Thomsen, Robert. *Bill W.* New York: Harper and Row, 1975.

Timberlake, Joseph. *Prohibition and the Progressive Movement: 1910–1920.* Cambridge, Mass.: Harvard University Press, 1963.

Ullman, Albert D. "Sociocultural Backgrounds Conducive to Alcoholism." *Annals of the American Academy of Political and Social Science* 315 (1958): 48–55.

U.S., Congress, Senate, Committee on Labor and Human Resources, Subcommittee on Alcoholism and Drug Abuse. *Report on Consumer Health Warnings for Alcoholic Beverages and Related Issues.* 96th Cong., 1st Sess. Washington, D.C.: G.P.O., 1979.

Vickers, Geoffrey. "What Sets the Goals of Public Health?" *The New England Journal of Medicine* 258 (March 1958): 589–596.

Walsh, L. E., Chairman, New York State Moreland Commission on the Alcoholic Beverage Control Law. *Report and Recommendations*. New York: January 1964.

Warburton, Clark. *The Economic Results of Prohibition*. Columbia University Studies in History, Economics, and Public Law, no. 379. New York: Columbia University, 1932.

Whitehead, Paul, and Ferrence, Roberta. "Women and Children Last: Implication of Trends in Consumption for Women and Young People." In *Alcoholism Problems in Women and Children*, ed. Milton Greenblatt and Mark Schukett, pp. 163–192. New York: Grune and Stratton, 1976.

Wilkerson, A. E., Jr. "A History of the Concept of Alcoholism as a Disease." Ph.D. diss., University of Pennsylvania, 1966.

Wilkinson, Rupert. *The Prevention of Drinking Problems*. New York: Oxford, 1970.

Williams, Alan F. "The Epidemiology and Ecology of Alcoholism." *International Psychiatry Clinics* 3, no. 2 (1966): 17–49.

Winslow, C.-E. A. *The Life of Herman Biggs, Physician and Statesman of the Public Health*. Philadelphia: Lea and Febiger, 1929.

World Health Organization, Expert Committee on Mental Health, Alcoholism Subcommittee. *Second Report*. World Health Organization Technical Rep. Ser. no. 48, August 1952.

Zylman, Richard. "Fatal Crashes among Michigan Youth Following Reduction of Legal Drinking Age." *Quarterly Journal of Studies on Alcohol* 35 (1974): 283–286.

Index